'TIS HIMSELF

413 South Brewer and Beyond

By George L. Hansel

Copyright © 2010 George L. Hansel
All rights reserved.

ISBN: 1439252513
ISBN-13: 9781439252512

ACKNOWLEDGEMENTS

There are many people who helped George's stories become this book and they deserve special thanks for their encouragement and hard work.

His mother Alma inspired him to be creative, and her stories, plays and poetry led him to have an interest in writing his own stories over the years. Many of those tales are now in this book.

His sister Arlene gave him his first diary and started him on his lifetime habit of writing the important things that occurred each day in his life. Arlene's skill as a proofreader was important to the book as she edited the first version with her red pen. She was a generous big sister, riding George everywhere on her bike until he was old enough to get places on his own. Although there was ten years' difference in their ages, they were always good friends.

Our son Doug and his wife Veronique were the principal editors of this book and spent many, many hours reading and re-reading the text. Veronique was able to guide us all through the pitfalls of publishing a book and it could not have come to completion without her help. Doug, as team leader, kept us pushing on and staying on task until the job was done.

Our son Matthew used his talents as a graphic artist to make some very old pictures appear as sharp and bright as possible. Many of the photos were important, but not usable as they were, so Matt spent long hours at the computer bringing them back to life to enhance the stories.

As principal typist and collector of stories, I learned more of George's colorful life than I had ever known before. Even after almost 52 years, there were tales I had never heard and there were surely many more.

To all of you who grew up with George, and many of you appear in these tales, thank you for being his friends. He loved you all.

Special thanks to the many grown up pals who shared the joys and pitfalls of hunting and fishing with George, especially:

Fred Welch, who was George's first hunting buddy in Wisconsin and who introduced George and me to the great game of Pitch.

Craig Malven, who shared his cabin in the woods with George and his friends and relatives and whose knowledge of the game in the area he passed on in long, detailed letters.

Jack Corbin, whose wife fixed great breakfasts and whose pointers showed George how to hunt quail in Tennessee.

Roger "The Turkey Pro" Raisch, George's nephew, whose knowledge of the ways of turkeys and deer in his farm made trips there memorable and whose energy and enthusiasm were catching.

David Denny, who could always be counted on to go hunting and fishing whatever, whenever and wherever, and with whom George spent countless days in the canoe on the Caney Fork River.

Rob Raney, who shared George's love of hunting and fishing, and whose dog Daisy joined with George's Dixie in many good duck and quail hunts

All George's friends, relatives and hunting companions meant so much to him. Each person he met was special to him and loved. Thank you for being his friends.

Shirley

TABLE OF CONTENTS

FOREWORD	ix
413 SOUTH BREWER STREET	1
BB GUNS	25
CAMPING	31
CENTRAL SCHOOL	39
CHRIS WENGER	47
HALLOWEEN TRICKS AND TREATS	49
HOW I LEARNED TO SWIM	55
BELT KNIVES AND TREBLE HOOKS	59
MINKS AND MUSKRATS	63
MUTT	65
OWWEEEES!	73
SUCKERS	87
SLINGSHOTS	89
THE TREE HOUSE	93
OUT TO PECK'S	97
COUSIN DON	119
WILLIE	127

SKUNK STORIES	131
TRAPPING	137
DUCK BLINDS I HAVE KNOWN	141
MEMORIES OF MY DAD	147
MY MOM	163
DOG TALES	169
FOXES BY THE DOZEN	195
MY DEMISE	209
LES AND SKIN HAPPENINGS	213
THREE IOWA MUSKETEERS	215
MY FIRST PIZZA	219
KANSAS MEMORY	221
MY CANOE	223
CAMPING ADVENTURES	231
SHIRLEY'S LUNKER	237
THE GREENFIELD FIRE DEPARTMENT	239
SHIRLEY'S BIGGEST CATCH	243
STUFFED STUFF	245
GUARDIAN ANGELS	251

CLAY BIRDS GET EVEN	253
BOUNDARY WATERS ADVENTURE	255
SAILING	259
THINGS ALONG THE WAY	261
A DUCK HUNTING SURPRISE	267
AFRICA - 1997	269
THE ORDEAL	275
IOWA FALL TURKEY HUNT	279
"MR. BIG"	283
A SPECIAL HAPPENING	293
IN CLOSING	295

FOREWORD

I was very fortunate to be born into a wonderful family, in a special place, at an interesting time. I was born on March 17, 1932, a Depression baby. I had a 12-year-old brother Dale, and a 10-year-old sister Arlene. I got off to a rough start since the doctor pinned my bellyband to me, and I did a lot of crying and little sleeping. Due to all the crying, they thought that I needed changing or that I was hungry. When they would pick me up, I would cry all the louder as the pin was hurting me. Don't you know, I have never caught up on all that sleep I lost?

    I have always wanted to tell or write the stories of my childhood as I lived and loved them, and I hope you enjoy them half as much as I did. Since I continued to have many interesting experiences, the stories have been greatly expanded beyond childhood, and I have included them as I want you to enjoy them, too.

    I had a special childhood, a wonderful growing-up, and a happy life. I have many people to thank; my parents, my childhood friends, my sister and brother, my hunting and fishing buddies, my sons, and all those folks who listened to me tell these stories through the years. Most of all I thank my wife, and I dedicate this book to her. She has always been very supportive and has helped me throughout our 50 - plus years of marriage. Thanks again, Shirley[3]. I love you!

    George

413 South Brewer Street, where I lived from 1934-1946

413 SOUTH BREWER STREET

I was born in 1932, and we lived in a pebble-dashed house in the north end of the town of Manchester, Iowa. I don't remember anything about that house, but my sister has told me some of the funny things that happened there. Anyway, when I was 2 years old, we moved to 413 South Brewer Street on the south side of town, in an area called Sandy Flat. The house had two stories, and it had a partial basement that had been dug out after the house was built. There was a separate two-car garage that had an upstairs loft with access by a pull-down stairs. This house was the fourth house south of the Illinois Central Railroad tracks. The land had a gentle slope to the south, but this lot was level, due to a three-foot wall on the north and an 18-inch wall on the south. We were two and a half blocks from the Maquoketa River, and one lot east of us was farm country. It was great. You walked north on the sidewalk to go to town or to school, and you walked the railroad tracks east or west to go hunting or fishing.

There were only three streets that crossed the railroad tracks, and Brewer Street was the only one that continued out into the country. Tama Street to the east went for maybe 500 yards, and it then jogged over and met Brewer Street. The streets were not paved, but they were graveled, and on occasion, they spread oil on them to hold down the dust.

The house layout consisted of three bedrooms upstairs, and the downstairs contained the kitchen, dining room, living room, a bedroom and the bathroom, which was located off the kitchen. There were two stairways, one down to the basement and another going upstairs to the bedrooms on the second floor.

My first story of living in this house was of my first bath there. I'm told that Mom had placed me in the bathtub with just a little water, and I was splashing that water and giggling and having a ball. She was in the kitchen and doing the dishes or something, and she came in to get me. She wrapped a towel around me, dried me off and set me down on the kitchen floor, out of all the water that I had splashed on the bathroom floor. I took off running through the house, and she used the towel to mop up the bathroom floor. Well, I ran clear through the house and out the front screen door, down the sidewalk and right out into the middle of the street. The gravel road may have hurt my feet because I stopped in the middle of the road. When Mom came looking for me, she thought that I was hiding somewhere in the house, and she couldn't find me. When she looked out the front door and saw me standing in the street, she screamed and came running after me. I thought it was great fun and started running away from her, going down the street. The neighbors heard all the commotion and came to see what was going on. They all got a big laugh out of it, as I didn't have a stitch of clothes on!

* * *

We kept a gun case, up in the upstairs hallway, and brother Dale had shot a hole in the north wall when he was cleaning a 22-caliber rifle. The hole was just at the top of the stairs as you started down. It was perfect for me to put my small finger in as I went up or down the steps. My hands were always dirty, too, so the hole not only got bigger each time I passed, but it got dirtier, too. Mom was always telling me to leave the hole alone, but I just couldn't. She would wash the hole and even took to pasting a piece of paper over the hole, but I could always find it. If I pushed the paper just a little, I could locate the hole. Soon the paper had a hole in it and we were off again, with a place to put my finger as I passed by.

* * *

I got very upset one time, when the house caught fire. Mom and brother Dale were cleaning the basement. They had a fire going in the furnace to burn up old newspapers. One of the burning papers went up the chimney, landed on the roof, and it caught fire. The neighbors saw and reported it. My sister Arlene was directed to take me across the street to get me out of the way. It put us where we could see all the action, and it upset me no end, and I started to cry. The fire was quickly put out by the volunteer fire department, and when Dad got there, he ran up to the front door where the Fire Chief met him.

The Chief said Dad couldn't go in, and Dad said he lived there and ran on past the Chief who was yelling at him all the way. Dad said he knew where the attic access hole was, and the Chief found out where it was too, by following Dad. It had been put out successfully, and all was well. Dad was a carpenter, so he fixed the roof and put a big wire basket up on top of the chimney so it wouldn't happen again.

Dale, Arlene, and me, aged 2

When I was about four years old, the folks gave me a pair of tin cork guns. You cocked the guns by folding the grip down away from the barrel, which pulled a plunger down the barrel where it stayed until you pulled the trigger. The cork was placed in the end of the barrel, and the plunger came forward and shot the cork out. During a big Sunday lunch, I left the dining room table and went into the living room to play. I set my toy soldiers up on the davenport and got the idea to knock them down by shooting at them with the cork gun. Somewhere I had found an old 45-caliber bullet, and I placed it in the end of the cocked cork gun. When I pulled the trigger, the bullet went off! There was a big explosion with smoke and fire. Everyone jumped up from the table and came running to see what had happened. I was sitting there in a daze in the smoke, and I had the handle of the gun in my hand, but the rest of the gun was gone. The lead bullet set the couch pillow on fire and the brass cartridge went flying across the room. I was okay, but scared, as was the rest of the family. The peened-over end of the rod that held the plunger in the gun barrel had been just right to hit the primer and set off the round. We found the gun barrel, and it was now just a flat piece of tin. That was my first lesson in gun safety.

* * *

Dad installed a stoker to feed ground-up coal into the furnace, and a forced hot air fan. The fan was to be in a big black box behind the furnace, and it was dark back in there. I was just right to poke my nose into whatever was going on, and I could walk where others had to crawl. Dad was heating molten lead with a blowtorch, and he was pouring the lead into little holes in the concrete floor. He had drilled the holes by pounding on a concrete cold chisel drill. He was filling the holes with the lead to anchor lag bolts into the floor to hold the fan box and the fan. Well, as I walked along, I saw the shiny little spots on the floor. I reached down to touch one and got a good burned finger, as the shiny spot was the molten hot lead. Mom was mighty unhappy with Dad for not watching me better.

* * *

I was potty trained, and I had to do a number 2, so I came into the house to the bathroom and when I finished, I flushed. Immediately there was a yell from the basement. It seems that the sewer pipe was plugged up, and Dad and brother Dale had taken the pipe apart to try to unstop it. Well, when I flushed, they were unprepared. They had told Mom not to flush the toilet, but no one had told me. Anyway, they got wet and dirty due to my actions. It turned out that Dale had cleaned a carp, and he had flushed the carp's bones down the toilet with some difficulty. The backbone had lodged at a pipe joint. Dad was most unhappy with Dale, as he should have known better, but I was young and innocent.

* * *

Dad was always making or building something around the house. One day he had put some planks across a couple of sawhorses to build a workbench in the back yard. He had tools, etc. on the planks, and I was hanging around, too. Somehow, I reached up and knocked a heavy bench weight off, and it lit on my big toe and smashed it. That started many years of ingrown toenails.

* * *

About this time I had a big bug collection. I caught so many different bugs, butterflies, and insects of all kinds that I couldn't find enough boxes to put them in. I put cellophane over all my boxes so you could see the bugs, and I put cotton in the bottom and pins to keep them from falling and breaking wings, etc. Mom always wanted to make sure they were all dead, as she didn't like bugs, especially spiders. I liked them all, once they were dead. The butterflies were beautiful, but some of the bugs were gruesome, especially the big beetles with hatpins stuck through them.

* * *

One of my jobs as a little boy was delivering bread. Mom was a great cook, and she baked wonderful bread. The neighbors found out about it and they wanted it delivered before breakfast on a

Sunday morning. Mom would get up real early and bake loaves of bread, rolls and coffee cake which we called candy bread. When it came out of the oven, she would wrap it in dishtowels, put it in a big basket, and send me off to deliver it. I had a regular route starting at the Blairs' and ending at the Ranns'. Each place would be waiting, and they would exclaim how good it smelled, and Oooh and Ahhh and thank me and give me the money, and off I would go to the next place where I would get the same reception. It was fun for me to see their reactions, and it did smell awfully good.

* * *

Howard Rann was the editor of the local newspaper, and he subscribed to about ten different papers. He would read all those papers looking for stories to put in his paper, and he always saved me the Sunday funnies. After Sunday dinner I would go to his house, and he would have the funny papers stacked in my favorite place, a bay window. The sun would be coming in, and I would usually spread the papers out on the bench seat and read them while kneeling on the floor. I didn't have glasses, then but I was nearsighted, so I could read okay. That's a special memory.

* * *

One time, Dad couldn't get the car started, and he attempted to push it out of the garage. I was there to help, and as the car started to roll, he jumped to the driver's side window to steer it, as it was too close to the north side. I was by then walking along between the car and the workbench. When he steered, the front end came over and trapped me between the fender and the bench. I was squeezed very tight as the car was rolling down the little ramp, and my body stopped it. Dad ran to the front of the car, and he literally slid the car sideways to get me loose. I had all my life experiences flash by me as I passed out. Dad carried me out into the yard and laid me down in the grass. They called the doctor, and by the time the doctor got there, I was awake but still lying down in the grass. The doctor checked me over and said I would live but, ever since that day I haven't been able to belch.

* * *

 Mom had a big garden out behind the house, and one Fall when the garden had been laid by, I was out there kicking clods of dirt and looking for something to do. I found some tall sunflower stalks sticking up, and they looked like good spear material. I kicked one over, broke off the clod of dirt on the bottom and the sunflower head on the top. The shaft looked like a javelin or a spear with a sharp point on the base where the clod had broken off. I hefted it and was looking for a target to throw it at, when out of the back door of the house came sister Arlene to call me for supper. Well, there was my target. I made a mighty throw, as it was a long way, and the spear went right towards the target. Arlene just stood there and didn't move. I don't think she thought I could throw it that far, but in any case, she did not dodge or go back in the house. The spear hit her right in the face. She yelled and said I had done that on purpose. Well, yeah, I had thrown it at her, but I didn't expect to hit her. Mom was mad at her for not getting out of the way, and I didn't get punished, but I felt bad for hurting my sister. We were lucky it hadn't hit her in the eye. She had a scar for a long time, but it might be in a wrinkle by now.

* * *

 The house had a forced hot air furnace and there was a main register in the dining room that was right above the furnace. It put out heat big time, and as I was always cold in the winter from playing in the snow, and my hands were always wet from snowball fights, etc. I would come in and plop down on that register and sit there with the hot air flowing all around me until I was warm and dry. I took to sliding down the wall as I was sitting down and the metal rivets in my jeans scratched the wallpaper. It soon looked pretty bad. Mom asked Dad what he could do about it, and Dad put a nice finished Masonite board about 3 feet wide and 5 feet high on the wall in front of the register. He put an aluminum edging all around it to finish it off. The board looked like 4- inch yellow tile, and it didn't go with anything else in the house or that room. People always asked what it was for. Mom wrote a poem to explain it and typed it out and posted it on the corner of the board, "It's not for pretty, and not for neat, but to lean against while you dry your feet."

'Tis Himself

* * *

There was a big field behind the houses across the street. A bunch of us kids were walking across this field, and it was tough going as the field had been plowed with a turning plow. It was all uneven. When we were halfway across, we came upon a big bull snake, and we surrounded him so he couldn't get away. We were shooting at him with BB guns and slingshots, but we weren't doing him any harm, as we wouldn't get close to him. We finally sent Sonny Barker home to get something that we could use to kill the snake. He came back with a pitchfork. No one would go close enough to hit the snake with it so we all took turns throwing the fork at him. It took a long time, but finally a tine of the fork went through his skin and pinned him to the ground. Now we could get close, and he was killed with a rock from a slingshot. What are we going to do with him? Well, skin him and tack his hide to Barker's barn, of course. I skinned him, and as I finished, the noon whistle blew for lunchtime. I rolled up the skin, which made a big roll about five inches in diameter and seven inches wide. I looked for a place to put it so I went in the barn and there was a coal bin there that had boards nailed to the exposed studs to keep the coal off the wall and plate. It was a perfect place to stuff the snakeskin, in between the studs and behind the boards. I was coming back to tack his hide on the barn, but when I got home, Peck and Dolly were there, and they invited me to come to the farm for the summer, so off I went.

When I got back, a few months later, just before school started, I jumped on the bike and rode down to Barker's to see what he had been doing. The back yard smelled really bad, and I asked him about it. He said they didn't know what made the smell, but his Mom was having a fit about it. They thought something had died in the barn. All of a sudden I knew what the problem was. I told him to get a flashlight, and we looked down in the coal bin wall. That snakeskin had turned to liquid, and it was very strong-smelling. No one had gone into the coal bin in the summer. We got the garden hose, washed it all out and solved the problem.

* * *

When I was in grade school, I got there several different ways. Most of the time I walked, and if I goofed off on the way and was late, I could always say the train held me up because the teachers knew I lived south of the tracks. On the opening day of trout season, I would have someone take me to the trout stream that ran through the fish hatchery. I would fish from daylight until almost time for school to start, and I would hitchhike to school with another fisherman who was coming back to go to work. On those occasions, I went to school in hip boots. I would go to the basement where the janitor would put my fish in a pail of water, and I would leave my boots, fly rod etc. all in the basement with him. I would go to school all day in my stocking feet.

On two occasions I went to school on ice skates. We had big ice storms, and everything was covered with a half inch of ice. You could skate right up the sidewalk. I put on my ice skates, and when I got to the Central School, there was a teacher trying to crawl on her hands and knees up the sloping sidewalk. She couldn't do it, as she would just slip back. I got above her and pulled her up. We went into the school and waited about a half hour. Since no one else showed up, she sent me home. I skated all the way back home, and my ankles were so tired I couldn't skate anymore when all the neighborhood kids came out to skate. I got shoe skates for Christmas, and it was a good thing. I couldn't have skated very far with the old clamp-on skates I had before that. I would clamp them on so hard that they cut notches in the edges of the soles of my shoes and bent the soles up into my foot, but they still wouldn't stay on.

Later when I got to use Arlene's bicycle, I rode that to school. She had won the bike, selling subscriptions to the local newspaper. She liked to fish, but she didn't like snakes. She would ride her bike all the way to the Quaker Mill to fish, with me sitting on the bar. She took me along to scare the snakes away. It was a good place to fish, and we always had fun. Mom took me to school in the car a few times when I was going to be late since I had overslept after running my trap line.

* * *

During the summer I slept on the south porch. The folks would put a cot out there, and I enjoyed it, as it was my own spot. I had all my stuff out there, too, my BB gun, football, baseball glove, etc. I would open all the windows in the summer to catch the breeze, as we didn't have air conditioning. When it would rain, the rain on the tin roof would lull me to sleep so hard that you couldn't wake me up.

* * *

The concrete wall along the south lot line of our house was perfect for shooting off carbide cannons. We made these cannons using special beer cans that had a puckered top and a beer bottle cap. The rest of the can was normal, with a flat bottom, but the top of the can ducked in to make it the size of a beer bottle.

To make the cannon, you drove a nail just 1/8" above the bottom of the can for a touchhole, and you drove a nail through the neck of the bottle to hold the barrel. The barrel was a 6 or 8-inch length of ¾ inch copper pipe with a hole bored through it about an inch from one end. You stuck the barrel in the neck of the can and inserted the nail clear through to fasten the barrel in the can. Now all you needed was the propellant, the projectile and the igniter. The propellant was carbide that we got for free at a repair shop. We needed very little, so the workmen always gave it to us. The projectile was a glassy marble, and the igniter was a match.

To operate the cannon, you would set it on the concrete wall, put a little water in the bottom of the can, put a pinch of carbide down the barrel, drop the marble down the barrel, light your match and put it close to the touch hole and KAWHAM! The marble was nowhere to be found. The timing had to be fast, for if your match didn't light, or you dropped the marble, the gas would build up too high, and you would blow up the beer can. Each can could only be used three or four times when all was done right, as it put a strain on the seam of the can. A new can was easy to prepare, needing only two nail holes as the barrel was transferable. The explosion was contained somewhat in the can, and it wasn't loud like a firecracker.

I'm sure Mom didn't know how dangerous this was, or she wouldn't have allowed us to do it.

* * *

Somewhere I should tell you about Mr. Lafferty. He ran a grocery store about where the Gamble Store is now. He was in business all during the Depression, and he allowed folks to run a tab or a bill for their groceries. Many couldn't pay, and it is said he kept many families fed during this period. Some eventually paid, but many didn't. Mom would send Arlene, my sister, or me to the store with a list of what she needed, and Dad would pay the bill on Saturday when he got paid. If I went along when Dad paid the bill, Mr. Lafferty would always give me a sack of candy. I liked jellybeans as they were big and didn't melt in my pocket. Mom always wanted the chocolates. They were little domed white stuff, covered with chocolate. The candy was in bins with sloping glass fronts, and I would stand and stare at all that candy. Mr. Lafferty was a true hero of his time.

The trains were very long during WW II since most of the cargo was war-related. When troop trains came through, we would all run to the train and give our troops magazines and newspapers that we collected and stored on Aunt Mildred's back porch. Her house was right beside the railroad tracks. It was fun, and the soldiers appreciated it. Maynard, Mildred's son, came through on a troop train, and he was yelling like mad as he went by his house, but we didn't recognize him or hear what he was saying. The train didn't stop until his car was way up by the depot, and he couldn't get off, of course. We had prisoner of war trains come through, too. They were usually singing and were either Italian or German. I would always try to get up close, because at the end of every car, an American soldier guard would get off the train with a Thompson submachine gun. I loved guns and would get as close as they would let me as I admired their weapon. When coal cars were on the freight trains and the train stretched way out in the country, I would see men climb up into the cars and throw coal chunks off into the ditch. They had burlap bags that we called "gunny sacks" to carry the coal in. Dad said they needed it to heat their homes.

'Tis Himself

* * *

Christmas time was a wonderful time at our house. We always had a nice tree with big electric lights. Dale and Arlene had real candles up at the pebble-dashed house, but that was before my time. We decorated our tree and sometimes we strung popcorn on a string for decoration. One year the city had bought too many pine boughs to trim the streetlights, etc. and they announced that anyone could come get all the boughs they wanted. Mom got a bunch of the boughs and she decorated our house and the church. Then she made our Christmas tree. Dad made the stand and a wooden pole, and Mom put the boughs on this with wire. It was a very nice tree.

Each year I tried to get a bigger stocking than I had the previous year. I first had my stocking, then Dad's stocking, and finally Mom's full length stocking. Santa always filled it, but the time I used Mom's stocking, it was mostly full of fruit. We didn't eat much fruit as it was expensive, but we always had it for Christmas. I wasn't very happy to have my stocking full of grapefruit and oranges. I wanted toys and candy. In later years, Dad always gave me pennies in my stocking. He saved them all year for that purpose, and there were always 3 or 4 dollars' worth. One year I got a new sled, and I came down the stairs and ran and jumped on my new sled and tore the buttons off my pajama top. One year Dad made me a machine gun because we were always playing war. It was special as it was on a pedestal, and when you turned a little handle, it clicked. He also made me a submachine gun and rubber guns (both pistols and rifles). We played with them a lot. We had good rubber in those days as inner tubes in tires were made of red rubber, which stretched and snapped back big time. In 1943, when I was eleven, my brother sent me a real cowboy leather belt and holster set. I wore it all over, and I took it off to go sledding and hung it on a bush. It got legs, and I came home without it. That night my sister went to the homes of all the kids who were there at the hill sledding, and the next morning, we found it on our front porch.

* * *

I was in Cub Scouts and Mom was my den mother. I then went into Boy Scouts, but that didn't last long. I was already camping out on the river for a week at a time and doing more scouting than our boy scouts ever did. The scoutmaster was our fat preacher, and to get your merit badges, you sat on his back porch and told him how you would cook a meal, etc. I had a cooking kit that contained a tin fry pan, two other pans, and a cup. I cooked a lot of venison hamburger in that fry pan as Mom was trying to get rid of it. Dad went deer hunting in northern Minnesota, and he would always bring back the biggest buck they got to show it off, as we didn't have any deer in Iowa. The deer was so old that you could hardly eat it, and it stunk up the house while it was cooking. Cooked out on my fry pan, however, it was fine! One time I was down on the riverbank below town where the dry run entered the river, and we caught a lot of frogs in the ponds of the dry run. I decided to cook up a mess of frog legs. I skinned them and put them in the pan and started to cook them, but they kept jumping out of the pan. Since I had so many, I let the first dozen go, but as they kept jumping out, I would pick them up, dust them off and put them back in the pan. When I felt they were done, we tried to eat them, but they were gritty from being in the dirt.

* * *

One year Howard Rann gave me a real steam engine for Christmas. It was a toy steam engine, but it was supposed to work and make real steam, and you could then harness that steam power to do all sorts of things. Dad tried and tried, but he couldn't get it to work. We took it back to the Gamble Store where it came from, and they said I could pick out whatever I wanted in the store to replace it. It was like a new Christmas because the steam engine had cost so much that I was able to get 6 or 7 other toys as replacement covering the price of the steam engine.

* * *

One time Sonny Barker showed up and said he had a new girlfriend. I wanted to know who, and he said it was a new girl that just moved to town by the name of Diane Bennett. Well, when I saw Diane for the first time, I decided she was way too cute for Sonny Barker, and I set out to make her my girlfriend. I would go over to her house, and we would cut Superman out of the Sunday funnies and paste him on cardboard; cut him out again and play with our action figures, making him fly all around, etc. Later, when I had gotten a football for Christmas, I carried it with me wherever I went. Barker and I found ourselves over at Diane's house again, and we asked if she could come out and play. She could, so we were waiting while she put on her coat. Barker climbed up in a pecan tree that was in her yard between the sidewalk and the street. He was saying all kinds of naughty things that he said he was going to tell her that I wanted to do to her, and I was getting really mad at him. I finally told him that if he didn't shut up, I was going to knock him out of that tree with my football. He kept at it, and I threw the football at him.

    I don't know what happened, maybe he tried to catch it. Anyway, I did hit him, and he fell out of the tree and landed on his back on the sidewalk. It knocked him out, and just at that moment, Diane came out. She wanted to know what happened, and when I told her, she wasn't happy with me. She took his knees, and I took his shoulders, and we carried him inside the house and laid him on the couch. She got a basin of cold water, and a washcloth, and sat down next to him. She put his head in her lap and put the cold wet washcloth on his head. I don't know how she knew to do this, as she was home alone. In a few minutes he came to, realized where he was, winked at me and groaned and wiggled his head in her lap. I told her he was okay, but she said he was in pain and delirious, etc. He groaned all the harder and ran his head around and around.

    Barker had the hardest head of anyone I ever knew. He came to my house one day and said he was going to the movies and could I go along. I told my Mom he was going and asked if I could go. She agreed and found the money, and we headed out the door. He started south but the movie was north. I asked where he was going. He said we had to go down to his house now to see if he could go. When we got to his house, we went into the kitchen where his Mom was, and he said, "Hansel is going to the movies, can I go too?" Well, she lit into him and said "No, because you have been bad all day and your Dad is going to blister you when he gets home." Sonny calmly walked over to the wall and banged his head against the wall so hard it shook the dishes in the cabinets. His Mom told him to stop that, and he just kept it up, saying he wanted to go to the movies. She looked at me, and my eyes were as big as saucers as I had never seen anything like that before. After his head hit the wall about five times, she said he could go, got him the money, and off we went. Sonny would also tell you he had a secret, and when you bent your head down to hear it, he would reach up, grab you by the back of your neck and crack your forehead against his. I would be standing there groaning and holding my head, and he would just laugh at you. Ugh!

* * *

We had two kinds of entertainment, the radio and the movies, but they were different from what they are now. One of the biggest attractions for kids was the Saturday morning radio programs like: 'Jack Armstrong', 'Terry and the Pirates', 'Captain Midnight', 'Sgt. Preston and Yukon King' and 'The Lone Ranger'. As kids, we wouldn't miss them, and we had to have the folks buy Ovaltine, etc. to get the coupons that we could send in and get prizes. On Sunday night, the whole family would be sitting around the living room while we listened to 'Jack Benny', 'Fibber McGee and Molly', 'Amos and Andy' and others. It was fun for all.

When we went to the movies, we were treated not only to the main feature but before that, we had a serial (cliff hanger), a cartoon, and a newsreel. The newsreel was usually about the war. We didn't eat popcorn in Wayne Dutton's theatre because everyone made a mess spilling it on the floor, so he didn't allow us to eat or drink. For a while we had two theatres, and you could have popcorn at the Castle Theatre. Dad would eat his popcorn during the short subjects, and his sack would be empty before the feature started. He said not to worry, as he would eat what he had spilled on his lap and bib overalls during the movie. You could get into the movie by bringing zinc jar lids or copper when they had special days to collect these metals for the war effort. We could usually scrounge the dumps and find the price of admission. When they had brass day, we were at a loss because most folks kept their brass doorknobs in case they met 'Injun Joe' in a cave.

* * *

When I was 10 years old, my sister gave me a diary for Christmas. In January there are five days in a row where I entered; "Went to school and got a rabbit". The snow was just right for tracking. The rabbits would eat the bark off the bushes around the houses at night, and then they would go out into Bank's field, which was planted to corn, and spend the day. The corn had been picked, and all cornstalks were knocked over. I would walk along the cornfield until I found a rabbit track that was headed out into the field, and I would follow it until it started to wander. I knew the rabbit was getting ready to find himself a place to spend the day. When the tracks stopped, I would know the rabbit was sitting under the closest cornstalk. I carried a club, and I would whack that cornstalk set, get the rabbit and go on home. I did that on my way home from school. Dad got a big kick out of it, as I didn't use a gun or dog or anything.

* * *

I spent a lot of time fishing below the Marion Street Dam. It is probably my most-remembered place from my childhood. One day Terry Schroeyer and a friend of his were up above me hiding behind some bushes. They took to throwing rocks at my cork. I got up, walked down the concrete wall I was sitting on, and came back with some rocks of my own. I could throw rocks and snowballs pretty good. I had a trick of making like I would throw a snowball at a fellow and when he ducked behind a tree, I would wait a second or two and then throw it. Invariably, I would get him when he looked out to see why I hadn't thrown at him. Well, that is what happened to Terry. I caught him throwing at my cork, and I told him if he didn't stop, I would throw a rock at him. He just laughed at me and threw another rock. When I went to throw at him he ducked down behind the hedge. I waited to make my throw and as he looked up, I hit him right on the forehead. He left crying, and I thought I would get in trouble, but I never heard anything more about it. I figured if he told his Dad about it, maybe his Dad told him it was his fault.

* * *

One day I was wading across the river beneath the railroad bridge and I was dragging a Hildebrant flicker spinner on my fly rod behind me. I caught a 5-pound walleyed pike! This was big doings, as we never caught walleyes in our river. Anyway, I didn't have a good way to carry him, so I put him in the top of my hip boot. Big mistake. He slipped down as I walked, and since his scales pointed backwards, they held him fast. I couldn't get him out of the boot until I got home and peeled the top of the boot down. Dad had fixed up a minnow tank on the north side of the house. It was a steel stock tank about four feet long and three feet deep. We would seine minnows and crawdads and keep them in this tank with water trickling in to provide oxygen. I put the walleye in the tank to show Dad; I kept him in there to show everybody. He died after a week or so in the tank. I asked Dad what happened, as he was eating the minnows. Dad felt that the chlorine in the water may have killed him, but he said it would be all right to eat him, which we did, and he was very good.

* * *

We had a pantry off the kitchen, and it had a bare light bulb hanging from twisted, yellow, cloth-covered wires. It didn't work, and Dad got up on a chair and was attempting to fix it. He hadn't turned off the electric power, and he was shocked so bad he couldn't let go of the wires. He was in a bad way. Brother Dale, the smart one, calmly kicked out the chair and Dad came tumbling down. Of course if Dale had grabbed a hold of Dad, he, too would have been shocked and unable to let go.

* * *

There was a fruit cellar in the basement where Mom kept all the vegetables she canned and where Dad, Dale and I kept our furs. Yeah, we trapped mostly muskrats, and we stretched them on wooden stretchers made out of wood shingles. When they were dry, we stored them in the fruit cellar, as it was cool and dry in there. We sometimes sold them to a little Jewish man, who came around buying furs, but I sent mine to Sears Roebuck, and I felt I got a better deal.

One day Mom sent brother Dale to the fruit cellar for a jar of piccalilli that she had canned. We were all sitting at the kitchen table waiting for him. When he got back and tried to open the jar, it exploded all over the ceiling, table and Dale. He said, "Fine stuff!" He had dropped the jar while in the basement, and that shook it up so it was ready when he tried to open it. We all sat there in shock for a moment, and then we began to laugh. Dale eventually laughed, but he wasn't sure we were laughing at him or with him.

* * *

Down below town, along the river, there was a slaughterhouse and a dump. We always checked the dump to see what was there that we could use for targets for our 22 rifles. Ed Frentress and I found that someone had thrown away some canned tomatoes. They were in glass canning jars with zinc lids. I told Ed to see if he could hit this one, and I threw it up high over his head. He aimed, shot, and hit the jar. The contents, spoiled tomatoes, rained down on him, and they smelled big time. He wasn't happy for a while until I convinced him that I hadn't known that the tomatoes stunk before I threw them. Not far away was a big owl's nest. I climbed up in the tree, checked out the nest, and found all kinds of hen pheasant parts lying all around. That momma owl was hard on pheasants. There was an owl chick in the nest, and he scared me at first when he snapped his bill at me. Somehow he knew that I was not supposed to be there. He was very small and covered with down. Lying on the side of the nest was a pocket gopher. I had never seen one before. He had beautiful fur, and I decided to take him home, skin him and keep his hide. When I got home, I went to the basement and stuck my knife in him. He immediately stunk up the whole house. Mom yelled from upstairs to stop whatever I was doing and get it out of the house. The furnace picked up the smell and took it all through the house and Mom had to open up all the windows to air the place out. That owl was allowing that gopher to putrefy so she and her little one could drink it. Ugh.

* * *

By the time I was in Junior High (7th and 8th grade), I was hunting, fishing and trapping at every chance, and I was having some success. Jeep, the beagle dog, was a hunter, and he made you a hunter. He would go all day, and he would wear me out. All of a sudden, I would be tired and a long way from home. I would have to catch the dog, put him on a leash, and start for home. By the time I got home, I was exhausted. I would clean my game, clean my gun, eat supper and collapse in bed. Mom said that I should go until I was only half tired and then start home, so when I got home I would just be tired. I told her it was a good idea, but that I didn't have any way to know when I was half tired.

* * *

Most of the time I hunted alone or with Ed Frentress or Norman Anderson. Sometimes I would take a boy along who was not a hunter, and I always got Mom in trouble. Their Mom would call my Mom and ask if her son was there. My Mom would say, "No," and that they had gone hunting. She would then be asked where they went, and when they would be back. Mom would have to say she didn't know. The other Mom couldn't understand why she didn't know where her son was or when he would be home. Mom would try to explain, but she always came away looking like she was a bad Mom when she could not account for me and my wandering ways.

* * *

Brother Dale had brought a German Luger home from the war, and it was stored in the cabinet under the gun case. He had demonstrated to Dad and me how smooth the trigger pull was, and that you never knew when the gun would go off. Dick Jones, a classmate, was visiting me, and I got out the Luger and cocked it and gave it to Jones with instructions to pull the trigger and see how smooth it was. When he was pulling it, I said that he should point it out the window as if he was going to shoot something, and then pull the trigger. Well, he did, and BANG! It went off. I told him to not pull it again, and I quickly took the gun and unloaded it. We never had a loaded gun in the house, and for some strange reason, Dale had left a loaded clip in it. Our ears were ringing because we had been in Dad's bedroom when the gun went off. I walked over to the window, which now had a bullet hole in it, and I raised the window, which gave me two holes. There was a bullet hole in the storm window, too. I then tried to line up the two holes, as I wanted to know what else got hit, i.e. the neighbor's house maybe. I could not tell where the bullet might have gone, so we went outside to look around. There was snow everywhere, and there was a boy going by. We asked him if he had heard a loud noise. He said he hadn't heard a thing. We then walked over to the wall along the north side of the lot and looked at it and at the neighbor's house, but we never found where the bullet went. It must have gone into the snow in the yard, and we were safe, except that Dad had to fix two windowpanes and I don't even remember he was mad about it.

* * *

Carl Anderson was the sheriff, and he had had two craftsmen in jail for a time. He had seen a kit to build a kayak, so he asked them if they would be interested in assembling it while they weren't doing anything else. They were willing and they built a very nice, one-man kayak. It had aluminum ribs and long ½ inch stringers. It was covered with canvas and painted many times. It would hold two kids or one man on its plywood floor. Anyway, Chuck Martensen got it from Carl and in 1946 I bought it from Martensen for $12.00. I loved it for a while. It would almost go in wet grass. I could paddle it in the gutter or road ditch after a rain. I would carry it all the way to the backwater and paddle around out there for hours. I had a two-bladed paddle and in some bays that were full of carp, I would hit a carp every time I dipped the paddle in the water. Once I trapped a big turtle against the bank, and he literally picked both me and the kayak up as he went under it.

I had the kayak down the river one day when a bunch of kids were swimming in the swimming hole. We had installed a diving board, and a little boy was out on the diving board, and he fell off. Someone heard the splash and realized what had happened, and Barker yelled for me to come help as I was up-river. I came paddling down and when I got under the diving board, I put my hands and arms in the water to see if I could find him. I didn't realize it, but my momentum and the current were carrying me downstream. It was a good thing, as I found him quite a ways from the diving board. I pulled him up by the hair, and he immediately tried to get into the kayak. He almost tipped me over. We got to the bank and he was saved, and I was a hero. Hah! It was all a God thing, don't you know.

* * *

I was duck hunting out of the kayak in the backwater, and a big goose flew right over me. I had Dad's 12-gauge shotgun, and as I aimed at it vertically, my right elbow was in the water. I knew I would tip over if I shot, so I let the goose go. We never got a chance to shoot a goose on the backwater, so I was unhappy.

* * *

When I got to the bank one day after duck hunting, I pulled the boat up and set it down and heard, plunk, plunk, plunk. Not knowing what the sound was, I picked the boat up and set it down again with the same result. When I turned it over, I found that beavers had cut willows off beneath the high grass and the sharp willows had penetrated the painted canvas. I now had six or seven holes in my kayak. I was getting unhappy with my wonderful boat.

* * *

Since brother Dale was in the military, he wasn't home to guard his Winchester Model 12 twelve-gauge shotgun. I started using it, and I bought my first box of 12 gauge shotgun shells for $1.40. A box of 22 shorts was 21 cents, according to my diary. Dale was mighty proud of that gun, as the action was so smooth it would fall open when you held it vertically and pushed the release. When he got home, he always said he had had a case of shotgun shells when he went away and now there was only one box left. Maybe???

* * *

The hunters in my duck blind were interesting. I hunted with Bob Davis, a jeweler who worked at Walt Rossman's Jewelry Store, and with Chuck Martensen. We all had Winchester Model 12 pump shotguns. Bob, the oldest, had a 20 gauge, Martensen had a 16 gauge, and I, the youngest, had Dale's 12 gauge. I shot a lot of game with that gun, but if I shot it straight up, like at a squirrel that Jeep had treed, the gun would give me a fat lip as the stock didn't fit me.

* * *

I trapped muskrats in the backwater the year I was 13 years old, and I made over $100.00. That was a lot of money back then. They wrote me up in the newspaper. Sixty years later, they put it in a short column again, and my cousin sent it to me saying that I was still getting publicity about that feat. I bought a High Standard, HD Military 22 caliber pistol with my trapping money, among other things.

* * *

Dad built us a new house up at 824 New Street, about a block from the high school, and we moved in just before I went into high school as a freshman. That ended my eventful life at 413 South Brewer Street. But there was more to come!

*My cousin Jan Renfrow and I
in front of the new home, 824 New Street*

*My folks got me my first BB gun to cheer me up
during my measles quarantine*

BB GUNS

When I was about 8 or 9 years old, I got the measles – big time! Mom was very concerned about me and she had made up a bed for me in the corner of the dining room. She hung heavy blankets over the windows to cut out the light as red measles were hard on the eyes, and my eyes weren't too good to start with. Let me tell you, it was dark in there.

The folks felt sorry for me, and Dad brought me a brand new Daisy No. 25, 50 shot, pump action, BB gun. It had a dark-blued barrel, and when he gave it to me in that darkened room, I couldn't see it. I was some thrilled, and I petted that gun every hour of every day. I slept with it, too, and it was never out of reach. Eventually, I got well and they took the "Quarantined" sign off the front of the house.

I had a lot of fun with my new BB gun, and I shot lots of critters. I got pretty good with it, as I recall. I had glasses by then, and I could see what I was shooting at. One time I was shooting at a target I had nailed up on a big box elder tree near the wall in front of our garage. Our next-door neighbor, Eunice Hilsenbeck, liked to wash her hair using the water from the pump just outside their back door. She would stick her head under the spout and pump the water right onto her head. She was bent over, rinsing her hair, when I shot, and she stood up and called me over to her. She reached down inside her shoe and picked out the BB I had just shot. I was scared she would be mad, but it didn't hurt her. She gave the BB back, and we recycled it back into the BB gun. I learned about ricocheting right there.

* * *

I was walking down the sidewalk on the south side of our house where Mom had planted a row of big Canna lilies between the sidewalk and the house. They were usually green, but it was apparently fall, as they were a rust red color at this time. I heard a splat sound in these plants, and I stopped to see what it was. When I didn't find anything, I moved on, and there it was again. I stopped and looked a second time and still couldn't figure it out. The third time I knew that someone was shooting at me with a BB gun. I looked around, and there was a barrel of a BB gun sticking out from behind an old outhouse that was beside a long shed at the back of the Hilsenbecks' lot. Well, I stepped into the south porch and came out with my BB gun. I quickly took aim at the gun barrel and squeezed off a shot. There was a yell, "Hey", and out from behind the outhouse came Marvin Johnson and five or six other kids with their hands up in the air. I had hit the barrel of his BB gun and put a dent in it, and they had all surrendered. Ed Frentress and his little brother came walking down the street heading for their place, and I crossed the street to talk to Ed. I was carrying my BB gun, and I didn't want folks to see it and worry, so to keep it out of sight and away from little brother, I put the butt stock on the ground and held the gun close against my side with the end of the barrel up under my arm. Somehow, little brother got behind me and reached out and pulled the trigger. Ouch – I had a welt under my arm for days, and I was glad I had on a shirt or that BB would have broken the skin and maybe penetrated me.

* * *

My aunt Mildred Renfrow lived four doors north of our house, and she planted a row of zinnias between their lot and the railroad right-of-way. I came along and saw a big bumblebee on the blossom of one of those flowers. I put the barrel of my BB gun right up close to him and shot him right in two. I thought that was pretty neat, and I reached down and picked up his head, looked it over real good, and then I picked up his rear end. It was even neater, as his stinger was pulsating in and out a little bit. All of a sudden that stinger came way out and went sideways and stung me on the finger. To this day I do not know how his head, which was lying on the ground, told his stinger where I was.

* * *

My buddy Mutt McCusker and I sometimes hunted birds in the "Bum Jungle" south of the railroad tracks on the west side of the river. The folks didn't like us to hang around there. In those days, there were always homeless men living there. They often came to our back door, and no matter what time of the day, Mom would always cook them something to eat. When I was only three or four years old, I would sit on the back porch with them while they ate. I was a depression baby and times were hard. Lots of men left their families and traveled on the railroad, fending for themselves to make it easier on those back home with one less mouth to feed. Many times they would ask if there was some work they could do, like cut firewood or spade the garden. Mom would always say no unless they insisted. I don't know how they knew to come to our house, but they always did. They would walk down the tracks to our street and come down the street, walking past all the other houses until they got to our place. Then they would come up our driveway to the back porch and knock on the door. Some folks said they had a code written on the bridge piling, but I've always thought that it was just by word-of-mouth.

* * *

Mutt had my lever action BB gun, and somehow he got his hand between the gun and the lever. While he was attempting to cock the gun, the lever slipped out of his hand and that spring-loaded lever came back and tried to close with his hand over the two curved prongs that stuck up to hold the lever. It drove those two prongs through his hand between his thumb and his first finger and he was fast to the gun as the curved prongs now held him instead of the cocking lever. He howled some, and finally jerked his hand free. We headed for home, and when we crossed the high railroad trestle over the river, he threatened to throw the gun in the river, but he didn't.

When my BB gun got a little age or use on it, it started to malfunction. It could have been the BBs, too, as they were not perfectly round. Anyway, they would stick in the barrel. I wouldn't know if I was out of ammo or not, so I would shoot again and again. Finally I would look and find I had lots of BBs in the spring-loaded magazine. I would have to take the gun home and tell Dad. He would fire up the blowtorch, and by heating the barrel, he would melt the BBs, and I could use it again. He would be unhappy with me if he found more than a few BBs stuck in the barrel. This started happening more frequently, and his heating up the barrel didn't improve the gun's accuracy either. About that time my cousin Don gave me a little Stevens "Little Scout" 22 caliber rifle. It was a single shot with a rolling block and no front sight. The front sight had been silver, soldered on, and when Dad started to chisel the solder out of the slot in the barrel, the solder curled up. Dad felt we should try that as a sight, and it worked just fine. I didn't need a BB gun anymore.

Ready to take my first BB gun camping

CAMPING

My first camping trip was when Chuck Gorman, who lived across the street, and I decided we would like to go camping. The folks said it would be okay, and both Mom and Dad had to get us the necessary equipment and provisions. For a tent, Dad came up with a canvas that had been painted with silver paint. He used it to cover fresh concrete sidewalks if it looked like rain. It was about 7' wide and 15' long. He told us to erect a ridge pole at the top, and put a bottom pole on top of the canvas at the back. We were to thread the canvas over the ridge pole with some hanging down in front. The roof would then be pulled out to the rear and held with the bottom pole. The rest of the canvas was the floor. Mom brought out an old quilt and blankets for our beds. This was in the 1940s before we had sleeping bags. Our spare shirts and our shoes would go into our spare pants, which would be rolled up to form a pillow. We would sleep in our clothes.

Mom gave us a cardboard box full of easy-to-prepare food – cheese and crackers, soup, beans and wieners, and buns, etc. We supplied our fishing gear, and I had my new Daisy model 42 pump action BB gun and my trusty Estwing hatchet. We were ready!

We wanted to row the boat up the river from Terrill Park to the mouth of Coffin's Creek and set up camp there. Dad said to be sure to locate our camp on high ground, and set it all up right away before we went fishing. He said to get the fire pit ready and wood gathered and make sure we cooked supper before it got dark.

Dad hauled it all to the park in the truck. We loaded the boat and off we went. There is not much current in the river, and I could stay out of that most of the time. When we got to the mouth of Coffin's Creek, we pulled into the creek and went as far as we could go. We tied up the boat, unloaded all our stuff, and went looking for a campsite. We chose a bare spot off to the south. It was on a little rise, so it was higher ground. There were no trees close, so we scrounged around to find dead trees or driftwood for our poles to hold up the canvas. We propped up and tied cross pieces and used a long, heavy

3" diameter tree with some of the bark still on it as our ridgepole. We laid the canvas on the ground for the floor, threw the end up over the ridgepole, and pulled it down a couple of feet. Then we pulled it out to form the roof and put logs along it in back to hold it in place. It looked good to us. It was sturdy and safe from the elements.

We put all our "stuff" under the "tent", prepared the fire pit, chopped and broke up driftwood for kindling and stacked it next to the pit. We had located the fire pit in front of the tent so heat would reflect off the canvas, but it was summer and that wasn't necessary. Also, the back of the tent was to the northwest to deflect the prevailing wind, but it was a nice day, so it was just precautionary.

By the time we had rowed up the river and erected our tent and had the fire pit ready, we were too tired to go fishing, so we just went ahead and built the fire and cooked our wieners and beans. We ate the crackers while we waited on the beans. By the time we were through eating, the sun was going down, so we let the dishes go until tomorrow and went to bed. We talked a while about our nice campsite, tent, etc. while the fire died out, and we went off to sleep.

During the night, a big thunderstorm moved in, and we had lots of lightning, heavy rain and very strong winds. Our tent blew down on top of us, and the ridgepole was right across my chest. It wasn't actually touching me, and the canvas was still over me, so I wasn't getting wet. I asked Chuck if he was all right, and he said he was, so we decided to just lay there until morning, as we knew we couldn't put the tent back up in the storm. We didn't get any sleep due to the thunder and lightning, and we were soon getting wet from below as water was on top of our canvas floor. I moved around as best I could to keep out of the wet spots. The big storm finally moved off, and in the morning, it was nice and clear.

We were up at first light, and everything was soaking wet. The cardboard food box and everything in it was wet and soggy. Our blankets, spare clothes – everything was soaked. Well, it didn't take us long to know we needed more food and blankets, so we decided to go home and get resupplied. We untied the boat and pulled it up on the bank and tipped it over to dump out all the rainwater. When we rowed out into the river, we were swept downstream fast, since the river had risen with all the rain, and I didn't have to row at all – just steer.

I had kept to the middle of the river and when we came to Terrill Park, I rowed hard for the bank, but we were swept on past. Downstream was the Marion Street dam, and we worried about being swept over the dam, but when we got close to the bank, we were able to grab tree branches and pull the boat to the tree and tie it off. We took off for home. When we got there, it was way before the folks would be getting up, but we woke them.

It turned out that Mom had been very worried about us in the big storm, and she wanted Dad to go rescue us. He wouldn't go as he said he did not know where we would be camped and couldn't find us in such a storm. He tried to convince her that we would be all right. She couldn't stand it and was so mad at him for not trying that she took my sister, Arlene, who was about 10 years older than me, and the two of them drove the car out in the storm to the Quaker Mill, which was upriver from where we were. They got out of the car and came down the river looking for us. They each had on a raincoat and were carrying a flashlight, but they were on the wrong side of the river. It was so dark and raining so hard that they couldn't see where they were going. They would stand in one place until the lightning flashed, and then they would go a little way and wait for the next flash of lightning to light the way. They were soon wet to the skin! They kept trying to yell to us, but the wind was blowing so hard it drowned out their yells. They finally realized it was futile to go on, since they were getting nowhere and not fast. When they turned around to go back, they had to wait for the lightning flashes to show them the way again. When they got home, they were very wet and tired, so it was no wonder they didn't want to get up early the next morning with our arrival, and we, of course, were safe.

After breakfast, it was decided that we should go back up to the campsite and rescue all our stuff and bring it back home, as it would take a long time to dry out the quilts and blankets. Also the river was high and muddy, so the fishing would be no good. We agreed. Chuck and I went back to the boat and found we had to wade to get to it. The river was so high it was out of its banks. We sat side by side on the center boat seat, each with an oar, as we tried to row upstream against the strong current. We just lost ground, and we landed farther downstream, retied the boat and went back home.

When Dad came home for lunch, we tried to convince him to help us rescue our stuff and his canvas, etc. He finally agreed, and got our outboard motor, and took us slowly upstream keeping out of the current as much as possible. When we got to Coffin's Creek, the whole area was flooded, and we motored right across the flooded land to a little spot which was our campsite. Dad was pleased that we had picked that spot. It was a little island now about twenty feet in diameter, but our stuff was high, if not dry. We salvaged what we could, and my new BB gun only had two little spots of rust on it. That first camping trip was short-lived, but a good learning experience, although harrowing for Mom who had let me go out on the river in a boat, even though I hadn't learned to swim.

* * *

My second camping trip was interesting, too. Chuck Martensen and I decided we wanted to camp for a week at the water gauge which was a small dam located a few miles below town. Dad hauled the boat and our gear down to Bailey's Ford, and we were to row the boat upstream to the water gauge. There were several big riffles below the water gauge, and we couldn't get the boat through them. It was just too much work, so we set up camp about a quarter mile below the dam. We had the same tarp for our tent, and after preparing camp, i.e. the tent put up and the fire pit dug and rocked and the kindling cut, we went fishing. We caught lots of stripe (yellow bass), and we decided to eat them for supper. By the time I had them cleaned, it was dark and we tried to cook them over an open fire, using a flashlight to see into the frying pan. It didn't work, but we ate the fish, and that night Chuck got sick. He was miserable most of the night, but he was okay by morning, and we didn't have to go home.

We fished every day, and one evening when I was standing at the edge of the river below a steep bank, a small, two-year-old beaver came swimming up the river right toward me. I flipped my fly line out toward him, and my Hildebrand flicker-spinner caught in his fur right behind his head. I was playing a beaver with my fly rod. He was working hard swimming against the current, and I was pulling him toward the bank. Since it was almost dark, and I was below the cut bank, he didn't see me until he was about 8 feet away. He immediately dove and went downriver fast, taking my spinner with him when my leader broke.

We caught lots of fish, and we wanted to take some home for the folks. Since we had no cooler or ice, the only way to keep them was to keep them alive. The bass and pan fish would all die, but we figured we could keep the catfish alive if we put them in gunnysacks in the water. We didn't have any sacks, so we walked to the closest farmhouse and asked the farmer if he would trade a mess of fish for two burlap bags. He was skeptical at first and wanted to know what was wrong with the fish. We told him "Nothing, and they are mostly still alive." When we told him why we wanted the bags, he agreed. We were able to keep the catfish alive in the sacks sunk in the bottom of the river with rocks inside the sacks with the fish.

* * *

On my third camping trip, Jimmy Klemp and I had Dad haul the boat all the way to the mouth of Turtle Creek which was way down the river. It was a good place to fish, and both Jimmy's Mom and Dad and my Dad had fished there several times with us from the bank. We always caught lots of crappies, so we felt we would eat fish all week. We rowed the boat across the river and set up our camp. It was very, very hot, and we couldn't catch a fish no matter how hard we tried. I had a little single shot 22 rifle my cousin Don had given me, and I shot a big carp that was sucking the top of the water. When we tried to clean him, he was hot and his flesh was soft and mushy. We didn't think it was fit to eat.

Since we didn't bring much to eat, we had to improvise. We went hunting and lived off the land. We had pancakes for breakfast every day. I had to cook them because Jimmy said he didn't like pancakes. He got over that as that was what we had. For supper we had squirrel or birds depending upon what we got on our hunting trips. We always managed to get something to cook, so we didn't starve.

When we ran out of drinking water, we rowed down the river to a group of cabins. There we asked a man, and he said we could have all the water we wanted. He had two daughters about our age, and they invited us to come back and go swimming with them as they had girlfriends coming down for a swimming party. We had to decline since we didn't have any swimming suits.

When Jimmy's Mom came down to fish and check up on us, we asked her to come back the next day and bring us some swimming suits. She did. She brought my Dad's swimming suit for me. My Mom had sewed up the crotch, and it had a belt so it pretty well fit me. She brought Jimmy his Dad's suit "as is," and the crotch hung way down, but he was covered in front.

We went back to the girls' cabin and joined a whole bunch of girls that were there swimming. They had a nice wooden pier that was about five feet above the water, and we were all jumping off the pier playing tag and chasing each other. I was standing at the end of the pier with my back to the water when one of the girls approached me. I did a turning dive, which impressed the girl's father who was our lifeguard. When I got to the ladder, I noticed most of the girls were in the water at the foot of the ladder but they weren't climbing up. When I looked up, I found out why. When Jimmy climbed the ladder with his Dad's suit hanging down, you could see all of Jimmy. I told him about it, and that night we used safety pins to pin up the crotch so he didn't show out.

We swam with them several days during the hottest part of the day, but we had to quit early so we could row back upstream to our camp and go hunting to see what we were going to eat for supper. One evening we were sitting on a log under a big tree. We were talking, and all of a sudden, a big fox squirrel fell out of the tree and landed right at our feet. The squirrel took two jumps and was back up the tree, and we couldn't see him for all of the leaves. We figured he must have fallen asleep listening to us talk and just fell out of the tree.

Oh, the good old days!

Alma and her "kits" (Arlene, Dale and me) during WWII

CENTRAL SCHOOL

Central School, as the name implies, was in the center of town, more or less. It took up a whole block. The building was in the middle of the block, and all around it was playground. It was a two-story building, and it faced south. There were two entrances on the south side and each was about a third of the way from the end of the building. Each entrance had concrete steps going up to an alcove where the doors were located. Inside the double doors there was a large wooden staircase that went halfway up to a landing and a turnaround, and then on up to the second floor. There was a big banister on this staircase, and on two occasions I got to slide down this banister, legally. I was always getting hurt, and when in a cast with a broken arm, etc. sometimes the teacher would take pity on me if I wimped around enough.

Grades 1 through 6 were on the west side of the building, and grades 7 and 8 were on the east side. On the west side, each of the grades had a classroom by itself. In Junior High, grades 7 and 8, each grade moved from room to room to get to the next class. It made the day go much faster when you got to get up and move to your next class.

There was a big tube fire escape on the north side, but it wasn't used when I went to this school, as it was in disrepair. The tube had come apart about a third of the way down from the top, and there was a gap about an inch wide in the bottom of the pipe. We used to climb up inside the tube or pipe and slide down out of it while we were playing on the school grounds on the weekends, when no one was around. If you climbed all the way to the top and didn't take evasive action when you reached the gap, you would tear the bottom out of your pants and maybe lose some skin too. If you weren't going too fast, you could slap your hands on each side of you and hump your rear end up and over the gap and save your britches.

Grades 1 through 6 had recess, my favorite thing, and we usually played speedball if it hadn't rained and the playground wasn't muddy. We played with a red rubber ball about 8 inches in diameter, and it was a little like soccer. When recess was over, they would ring a bell, and everyone would line up at the entrance in front of the steps. When the bell rang again, you marched into the school. One day I was in line about in the middle, and Sonny Barker, my neighbor and friend, was at the back end of the line. He saw the teacher wasn't looking so he sneaked up and pushed me out of line. When I looked back, he was standing in my place. Well, he was smaller than I was, so I wasn't about to settle for that. I walked over and pushed him out of line and took my place back.

The problem was, the teacher, Miss Schepker, was looking and she saw me push Barker. She came over to me and grabbed my by the arm and pulled me out of line and proceeded to tell me what a bad boy I was and didn't I know any better, etc. etc. I was yelling at her that he had done it to me first, but she wasn't listening. After some time, I wasn't getting anywhere, so I announced to her that I was going home. She said, "No, you're not", and I said, "Yes, I am", and I started walking towards home. After the first two steps, my feet came off the ground as she had a hold of me. I kept announcing that I was going home, but she was holding me back, so I punched her right in the belly with my loose arm. She let go, and I took off for home. There were two gas stations on Main Street that I had to pass. I knew the men there realized that I was supposed to be in school and were wondering what had happened. The closer I got to home the slower I dragged my feet, as I now was going to have to tell my mother what had happened and that I had hit a teacher. I was in deep trouble for sure. Mom saw me coming up the front walk, and she asked me what I was doing home. I told her the whole story, and I was about to cry when I got to the part where I had hit the teacher. Mom told me that Miss Schepker had called her, saying and that she now knew what had happened. She wished that I would forgive her for not listening to me, and she wanted me to come back to school. I didn't want to go, as I was embarrassed and ashamed for having hit a teacher, but Mom finally convinced me to go back. I dragged my feet going in that direction, too.

* * *

In about third or fourth grade we had a math test. I was pretty good at math, but this time the teacher put the problems on the blackboard behind her desk. I could see her standing up there, but I didn't know what she was doing. When she picked up the papers mine was blank. She sent a note home with me, and at supper that night, Mom read it to Dad. It said that George might have trouble seeing. There was a large Farmers and Merchants Bank calendar on the wall above the kitchen table. Mom had me look at it and spell Farmers. I said F A R M E R S, and then she asked me to spell Merchants. I started out okay, but then I took my eyes off the calendar, as I looked skyward to try to remember how to spell Merchants. She then wanted to know what day or the week the 25th was on. Since I couldn't see the numbers, I was lost. I ended up in Dr. Wayne Hall's office. He was the optometrist, and he ordered me some glasses. When I got them, I was amazed. When Mom and I went down the enclosed stairs and got to the landing and through the door to the outside world, I immediately was seeing signs everywhere, advertising everything. I had never seen them before, and I said to Mom, "Can everybody see this good?" When I would go to the movies with the kids, we always sat in the front row, but now I could see words and people on the screen, whereas, before glasses, there was just a smoky screen with no shapes at all.

My cousins Lee and Allyn and I with the machine gun my Dad had built.

Another time I went home unhappy wasn't due to a teacher. I had a toothache, and Mom had made me an appointment with the dentist. Dr. Goen's office was a block north of Main Street on Brewer Street, so it was not very far from Central School. I left school for the appointment, and that is where the story began. Dr. Goen found the right tooth, and he gave me a shot to deaden the pain. He waited a few minutes for it to take affect. When he touched the tooth again, I yelled, so he gave me another shot and waited some more. When I yelled the next time, he knew we had a problem. He prepared to pull the wisdom tooth that he knew was impacted. He also knew that it was going to hurt me. Since it had four roots, it was not going to let go easily either. Anyway, he climbed up on the dental chair with his knee between my legs and his hand on my forehead. With the grimmest expression on his face, he proceeded to jerk this way and that way until it finally came out. By that time, I had yelled my head off and was mad all the way through. He had scared me and hurt me, and I wanted to get out of there at once. He showed me the infected sack that was in between the roots of the tooth, but that didn't mean anything to me. He wouldn't let me leave for a few minutes until I settled down, and he could see I was all right. When I got home, I told Mom all about it, and after I was through she said that Dr. Goen had called her and explained how bad an extraction it had been, due to the infection and the Novocain not taking effect. Nevertheless, I didn't like him for a long time. He had a nice daughter in my class, though.

* * *

When in 7th and 8th grades, we got to go to the High School gymnasium for physical education. I disliked that very much as all they ever did was play basketball. The teacher/coach would pick two teams, and they would scrimmage while the rest of us sat in the bleachers. I was always a sitter. I have a diary that my sister gave me, and it is full of entries "darn coach" meaning that I had spent all P.E. on the bench.

* * *

I was in 7th grade when my brother Dale flew over the town in a Bell Air-Cobra, P-39 pursuit airplane. The plane had a big belly gas tank underneath it, so he couldn't turn very short. He had to go way out in the country to get turned around and fly over again. He was supposed to fly over the day before, but the weather wasn't cooperative, so he came a day late. He was in the Air Force Ferrying Command and was delivering this plane from one end of the country to the other. Anyway, the teacher let me go out on the fire escape to watch, and all the other classmates got to stand at the windows. I only saw the tip of one wing go over the schoolhouse, but I knew it was him. Dad was in the coffee shop downtown, and it was cold out. He would hear the roar of the plane's engine as it went by, and he would go outside and stand around. When Dale didn't come back, Dad would go back inside. That happened several times, and each time Dad felt that was the last time, so he would go back inside. He never did see the plane. Mom was downtown, too, but she did see it each time.

*　*　*

Ted Ortberg and Ted Crawford, two eighth graders, were teasing Billy Snyder out behind the school building near the furnace where no one could see them. Billy was in a bad way, and I stepped in to stop it. I told the two Teds to pick on someone else, so they thought I would do. I was taller than Ortberg, but Crawford was a big boy, much bigger and heavier than I was, and I was scared. My knees were shaking, and I looked down to see if it was showing, but thankfully my pants were roomy enough to cover it up. I stood them off long enough for Billy to escape. We didn't get into a fight, for if they had beaten me up, they would catch it from the teachers.

*　*　*

Brother Dale sent me some firecrackers from China, so I took two of them to school to show them off. Right away Barker wanted one but I wouldn't give him any. He finally said, "Would you give me one if I set it off in class?" Well, sure, so I gave him one, and he put it in his pocket. After the first class, we got up and went out in the hall for the next class. I wanted it back, and he said "No, wait, I'll do it in the next class." This went on again for the next class and I let him keep it for the third class. A substitute teacher was teaching that class, and we were learning about transportation, such as trains, trucks and boats. Barker raised his hand and asked the teacher if she would like to hear the sound a big flat-bottomed barge made when it hit the water. She said "Can you make such a sound?" and he said he could, so she agreed to let him. He told her to turn around. She swiveled her chair around so she was facing the blackboard. He got up, went to the radiator, pulled out the firecracker and put it on top of the radiator. The girls all drew in their breath as he calmly lit a match and applied it to the end of the fuse of the firecracker. The fuse lit, but promptly went out from being in and out of so many pockets; most of the powder had fallen out of the fuse. He lit another match and BANG! It went off. The teacher whirled around in her chair, reached into her desk drawer and got out the paddle. The two of them went out in the hall, and we all counted the 8 swats he got while bending over and holding his ankles. They came back into the classroom, and she sat down at her desk. Sonny stood beside his desk as he didn't want to sit down, and she didn't insist that he did. We didn't get much done in that class. We were all looking at either the teacher or at Barker standing beside his desk.

* * *

One nice, warm day in the winter the teacher let us go outside. The snow had melted next to the building on the south side. The girls were standing in that spot while the boys were all lined up on the sidewalk that had been shoveled off and was dry. Now, you weren't allowed to throw snowballs on the school grounds but some of the girls started to make snowballs and throw them at us boys. No problem, we thought. We could easily duck the snowballs and not get hit. We were waiting for the girls to get caught throwing them. The girls got tired of us ducking, and they ganged up, all of them throwing at one boy, making it impossible for him to duck them all. The boys took issue and began throwing snowballs back. In the heat of the battle, the teacher looked out the window and caught us. She could see all the boys out at the sidewalk, but she couldn't see all the girls. When the teacher got us all back in the classroom, she said that all the students who were throwing snowballs were to come to the front of the room. We got up and lined up across the front. There were both boys and girls. One girl, Flora Mae Ausmus, didn't come up, and she had been an instigator from the beginning. The teacher asked if that was all and I said, "How about it, Flora Mae? Don't you want to come up and join us?" She looked at me with her most innocent look, and said, "Who, me?" I told her I thought she should join us, and to this day, she has never forgiven me. At a class reunion, I asked her if she remembered it, and she huffed and walked away. I guess we are still not friends.

After eighth grade, if you passed, you left Central School and went to Manchester High School and another adventure started.

CHRIS WENGER

Every boy should have an old man to take him fishin'. I had two grandfathers, but all the time I knew them, they were always working. One was a farmer and the other a carpenter, and I never went anywhere with either one of them - just us, that is. However, across the street and down one house lived Mr. Chris Wenger, an old man that went fishing a lot. One day he asked if I could go along, and when my mother said it was okay, we started a very fine friendship.

He fished up at Coffin's Creek most of the time, and we had to walk to get to the stream as it ran back behind the farms and rarely crossed the road. I was too young to actually fish, but I helped by catching the bait. There was a low area near the creek that always had frogs in it, and Chris would have me catch him some frogs. I would sneak up and try to grab them, and they would hop away. Chris would give me lots of encouragement by saying "Git him, Porgie, git him, Porgie". When I was little, everyone called me Porgie after the poem, "Georgie Porgie puddin'n pie", since my first name was George. I was named after my grandfather on my father's side. His name was George Washington Hansel, as he was born on the 4th of July. Later, when I was older, they just called me "Porge".

Anyway I would catch him some frogs, and he would put them in the minnow bucket he carried, and we would go to the creek. He had a favorite fishing hole that was a secret, but I don't think anyone else would fish it anyway, as it was hard to get to. It was a spot along the creek that was full of small trees all growing close together. It was maybe 30 or 40 feet along the bank, and since the trees grew right up to the bank, it was always shady there. It was wet underfoot too, and Chris wore rubber knee boots so he wouldn't get his feet wet. He always told me to stay back away from the bank so I wouldn't fall in, but I figured it was so I wouldn't make any noise and scare the fish away. I just naturally made noise at that age. Chris would sneak through those trees with his fish pole in front of him, and he would lower one of my caught frogs into the water, and in just a minute or so there would be a nice two-pound smallmouth bass flopping on the bank. He couldn't let 'em fight much as they would get snagged up in the brush. He caught a lot of bass in that area. He also caught crappie on the minnows he brought along, but he said he would rather catch the bass on the frogs I got for him.

One day when we were heading back to the creek, we came to a barbed wire fence that had some sheep's wool caught and wrapped up around a barb. Chris told me to see if I could get some of that wool off the fence as he felt he could catch a fish with it. I said, "Sure", and reached for the wool and suddenly pulled my fingers back, as I felt a sting, and I thought I had touched the sharp barb. He said, "Git it for me, Porgie" so I tried again more carefully. Again, I felt a sharp pain go up my arm and that time I knew I didn't touch the barb! I looked puzzled at Chris, and he was doubled up laughing. He said it was an electric fence, and it had shocked me. I didn't understand what he was talking about, but I learned nevertheless. He didn't catch any fish on the sheep's wool either, as it stayed on that fence.

In the spring Chris would bring home big white suckers, a fish most other people threw away, as they were full of little hair like bones. Chris would cook them and then put the meat through a grinder, little bones and all. He would add pickles and mayonnaise and spread it on bread and make wonderful sandwiches that he would share with us.

Mr. Wenger was a wonderful man to me just when I needed him. As far as I knew, no one ever called him anything but Chris. I never got to tell him how much I enjoyed those fishing trips he took me on, but I think he knew.

HALLOWEEN TRICKS AND TREATS

Halloween has changed over the years. At the turn of the century and during the depression, no one had money to waste, so no one bought candy to hand out to trick or treaters. No one ever "rolled" a tree, as toilet paper was the catalog in the outhouse. No one threw eggs at a house either, as what you didn't eat was a cash crop. Soaping windows got popular later when people quit making their own soap.

However, everyone looked forward to Halloween to see what mischief the kids would get into. That's right, Halloween meant Mischief! The young folks were sure to do something on Halloween night unless their folks were ultra strict, and kept them in.

My Dad told me that when he was a boy, one Halloween night he and his brothers and some neighbor kids, completely disassembled a buggy wagon that was in a garage, and reassembled it up on the roof of the garage. Of course, the owner had to reverse the process to get the wagon down. Dad said no one ever broke anything or did anything maliciously, and that was the intent. You had to come up with some trickery that didn't hurt anyone, but was fun. It might take work to do and to undo, but people were used to work. It was like a practical joke. Everyone liked it, as long as no one got hurt.

One of the things that always happened on Halloween night was tipping over outhouses. Everyone had an outhouse, and they were built very sturdy as you knew, come Halloween night, it would be lying on its side. Also it had to be built light enough to move. When the hole under the house got almost full, you dug a new hole and moved the outhouse over it.

* * *

When I was a boy in the late 30's and early 40's, we went trick or treating a little, but we didn't have masks and costumes, so you had to go where the people didn't know you. We once went to the house east of Munson's, and an elderly couple came to the door and invited us all in. They gave us big old sugar cookies out of a cookie jar that hadn't been opened for ages, but that was all they had. We were all embarrassed. We were in their home where we didn't belong, and they wished that they had something better to give us. Some of the guys went under the big bridle wreath bushes on either side of their front door, and soaped their windows, but I made them scrape off the soap with our razor blades, as the folks had given us what they had.

* * *

One Halloween night, we were sitting on the bank next to the railroad tracks across from the Renfrows' place, and we were trying to come up with some devilment for us to do. Chuck Gorman said he had heard of a really neat trick that we might try. What you did was defecate in a paper sack and put it on someone's front porch. You then set the top of the sack on fire, rang the doorbell, and ran. The man would come to the door, see the burning sack, and immediately come out and stomp out the fire. It sounded wonderful. All we needed was the where-with-all and the victim.

Well, we had a man in our neighborhood that didn't like us. He had a big yard with three huge pine trees that were absolutely perfect to play "hide and go seek" in. You could just run into those big pine branches that came all the way to the ground, and the tree would just swallow you. But we didn't get to play there. The man had two daughters that never played with us, and they went to the Catholic school, so we rarely saw them, and then only at a distance. One day, Sonny Barker, told me that the oldest daughter was his girlfriend, and he was going to see her naked! I said, "Bulls—t", and he proceeded to tell me how it was all going to come about. It seemed their bathroom window was near a corner of their house, and a downspout came down right close to it. He said when he saw the light on in the bathroom, he was going to climb up the downspout and look in the window, which was always open a few inches for ventilation. Anyway, he hadn't seen her naked yet, but it was just a matter of time until she took a bath.

Well, we walked over that way to check it out, and wouldn't you know, the light came on in the bathroom. Sonny took off running as fast as he could go, and I was right behind him. He quickly climbed up the downspout by holding onto the pipe and putting one tennis shoe on each side of it, and up he went. When he looked in the window, he turned his head to look down at me, and with his mouth right close to the open window, he whispered, "It's her old lady". There was a scream from the bathroom, the light came on at the back door. He jumped down and we both went running for the pine trees. No one came out while we were hid in the pine trees, and I gave him the devil for almost getting us caught. It turned out he had tried it before, and they were on to him.

Needless to say, that man was our victim. Gorman went home to get a sack, and I went to get the matches. Sonny, who lived too far away to get anything, was elected to do his duty in the sack. When all was ready, we slipped up to the screened front porch and I carefully opened it by holding the spring away from the door so it wouldn't make any noise. Barker went up on the porch, set the sack down, lit it on fire, rang the doorbell, and we all ran into the pine trees. The man came to the door and opened it, saw the burning sack, and he calmly opened the screen door, put his foot behind the sack, and scooted it right off the porch and out into the yard. Then he went back into the house and closed the door.

We didn't know what to think. What went wrong? Didn't we do it right? We finally figured out that the man had heard of the trick before, and knew just what to do. We felt the man had gotten the best of us somehow, and we wanted to get even. I had a skinned woodchuck hide at home that still had fat on it, and it smelled. I went home and got it, and Barker and I stitched it to the man's screen door with wire. It wasn't much, but it was the best we could think of at the time.

We went back to sitting on the bank by the railroad tracks, trying to think of something else we could do. Finally, Gorman said that tipping over outhouses used to be what everyone did. Well, everyone in our neighborhood was on sanitary sewer, but one house, the O'Dells. They still utilized an outhouse that was located on a vacant lot, next to their house.

We gathered up all the kids that were out and headed for the O'Dells. There was Chuck Gorman, the oldest and biggest, Sonny Barker and I, who were the same age, a year behind Gorman, and assorted younger kids, the Renfrows, etc. We went down the street until we got to Chuck Gorman's house, and we cut through to the back lot line, and crossed the fence and went down the cornfield until we got to the O'Dells. We didn't want anyone seeing us, so we had to approach from the rear of the property, the cornfield, where it was dark. It was so dark we could hardly find the outhouse, but we managed by using the streetlights to silhouette it. We helped the younger kids over the fence, and made a stealthy approach on the house. When we got up to the outhouse, we were amazed at the size of it. It was huge. We started to push on it and when it didn't move, we complained to each other. There came a yell, "Hey," from inside the outhouse. We all ran back toward the corn, and not having enough time to get over the fence, we all laid down in the grass. Mr. O'Dell came out of the outhouse, fixing the suspenders of his overalls up over his shoulders, and he went on into his house. We stayed lying down for a while, thinking he was probably looking out a window at us, until we realized he couldn't see us.

We sneaked back up to the outhouse and Gorman, Barker and I, got on one side and pushed. Nothing happened. It was like pushing on a brick wall. We talked it over and said if we dug our feet in, it might help to give us some purchase. We kicked divots out of the grass and gave it one last try with all three of us pushing together. Would you believe it just barely moved? But it had moved! We now pushed again with renewed vigor, and it slowly started to come up, but as the outhouse moved away from us, our arms were too short to keep pushing. Chuck reached down and got hold of the bottom of the house, and we asked him if he could hold it. He didn't know, but we said if he could, Barker and I would run around and jump up and grab hold of the roof to pull it over. Chuck held it and together Barker and I jumped up, and caught hold of the roof. It did the trick. The outhouse slowly came on over and Barker and I jumped clear. As the outhouse hit with a crash, we all ran for the street.

However, Chuck, who had hold of the sill and was lifting mightily, was pulled out over the hole as the outhouse went over, and he fell in. He landed on his hands and knees, and was about five feet below ground level. We heard him yelling to get him out of there. We ran back, and he raised up his hand for us to pull him out, but no one offered! We went looking for a hoe or a rake or something that had a handle on it, to help pull him out. He managed to climb out while we were looking, and he was trying to clean himself up when we got back.

Chuck decided he wanted to go home, and he started up the sidewalk on one side of the street, and we all crossed the street and went up the other side. It seemed no one wanted to be near him, and we all went home, as we had lost our appetite for outhouses and Halloween. The next morning before school, I ran up to the Renfrows and looked to see if the hide was still on the screen door across the street, but it was gone. Then I ran the other direction to the O'Dells, and there stood the outhouse as if nothing had ever touched it. All of our good work was for nothing, it seemed.

HOW I LEARNED TO SWIM

We lived 2 ½ blocks from the Maquoketa River, and from an early age, I "ran the river". The Marion Street dam was one of my favorite places, as it was good fishing, and I could jump from rock to rock or wade the rapids and fish many different places all the way across the river. There were some deep holes, but I never thought of falling in.

When I was about eleven years old I was trapping muskrats in the backwater of the dam. That area was on the other side of town. I lived on the south side and the backwater was on the northwest side. I would ride my bicycle and tend my traps before and after school. The most important time was early in the morning as the "rats" were active at night and it was important to get there early so they couldn't get away if they had not drowned. I would ride my bike to Terrill Park, get in our wooden rowboat and row across the river and out among the islands where I had set my traps. One day, I was late and Mom said she would drive me in the car and wait for me and then drive me to school, as there wasn't time for me to do anything else. Of course it was pitch dark, way before dawn, when she let me out at the park. I got in the boat and rowed out across the fog covered river and Mom stood there listening to the creak, splash of the oars as the sound got dimmer and dimmer the farther away I got. She started to worry and was listening real hard hoping to hear something that would signal to her that I was all right. It just so happened that a beaver came swimming along right where Mom was standing and when the beaver saw her move, he slapped his tail on the water and it scared her half to death.

She didn't say much when I got back as we were running out of time. I put my boots and rats in the trunk, put on my shoes and she dropped me off at school. That night at the supper table, she unloaded on Dad and me. She told of me rowing out onto the dark, foggy river and the beaver etc. and she put her foot down and said, "If that boy is going to 'run the river', he is going to have to learn to swim. It made good sense except right then was not the time to learn. We didn't have a swimming pool in town and it was November and the water in the river was too cold. So I promised to be careful until next spring when Dad agreed he would teach me to swim.

There wasn't a good swimming hole around, but when the weather warmed up in the spring, Dad took me to the Mill Pond above the Quaker Mill north of town. There was a cul-de-sac at the end of a gravel road that stopped overlooking the water. It was just south of a little development called Sunset Beach. We had cut off jeans or some such outfits that Mom had fixed for us to swim in. We climbed down the steep bank and waded out in the water to about waist deep. Dad then went out a little farther and he swam past me doing what he said was the Australian crawl. He then came back to me and said I should try it. He had me lay out on the water while he held me by the waist. He told me to kick my feet and when I had them going good, he told me to make my arms go. When he felt that I was making the right motions, he let go of me and I immediately sank right to the bottom. I came up sputtering and wiping the water off my face with my hands. I hadn't expected to get dunked. He smiled and said I should try the sidestroke. He swam by me doing the sidestroke and then he held me like he did before, while I got my feet and arms going doing the sidestroke. When he let go, I sank right to the bottom again and came up gasping and unhappy. He then told me about the dog paddle. You kick your feet like before, but you cup your hands and make them go in a circle under your chin. He showed me and then he held me by the waist as I tried it. Again, when he let go, I sank right to the bottom. Well - that was it. He told me to practice until I could swim. We got out of the water, to my delight, and went home.

I don't remember ever practicing, but later that summer, a bunch of us boys were wading down the river carrying rocks to throw at any fish that we might drive out of hiding in front of us. It was very hot and when we came to a drop off, I jumped right in. To everyone's surprise it was deep, over my head. I came up dog paddling but I couldn't get back to where the boys were standing as I was going against the current. My buddy Barker yelled, "Hansel, you can't swim". I finally realized that I was fighting the current, so I turned sideways and headed for the bank. An older boy, who could swim, jumped in and tried to come to my aide, but I made it to the bank ahead of him. I could swim and I hadn't known it. Wheeeoooow!

    I was tall and skinny and I couldn't float. When I got married and told my wife I couldn't float, she scoffed at me and said everyone could float. She told me about the egg float where you pull your legs up and hold them with your arms while you put your head under the water and you are supposed to float with your back just at the water surface. I told her it wouldn't work for me but she wouldn't believe me. We went to a swimming pool and I showed her. I got in the pool and went through the motions to do the egg float. I let out my air and sank right to the bottom. I stretched out on the bottom and with my head propped up on my hand and elbow I waved to her with the other hand as she was sitting on the edge of the pool. She believed me then, even though she didn't want to. I told her I didn't have any fat on me and that it was fat that made you float. She said my problem might be lead in my britches or a thick head etc. etc

BELT KNIVES AND TREBLE HOOKS

My dad was a carpenter and he always carried two pocketknives. One was average size and was a general-purpose knife with three blades. The other was a little thing with pearl handles and a thin pointed blade. It was his "sliver getter." He would have a sliver that he couldn't see, and he would merely cut a plug out of his calloused hand in the vicinity of the sliver, and all was fine.

I made the mistake once of telling him that I had a sliver I couldn't see, so he tried the same treatment on me, but I didn't have any calluses. Blood spurted, I yelled, and he apologized, but he was never allowed to come near any of my slivers again - I kept them to myself.

* * *

I started hunting and trapping in grade school, and Dad got tired of skinning my game, so he showed me how. He gave me a pocketknife and I've always had one in my pocket ever since, all through high school, etc. Everyone knew I had it, and no one cared, but times were different then. The teachers or janitor would even ask to use it, since it was always sharp – ready to skin muskrats or whatever.

Well, a belt knife was something else. I had several, and lost them all. One was brand new with a leather handle that I took to my uncle's farm near Jesup, Iowa. I was lying on my back with my hands crossed above my head on the back of one of the two big draft horses, as my cousin Don plowed corn. The hunting knife fell out of its sheath. I walked the cornrows for two days trying to find it, but it was apparently plowed under.

Another one was accidentally kicked into the river as I sat fishing on a narrow concrete wall below the dam in my hometown of Manchester, Iowa. My buddy, Mutt McCusker, tried to go around me and kicked it into the water. It was deep right along the wall due to the cut in the rocks for the footing, and the knife was never found, even though I tied half a dozen telephone magnets together on a long pole and lowered them into the water where I had marked the spot on the wall.

Mom took one hunting knife away when she looked out the kitchen window and saw me making like an Indian, crawling across the yard with the knife in my teeth as I sneaked up on a young blue jay. All of my hunting knives were new because I never had one long enough for it to get old.

One time Willard Hawker and I were fishing in the river below town, and I had a trot line out. It probably had ten or twelve hooks on it, and on the end was a brick for the weight. The bank end was tied to the brush, and I would whirl the brick around in a circle and throw the line out into the river.

The end hook nearest the brick happened to be a treble hook, and I had baited it with angleworms from the garden. I whirled the brick around, and when it was going good, I flung it out toward the center of the river, but it never made it. One of the treble hooks caught in my right hand index finger, and that brick jerked the hook clear through the finger until the point was sticking out through the nail. Now, I howled some, let me tell you, but I finally calmed down enough to ask Hawker to cut the line with my belt knife. He obliged me by pulling on the line and sawing away with that dull knife. He finally got it cut off, but I didn't know when, because I had passed out.

I made it home with hook and line, and Mom took me to the doctor. By then it didn't hurt much, but the doctor took care of that. He calmly took a pair of pliers and proceeded to jerk the hook on through the nail before I knew what he was up to. I started yelling all over again, but he cut off the barb and backed the hook out and gave me the now two-pronged hook with the worm still wiggling on it. I dried my tears and stashed that hook behind the wooden steps to the south porch of our house at 413 S. Brewer Street. I checked it a couple of times in later years, and it was always there with the dried up worm on it, too.

* * *

Then there was the time my wife, Shirley, and I were fishing for muskies on a lake in northern Wisconsin. We were in a canoe on a flowage filled with stumps and downed trees. I was throwing a jointed pikie minnow, one of those big plugs with big treble hooks, and I had cast out over a couple of logs. As I was cranking the lure in, I jerked my rod tip to make the plug jump the logs. It did, but I had jerked too hard, and here came that pikie right at me. I ducked and that big plug landed on my back, with one treble hook in my scalp and the others in my jacket.

I was held fast. I could not straighten up or move in anyway without moving those hooks. Shirley, in the front seat, had to paddle us to the bank, get out of the canoe and wade back to me to try to help me out of my predicament. It turned out that the hooks were so big, my skull stopped one before it went in past the barb, and she could just pick the hook out once she bunched up the jacket to get some slack. Wheeeyouuu! That was close.

MINKS AND MUSKRATS

Years ago, before I was born, my Dad had a trap line on the backwater of the Marion Street Dam in Manchester, Iowa, and he had set a trap in a hole near the edge of the bank. When he came along, he found the trap was pulled into the hole as far as it could go. Not knowing how well the animal was caught, he tried to distract it by pushing a willow switch down into the hole so he could pull him out. As he slowly was able to pull the trap out, he found that his trap did not have the animal at all, but it had caught the ring at the end of someone else's trap! That trap and the animal were still down in the hole. He kept poking with the stick and pulling, and he finally brought out a big mink. He was very pleased as we saw few mink in the backwater, and they were worth a lot of money.

Not wanting to damage the pelt, he decided to give the mink a "heartburn" to kill it, as he often did muskrats. He tapped the animal on the end of the nose with a stick, grabbed it around the neck with one hand and attempted to dislodge its heart with the thumb of the other hand. The mink, being very agile, promptly bit him on one wrist, and when he let go with that hand, it bit him on the other wrist. Dad dropped the mink, which jumped into the water and dove out of sight. Dad was heartbroken, but the mink was still dizzy from the tap on the nose, and it came up and swam around in circles until Dad was able to collect it with his gun. Wheeyou! That was close.

* * *

Dad also did something that was strange and dangerous while trapping. He would, when the situation presented itself, catch muskrats alive in his bare hands. If a muskrat was swimming toward a run that led to its hole in the bank, and Dad could get there first, he would run up, stick his hand in the run with his thumb and first finger pointing toward the bank. When the muskrat touched his hand, he would grab it and hold it by the neck. He never got bitten that I know of - but I did!

I was trapping up on the backwater and was riding my bicycle every morning to tend my traps, as we were still living on South Brewer Street. The backwater was northwest of town, and we lived southeast. Anyway, I had waded out to a muskrat rest station that was built up in a cluster of trees out in the water. I had opened up the south side and had set a trap inside and closed up the hole I had made. When I came along the next morning, I waded out and opened the hole up, but I couldn't find the trap. I stuck my hand and arm way in, and felt a snap. I thought the trap had caught my hand, so I quickly pulled it out. There was a cut on my right hand index finger. It was deep and I could see that little white bone in there, but there was no blood. My hands were so cold, the blood wasn't flowing. I climbed up into the trees and there, sitting outside, sat a muskrat in my trap. When he had seen my hand approaching, he just gave it a big bite.

I rode my bicycle all the way home with three muskrat tails in each hand, and that finger stuck up in the air like your pinkie when you are drinking tea. When I came into the warm kitchen, I told Mom what had happened, and I passed out. When I came to, Newell Tinkey, my sister's boyfriend, had bandaged my finger, so I gathered up my muskrats from off the kitchen floor and started down the basement stairs. I got halfway down, passed out again, and fell to the bottom of the steps. Mom came to the top of the stairs and shouted down at me, "You pass out again, and I'll cut your ears off!" Yeah, she did. I just said "I didn't mean to".

MUTT

I want to tell you about a grade school friend of mine named Mutt McCusker. He was a mighty good friend, and he would do anything for you, even though he had nothing. He was raised by his grandparents, and his granddad was a retired carpenter. When his grandma did the laundry, all the clothes I ever saw on the clothesline were overalls.

They lived in a little house on an alley between Tama and Madison Streets, south of the railroad tracks in my hometown of Manchester, Iowa. Goodman's Junk Yard was on the west side of the street below the tracks and Mutt used to hang around there a lot. It was an interesting place, but I was always afraid to go there.

Well, Mutt, whose real name was Junior, was always dressed in one garment in summer, a pair of overalls. He had no socks, no shoes, no shirt and no underwear. His overalls belonged to his grandfather, and they were, of course, too big. His Grandma had shortened the suspenders by sewing them up, and the overalls had been washed so many times the buttons were gone from the sides. When you walked down the street with Mutt, he was just rattling around inside those overalls since they were so big on him. The overalls were stiff, and if Mutt was walking in the front of them, there was a lot of room behind him. If he was walking in the back of them and you were beside him, and looked in the side slits, you could see all of Mutt.

* * *

One day we were walking down along the side of the Dry Run, a wet weather stream that drained the east side of town. Chuck Renfrow, my cousin, was in the Dry Run, which was dry, when he came to a hole that was filled with water. The water didn't look very deep as it was very clear water. Anyway, Chuck stepped off into the hole, and he went in over his head. Mutt and I were up on the bank looking down at Chuck in that clear water. He looked so funny. His hair was floating out away from his head, and his arms were flaying out from his sides like he was trying to hit something. We stood there a moment as we had never seen anything like that. The next think I knew, Mutt jumped off the bank, and reaching out, he grabbed Chuck and pulled him in. Oh, yeah! He was drowning. It all happened so fast Chuck hadn't had time to swallow much water, but Mutt sure came to a lot faster than I did.

* * *

We were all out in Bank's field playing one day, and two or three of us had bows and arrows. My Dad had made my bow for me, out of an old hickory fence post that was underneath Grandpa's bench at the shop. He had soaked the bow in our cistern and had bent it around a frame he made, to give the bow a curve. I had made the arrows by ripping 3/8th inch strips off a board and using an old wooden ¼ round molding plane to run over each edge to make them mostly round. I had an old Eversharp pencil point on the end of the arrow for the point, but the arrow had no feathers.

We would sneak up on the green clumps of grass in the pasture and shoot into them in the hopes a rabbit would be sitting in there. The green clumps were there, of course, because the cows had been there first and had made a deposit that fertilized that spot. Anyway, we would shoot and try to hit the clump. One day, we tried that and three pheasants took off. I pulled up my bow and shot at the rooster. The arrow went out ahead of him, and way up over him and then it turned over. As it came down, it hit the pheasant right in the back of the head. We took off over there where the pheasant had fallen, but he was just stunned. Mutt ran him down and whacked him with his bow. We were some surprised, and I was proud to have hit him. I decided to take him home to show Dad, and I wanted all the kids to come with me to testify, as I knew Dad would be skeptical of such a feat.

Since it wasn't pheasant season, we couldn't go around carrying a pheasant, so I skinned him, and Mutt said he would carry him. He put the bloody pheasant inside his britches and carried it behind the bib of his overalls with his arms crossed across his chest to hold him there. When we got to my house, Dad hadn't gotten home from work yet, so we all stood around until he drove in. When he got out of the truck, I blurted out that I had shot a rooster pheasant on the fly with a bow and arrow. Dad said, "Yeah?" and all the kids said, "Yeah!" Dad said "Where is he?" and Mutt said, "Right here." When Mutt went to pull the skinned bird out of his pants, his eyes got about as big a saucers since the blood had dried, and the pheasant was stuck to his skin. Mutt kept pulling, and with a tearing sound, the bird came loose. It left a bloody imprint on Mutt's chest that he had trouble washing off at the pump, without losing his pants.

* * *

We fished a lot in the river which was only a block from Mutt's house, and two and a half blocks from mine. Under the railroad bridge was a big sewer pipe that dumped all the sewage from the town into the river. We had no sewage treatment plant at the time. Big carp were always sucking the foam that floated on top of the water there, and we were always trying to catch them. One of us would crawl out onto the end of the pipe and try to drop a hook baited with a worm into a carp's mouth. One day I was out on the pipe and the carp were close to the bank, so Mutt tried to reach out from the bank with his pole. Kersplash! He went right into the water as he had stepped on hardened foam that had been colored black like dirt from the train's coal smoke. Now he was waist deep in sewage, and he wasn't happy.

* * *

The railroad tracks crossed the river on a high steel bridge, and Mutt and I used to climb out on the bridge, underneath on the steel braces, and fish off the pier in the center of the river. It was tricky, but we didn't have enough line to reach the water from the top of the bridge. We saw men who would fish off the bridge, and every now and then, they would reel a catfish all the way to the top of the bridge.

One day Mutt and I were coming across the bridge after being down in the woods below the tracks, and a train caught us. We tried to run to the end of the bridge, but the train was coming too fast. We had to come up with another alternative. It was too high to jump off, so we did the next best thing. The bridge had a walkway all along the south side that we were walking on, and it had a railing made of creosoted 4 X 4 posts with a looping cable stretched between them. Mutt and I sat down on the walkway with a 4 X 4 between each of our legs, and we hung onto the cable for dear life. That train wasn't going to suck us in under the wheels. The engineer blew and blew his whistle at us, and when he went by and I looked up at him, he was laughing at us, but we were sure glad we were hugging those posts.

*** * * ***

One spring Saturday, Mutt and I had a bonanza when we went fishing. We kept filling our stringer with crappies we caught underneath the railroad bridge. We would bring them home and put them in a copper wash boiler filled with water. We had made several trips, and the boiler was full of fish when Dad got home. He was pleased, surprised and disappointed all at the same time. He was disappointed that we hadn't taken some time to clean the fish which, of course, he had to do, with us helping him a little. Since the next day was Sunday, Dad wanted us to take him fishing in the same spot. We caught a few, but not like Mutt and I had done the day before. I caught about a 14-inch-catfish, and I asked Dad if I should keep it. He said, "Sure", so I put it on the stringer. Of course, I knew that catfish season wasn't on yet, and I assumed Dad did, too. When we were cleaning the fish, I mentioned that the season wasn't open on catfish, and Dad was very upset with me. He hadn't paid any attention to the seasons and didn't know we were breaking the law.

*** * * ***

Mutt and I used to go to Boy Scouts together, and afterwards we would go down to Mr. Slack's Ice House to try to catch some pigeons. When I was a kid, they still cut ice out of the river and stored it in icehouses. Men would use what looked like a one-man tree cutting saw to saw ice in the river into blocks, and then they would push and pull it up wooden ramps into two big barns or icehouses. The ice would be stacked in layers, and every couple of layers would be covered with sawdust. It kept ice for a long, long time. Anyway, pigeons would roost inside the buildings way up at the top, as there was no other place for them to sit. The walls of the icehouses were insulated and finished off with wood boards, so the pigeons had to sit at the top. Our ploy, which worked surprisingly well, was to shine a flashlight up at a pigeon and shoot at him with a slingshot. If you hit the pigeon or close to him, he would start to fly. You immediately would shine the flashlight down at the floor of the building in the corner (on top of the sawdust covered ice). The pigeon would fly around, running into the wall, eventually getting lower and lower until he landed on the floor by the light, and you grabbed him.

One night after Scouts, we were headed down the street toward the icehouses, when a rabbit ran out of Terrill Park across the street in front of us and between the houses. I took off after the rabbit, and Mutt ran around the other side of the house. The rabbit cut his way behind the house with me right behind him. Mutt was coming down the driveway when the rabbit ran right in front of him. He kicked it, and got it. We were both standing there puffing and exclaiming that we had run down a rabbit all by ourselves when I looked down and saw a little three-cornered tear in my good new blue pants. Mom would skin me! I pulled open the little flap and looked inside and saw blood. Before that point, I didn't know I had been hurt. I pulled up my pant leg and WOW! There was a vertical gash about 5 inches long, half an inch deep and ¾ inch wide. All of a sudden, I couldn't walk.

George White was with us, and he was older. He carried me piggy-back about 5 or 6 blocks to Dr. Stepp's office. He was an old doctor who lived in back of his office that was across from the library. He was home, and he came to the door and took care of me. The wound needed stitching, but he put five clamps in it to hold the two sides together, and then bandaged it up. While he was doing all this, Mutt was standing right beside me. He looked down at me lying on the table and said that I could hold his hand and squeeze it if the doctor was hurting me. Well, it hadn't hurt yet, but I felt I had to make Mutt think it did, so I squeezed his fingers in my grip to make him wince or in some manner show I was hurting him. Would you believe he never let on that I was hurting him one bit? Eventually I got tired and quit. Much later he told me that I had really hurt his hand, but he could not let on because I was the one that was hurting. I was an active child, and the clamps quickly pulled out, and I have a dandy big scar on my leg to go with all my others.

* * *

One night when we were after pigeons, we were at the Congregational Church. There were always pigeons that roosted on the downspout where it ran almost horizontal from the wide gutter back to the inside corner of the church and then down the wall to the ground. It was a long way up to the roof, but Mutt took off, climbing up there by putting one foot on each wall and hanging onto the big eight-inch downspout. He had gotten about three fourths of the way up to the pigeons when the downspout pulled out of the wall, and the whole thing leaned out away from the building and came crashing down, Mutt and all. He yelled, "Yeeaahhh", and landed in a pile of downspout sections. I was afraid he had gotten hurt, so I ran towards him, but I couldn't catch him as he was up and beating a quick retreat before someone came out after hearing all the commotion.

* * *

We were below the Marion Street dam one day wading in the water on the millrace side of the long concrete wall. We were trying to flush fish out of their holes so we could then throw rocks at them in an attempt to catch them. Mutt stumbled upon an old milk can under the water, and he set it upright and continued wading to keep up with the rest of us. When we reached the mill house with no fish, we got out of the water and came walking down the long concrete wall. We still had our rocks in our hands, so we pegged them at the top of the milk can that was sticking up out of the water. One of the rocks hit the can, and there was a splash inside the can. We all jumped back into the water and waded out to the milk can, and we gave Mutt first reach in, as he was the one who had set up the can and trapped whatever was inside. Mutt tried a couple of times to stick his hand in the can, but he was afraid of what might be in there. I shoved him aside and, sticking my arm down in there, I came out with about a three-pound catfish. Of course, the fish was mine as I had caught him!

Mutt

* * *

One time when we were down in the bum jungle below the railroad tracks on the west side of the river, we almost got into trouble. We were chasing a catbird and trying to hit it with our slingshots. Mutt had a few ball bearings he had gotten from the junkyard, and he shot one at the catbird and missed. The sun was coming down through the leaves in the trees in shafts of light, and that silver ball bearing shone every time it crossed a sunlight shaft. That ball bearing went clear across an open area and hit a bum right in the back of the head. The man fell into the fire where he was bending over stirring whatever he was cooking. Two others jumped up and pulled him out. We thought we had killed him, and we made ourselves scarce. We checked the papers and quizzed everyone about it to see if the man had died, but we never heard about it. Needless to say, we were two scared kids for a while.

Mutt moved away before we went to high school, and I never heard from him again. I would sure like to know if he is still alive, as I would travel a long way to see him. We had some fun times, I can tell you.

Arlene caring for me after I scalped myself on a swing set

OWWEEEES!

When I was little, I was always getting hurt. Some said I was prone to accidents, but I think I was just a very active child and not aware of the circumstances. If it looked possible to do, I did it, sometimes suffering the consequences.

Of course, some of my accidents/injuries were not my fault. I am told that when I was brand new and had just been born, the doctor pinned my bellyband to me. That's right, he stuck the safety pin into the bellyband and me and back out and fastened it. Every time I moved or they moved me, I cried. It was a couple of days until they found it, and I was always crying. They would try to feed me or change me, and I would cry every time I moved, when being burped etc. I lost a lot of sleep during those days, and I have never to this day caught up on my sleeping.

One of my earliest accidents was when my cousin Maynard Renfrow gave me a ride in a wagon that he was pulling behind his bicycle. He got to going fast, and when he turned off the sidewalk to go out Hanson's cinder driveway into the street, I got tipped out. My hands and knees were full of cinders, and some of those cinders took years to work their way out.

When I was in kindergarten, there was a big swing set on the playground, and it had three-inch pipe legs that held up the pipe that the swings hung down from. These legs sloped out for stability, and kids would put their hands on the pipes and slide down them while their feet scooted ahead of them in the dirt. Over time, this dug the dirt out, making a little bowl under the pipe. When it rained, the water would wash into these bowls and fill them up. One morning when I got to school, there was water standing under each of the legs, and all the pools were a different size. The girls were stepping over the smallest pool, and some of the boys were jumping over the next larger one. I felt that both of those puddles were too small to mess with, so I took a run and jumped over the third largest. One or two of the other boys jumped it too, and I felt I could outdo them if I could make it over the biggest puddle. I measured it with my eyes, and I knew I would have to take a long run in order to get up enough speed to carry me all the way across, but I knew I could do it. All the kids were watching as I made my long run and mighty leap. I landed right in the middle of the puddle, as I had jumped so high my forehead hit the sloping pipe. It almost knocked me out, but I was numb and not even aware that I was sitting in the water.

The kids all screamed and carried on because my face was all bloody. My whole forehead had been skinned, and the bloody skin was hanging down in front of my eyes. I had been scalped and the flap of skin was hanging down over my face making it look like my whole face was a bloody mess.. When the teacher came, she led me into the school where she flipped the flap back up, covering my forehead. She put it all in place and covered it with a bandage and taped it down. They called my mother who had to get someone to bring her to school since Dad had the only car. Mom came to take me to the doctor. The doctor very gently took off the tape and peeked under the bandage at the wound, and then he covered it right back up. He said the teacher had done a wonderful job, and it was already starting to heal. The remaining scar isn't even noticeable, as it is right at the hairline.

* * *

One time when I was little and running around, I saw some kind of activity going on out in the middle of Bank's field. This big field was located across the street from my house, and it ran behind all the houses over there. A bunch of us kids were trying to see what all the people were looking at, but since we were short, we couldn't see over them. I got the bright idea of climbing the fence and sitting on the fence post. Of course, when you sit on the fence post, which is higher than the fence wire, you have to reach down to hold onto the wire so you won't fall off. I was holding onto the top wire, which was a barbed wire, when I fell backward right off the post. The barb in the wire grabbed my little finger and almost cut it off. I have a nice scar that goes around under the little finger of my right hand from one side to the other.

Owweeees!

* * *

I was playing cowboys and Indians up at Grandpa's house in the north end of town and I was crawling on my hands and knees in the ditch alongside the M&O Railroad tracks. My knee came down right on top of a broken beer bottle. The bottom of the beer bottle had been sticking up, and the broken glass went in under my kneecap. When I cried out and stood up, the beer bottle was sticking out of my leg, and it had to be pulled out, as the glass was way in. That knee has a nice scar around the bottom of the kneecap to go with the cinder scars.

* * *

Dad was working on fixing something in the back yard, and he had sawhorses set up with planks across them to form a workbench. I was helping, "natch", and somehow I reached up and knocked off a heavy bench weight, and it fell and smashed my big toe. I've done that four times that I know of, smashed my big toe, that is. In high school I had a really bad ingrown toenail due to a smashed toe. When the doctor lifted the nail off my big toe several days after I smashed it, he told me I would never have a toenail on that toe again. He was wrong, and much later, when the sides of the toe had grown into the nail area, here came a new toenail. It was constantly sore on both sides of the new nail, as it had to gouge out the meat of my toe to make room for it. When I would stop too quickly in the hall, or playing basketball, it would just about kill me. It took a long time for that toenail to grow out. Right now, I have a very thick toenail trying to grow out from a bench weight falling off the bench in my garage, when I was attempting to fix something for my sister, Arlene. You'd think I would learn.

* * *

Of course, I had ingrown toenails from wearing a pair of Brazilian boots brother Dale had sent me from his travels in the war. They were wonderful boots, and they were lined on the inside with smooth leather. I wore them long after they were too small, and my mother finally noticed me limping. She thought I was some kind of a nut to wear shoes that hurt my feet that much, as my toes were bleeding. Hey, I liked those boots!

* * *

One time I underwent surgery to remove my ingrown toenails. They gave me laughing gas, but I didn't laugh. The doctor told a nurse to get some help to hold me on the operating table, and I heard him. I told him that I wouldn't jump or kick. Mom was in the room to comfort me until I was under, and on the way home, I told her I heard what the doctor said, and what I had said. She laughed and told me what really happened. She said I was yelling, and my arms and legs were going all over the place. It had taken four people to keep me on the table until I calmed down. She said she had to leave the room, but she was afraid to, as she felt they would hurt me as I was hurting them.

* * *

As kids in grade school, we got the idea of having a track meet. There was a vacant lot between Hilsenbeck's and Hanson's, and it had been a garden. The dirt was fairly soft there so we could broad jump, pole vault, etc. For our high jump, there was a barbed wire fence to jump over. I made a gallant jump, but my leg caught on the wire and I fell. I started bawling and headed for home. By the time I got home, the hurt was mostly gone, and I had quit crying. Mom was on the telephone talking to someone, and I heard her say, " I have to go. George has broken his arm". I started crying again. I later asked her how she knew my arm was broken, as I hadn't told her what the problem was at that point. She said my arm was bent the wrong way.

* * *

When I was little, I also had terrible earaches. My ears would or wouldn't drain, and I couldn't lay on them, so I got no sleep. Finally, after the folks couldn't live with me, the doctor said I should have my tonsils out. That gave me the worst sore throat I have ever had. Mom tried to feed me gelatin that was cut in little cubes, and I couldn't eat it as the edges of the gelatin cut my throat.

Owweeees!

* * *

One summer, we traveled to Sutherland, Iowa, to visit my aunt and uncle, Leona and Ray Davis and my cousins. Leland, the oldest boy, was a year older than me, and he was always making something. He was good at it, too. This particular time, we made corncob darts. You took a nicely-shaped corncob, stuck a big nail in the heavy end and some chicken feathers in the other and you had a dart that would stick in the side of the garage. We drew a target on the side of the garage and threw the darts at it, but the thing I remember most about it is when he threw his dart at me. I don't remember if we were mad at each other at the time but he hit me right in the chest, and the dart stuck in me! I started bawling and pulled the dart out. The two Moms came running to see who was killed, as I could cry loud, don't you know. By the time they got there, I had stopped crying and Leland was now crying, as he just knew he was going to get a licking for throwing the dart at me. The mothers went to him to see what the matter was, and he just pointed at me, as he was trying to get his breath. Fortunately I had wet eyes and a hole in my chest with a little blood coming out, so I could get the attention I deserved.

* * *

Sometime in grade school, I started gluing feathers on my arrows. I split chicken or goose feathers and glued them on the wooden arrows I would make in Dad's shop. The problem was, I shot the arrows off my hand, that is, I didn't have an arrow rest. I just rested the arrow on my hand. This worked fine on featherless arrows, but on the feathered arrows, the feathers would come loose, and the sharp glue would cut my hand. I put up with it until one day the whole feather was driven into my hand. I came home with half the feather in my hand and the other half sticking out. I have a nice scar on my left hand from this incident, and Dad put a little piece of wood on the side of the bow to act as an arrow rest so it wouldn't happen again.

* * *

I received a snorkel, mask and swim fins as a gift one year, and I took to swimming under the water in the river. The water was normally so dirty or full of algae that you couldn't see much except in the spring and fall. When the water was cold, you couldn't stay in very long. When we could see, we saw lots of fish in the holes under trees etc. I once saw a carp that I swear was bigger than I was. Well, I wanted to catch some of those fish, and I made myself a spear gun. It was powered by rubber bands, and it had a trigger, sear, and trigger guard off a very old junked rifle. It worked fine if you could get close enough to the fish. I don't remember spearing anything with it, except myself. I was standing on the river bank up by Tripp's bayous, getting ready to come down the bank and enter the water, when I dropped my arrow. It was a solid brass curtain rod, and I had flattened the end so it could be filed to a point, and I cut a big barb in it to hold the fish. It had a notch in it, too, to hold the cable from the rubber bands, and another notch for the sear to stick up into, to hold the arrow on the spear gun. Anyway, I was carrying an armload of gear and as the arrow started to fall out of my arms, I thought I would just let it go, as it was falling down the bank where I was going anyway. The arrow was falling backwards, and the barb caught in my leg and tore a nice deep hole, as I had made a nice big barb.

* * *

When I was in high school I went out for football, basketball and track. I liked football, but I was no good at offense. So, I liked defense best. I was tall and skinny and played end, but I wore thick glasses. I had the first eggshell helmet on our team. The coach got it and took it somewhere and had a wire grid put across the front of it to protect my glasses. The folks got me hardened lenses that were so thick and heavy the nose pads made deep holes in my nose. They worried about the other teams' fingers, so they put black tape on the wire to protect their fingers. The result was that I couldn't see the football up in the air at night in the lights. Consequently, I was an end that never caught a pass in a football game. It was no use to throw it to me, as I was not going to see it with my helmet on. On defense, it was another matter. They didn't run around my end without me knocking someone down, hopefully the ball carrier. Of course, there were risks. To me, of course.

My senior year, which should have been my heyday, I was kicked in the mouth in practice and had my bottom teeth go through my lower lip. The next Friday night's game, I wore a boxer's mouthpiece, and a ball carrier came around my end, and I had him dead-to-rights. I was about to tackle him when, for some strange reason, he turned into me instead of away from me. His thigh pad and my face came together, and it resulted in a broken nose. Mine!

For the next Friday night's game, I wore a boxer's mouthpiece and had my nose all taped up. That night, a guy clipped me and gave me a bad knee for the rest of my life. My knee swelled way up, but it wasn't water on the knee. It was legitimate swelling. Still, every time I bend that knee too sharply, the fibula jumps out of place, and I have to slowly straighten the leg out until it jumps back into place. Fortunately, it doesn't hurt too badly. A surgeon in the Army offered to repair it for me, but when he diagramed it for me and told me what he would do to fix it, I was too scared to let him do it.

One day, in football practice after school, I put "Heet" on my sprained ankle. I put a wool sock on and laced up my high top football shoes and went out to practice. It wasn't long until I sat down on the ground and began to tear the laces out of my shoes. The coach came over to see what was wrong, and when I got my shoe and sock off, my foot was as red as a beet. Everyone had a big laugh about it, but me. I went into the locker room and tried to wash it off, but I didn't have any luck. I learned to leave wool socks alone too.

When I went to college, I went out for football as a walk-on. We were waiting to draw uniforms, and we were playing touch football when I turned too quickly, and my knee twisted and swelled way up again. They took me to the University hospital where the doctor and several interns started examining me, and the doctor announced that it was water on the knee. I told him it wasn't, but he proceeded to stick hollow needles into the swelling and attempted to draw out some liquid. When it didn't work, he got a bigger needle. When that didn't work, he left the needle in and got a bigger syringe. When that didn't work, he got a bigger syringe. About there, I passed out. When I came to, my legs were crossed and they stuck out stiff as a board. The doctor looked at me and said, "It's not water on the knee". Anyway, I had to hobble around to class the next week or two until the swelling went down, and that was the end of my college football career.

* * *

When I was in the Army in Fort Sam Houston, Texas, I was in the Medical Service Corps training to be a Sanitary Engineer. We were playing basketball outside in an open basketball court when I broke my hand. When I was in the hospital emergency room waiting for them to take care of me, they brought in two much more serious cases. One young man had scalding hot coffee spilled all over him when he and another fellow were trying to move a small field table that had a big coffee urn on it. The next man had fallen into an open, never used, latrine pit, while on night maneuvers. He was alone without a flashlight, and the pit was full of scorpions. Every time he would try to move to get out of there, he would be stung two or three times. He didn't know what was doing the stinging, but he was hurting. By the time they found him and got him to the hospital, he was in bad shape.

They finally had time to put a cast on my hand, but it was almost midnight before I got back to the barracks.

There were lots of officers at Fort Sam, which is the Army Medical School. When we stood inspections, we might have six or eight officers in a row come past. Of course, the first officer was always the ranking officer, and it was either a Colonel or a General. I knew that when they got to me, they would question what happened when they saw my hand in a cast and my arm in a sling. I was ready. This General stopped in front of me and said, "What happened to you, soldier?" I looked straight ahead, right over his head, and said in a loud voice, "Sir, I broke my fourth metacarpal participating in organized athletics". He smiled and said, "Fine", and I said, "No, Sir". He continued down the line and then turned back to me and asked, "In the line of duty?" and I said, "Yes Sir!" still looking straight ahead. We both got a kick out of it, as did all the other officers in the inspection team.

Of course, when he said, "Fine", he meant that he liked my report, but I didn't take it that way.

*　*　*

When I got out of the Army, I took a job in Milwaukee. Wisconsin. My buddy Craig Malven, who was from my hometown, was deer bow hunting up in Jackson County and we used to meet there, and camp and hunt together. One morning, before daylight, he let me out of the car to go up on this high ridge. I was to take a stand and hunt until about nine o'clock, and then make a slow drive down the ridge toward the road in hopes that I would spook a deer out where others could get a shot at it. Well, when I got out of the car, I laid my bow on the ground while I slung my ditty bag over my shoulder. I reached down, picked up my recurve bow and let my hand just slide down the limb of the bow, and I felt a slight drag on my hand. I did not have a shield over my broad head arrows, and I had cut my hand, big time. The taillights of Craig's car were still in view, but I had no way of letting him know of my problem. Since I didn't have a flashlight, I didn't know how bad I was cut, but I was leaking badly all over everything. I tried to put my hand in my mouth to stop the bleeding, and that is how I found out how big the cut was, as I could run my tongue along it. I got out my handkerchief and managed to get the bleeding stopped. I just sat down up on the ridge and waited till the appointed time since I didn't know where anyone was until we set up the ambush at the end of the ridge. I lived.

*　*　*

In 1970 we moved to Nashville, Tennessee. I have continued my prowess at becoming injured to this day. While duck hunting out on J. Percy Priest Lake in front of the house, I somehow broke a tendon in my left hand little finger while putting out the decoys. I was sitting in the blind in the rocks with a cup of coffee, when I noticed my little finger was crooked. My hands were so cold I hadn't noticed that it had hurt, but I'm assuming it must have. The doctor put it in a splint, but he said the chance of it reattaching was very small. He said if it was on my right hand, he would recommend surgery to straighten it out, but he felt the left hand could do all right with a crooked finger, as I was right handed. It is still crooked, natcherly.

* * *

My son, Matt, and I shingled the roof of our house and I was bending a long piece of aluminum to form a valley. When I got it bent to my satisfaction, I got my hammer and nail apron and reached down to pick up the valley to carry it up the ladder to the roof. I received a vicious cut on the end of my index finger from the edge of that aluminum. It took a long time healing, and I had a dent in the end of that finger for years. It finally rounded off, but I remember it!

* * *

I found a short piece of aluminum cable in the back yard, left over from some construction project, and it was covered with a tough plastic coating. I got out my knife to cut the plastic off, as I felt I could find some use for the aluminum wire. I made a slice, but the tough plastic didn't cut. The cable rolled just a little - just enough to allow my hand to receive the cut and I went to the emergency room. I was at Vanderbilt Hospital, and I became very unhappy with my treatment. The young doctor or intern, proceeded to scrub the open wound with a bristle brush. He ran that brush vigorously, right down into the wound, and I was hurting big time. I had never seen anyone treat a wound in that manner. It eventually healed, and I don't remember that it got infected. Another scar.

* * *

I have another scar along my thumbnail on my left hand. It is from a fairly recent incident, when I was up on the garage roof one winter, attempting to get a shingle to lie down. Our big ham radio tower and antennae has four guy wires, and one of the wires goes over the garage roof. It caused the shingle to be cut and buckled and I felt I could make it lay down. I was attempting to nail it down when I hit my thumb with the hammer. Now I have hit my thumb many times but not like this. It was cold, and I hit it hard, as the shingle was out over the eave, and it was bouncing. Anyway the skin broke and the flesh separated and all that was holding it on, was the skin on the underside of the thumb. It has been a couple of years now, and that part of my thumb has healed, but it doesn't feel like it belongs to me. I guess that area is full of scar tissue with no feeling in it. You can see the scar though, which reminded me to tell you about it.

SMOKIN'

I don't know how old I was, maybe 7 or 8, when a bunch of us kids in the neighborhood got to talkin' about tryin' smokin'. We lived in the southeast edge of the small town of Manchester, Iowa, in an area called Sandy Flat. Sonny Barker's dad smoked cigars, and my dad smoked cigarettes. Both of us boys knew where our fathers kept their supply, and we could 'borrow' some.

Out behind Barker's barn was a chicken house that was no longer used for chickens or anything else. It was empty and invited us in to try our hand at smokin'. Sonny went in to get the cigars, and I went home to get the cigarettes. Dad kept a carton of Avalon cigarettes in the little cupboard under the gun case in his bedroom. I helped myself to a pack and got some matches, too. We all met at the chicken house and went in and sat down on the floor. There were probably a half dozen of us, but only the big boys tried smokin'. As I remember it, that meant that only Ed Frentress, Barker and I smoked, but there could have been another smoker. We didn't know anything about inhaling. We just puffed away trying both cigarettes and cigars, trying to outdo each other with the biggest puff of smoke. The chicken house got so filled with smoke that we were laughing about it. We couldn't see each other even though we were sitting side by side in kind of a little circle. It was a very small chicken house with windows on one side. When one of the kids went out and looked in, he couldn't see us due to all the thick smoke. Even though we weren't inhaling, we were still breathing, and needless to say, we all got sick. I still remember being green around the gills and Mom having a fit about it. I couldn't figure out how she knew we had been smoking, but, of course, we must have smelled to high heaven, in addition to being sick.

* * *

Sonny had a good back lot to play in. His dad was in the American Legion and had gotten a real World War I water-cooled machine gun on a tripod. He had set it up for us on the edge of a foxhole we had dug on a little knoll behind the chicken house. The gun was welded shut, so it was inoperable, but it did swivel on the tripod. However, the thing that kept it from being played with was its un-portability. It was very heavy: and none of us could budge it. Since we were active kids and always on the move, we went off and left it most of the time.

* * *

Up at my house, at 413 South Brewer Street, we had a barn, too. It was really a two-car garage with a full-sized loft up above and a pull-down stairs. The stairs were counterweighted with a rope and window weights in the walls, so even a boy could pull the stairs down. In back of our barn/garage, our neighbors, the Addlemans, had a little garage that backed right up to our garage, with a little space between, about 18 inches wide. Dad was a contractor, and he kept galvanized water pipe stored between the two garages, up on blocks. Between these garages was a good place for boys to get out of sight, too.

Anyway, one day Barker and I decided that I should sneak another pack of cigarettes for us to smoke between the garages. Again the smoke got so thick that my sister, Arlene, thought that the garage was on fire. She came out to investigate. We heard the screen door slam and knew someone was coming. We put out our cigarettes, and I dropped the butt behind the pipes. The other boy just left his on top of the pipes. Arlene said, "I caught you smoking," and since we were no longer smoking, I said, "No". She said, "Yes, I did and that's your butt." Since it wasn't my butt, I said, "No" again. Anyway, we were caught, but she didn't tell our parents, for which we were very thankful!

SUCKERS

In the spring of the year, fish run up the rivers and the creeks to spawn. There was a time when the suckers congregated below the Marion Street dam by the hundreds. As kids, we were always fishing there, and one day we got the bright idea that we could snag these fish. We put on treble hooks and cast out into the pools, and about every fourth or fifth jerk, we might snag into one. Sometimes we would only get a scale, but every now and then, we would catch one.

This system was much too slow, and we got to wading in and catching them with our hands. They were so thick that, in the pockets or holes out of the fast water, the bottom was covered with suckers. They were all about 14 inches long and laying in there, shoulder to shoulder.

I was tall and skinny, with big hands, and I would catch one in each hand every time I waded in. Well, we would climb out of the water with these fish and dash them on the rocks to kill them and wade back in for more. Soon the rocks were covered with fish.

Now, this dam is right downtown, and we had lots of folks on the bridge watching us and cheering us on. Then someone called the sheriff, who came down, saw what we were doing, and called us all out of the water and told us this was illegal. Fish had to be caught with hook and line. He made us throw all those dead fish back into the water. Of course, we were smart enough to throw them into the quiet pools so we could snag them out with our poles and treble hooks. Then we went home and got a couple of coaster wagons, loaded them up with suckers, and set out to sell them by going down the street yelling, "Fresh fish for sale!"

We sold very few, however, as most of the folks ignored us. The few that came out and looked wanted to know what was wrong with the fish. They felt to have that many, meant they had been poisoned or seined or gotten in some illegal way. They just couldn't believe we caught them with hook and line, because they had bruised places on them from the rocks. Of course, some might have recognized them, and knew that suckers were full of little hair like bones, making them hard to eat. In spite of few sales, it was a good day's work for kids.

SLINGSHOTS

We made slingshots and did a lot of practicing with them. They were really good slingshots as Dad helped me make them. He even picked out the crotch in a plum tree and sawed it out. We had good, red rubber inner tubes for the rubber bands and an old shoe tongue for the leather. At first, about the only things we could hit with our slingshots were robins. Yeah, it was against the law to shoot songbirds, but they were so easy. They would let us walk right up to them and whomp 'em good with a rock at a range of about 4 feet. We would quickly pick them up, put them in a pocket and hurry on down the street. We took to storing our dead robins on the pipes between the garages, just to see how many we got. One day Dad went to get some pipe, and he came looking for me. When he found me, probably at mealtime, he took me out between the garages and pointed at the decomposing robins, saying, "What's this?" I, of course, said, "Robins." He said, "No more", and I said, "Yes, sir", and that was that.

* * *

We did a lot of hunting with slingshots. We got pretty good at hitting what we were aiming at, as long as we had good ammunition such as marbles or good round rocks. Dad had three crews working for the Illinois Central Railroad, tearing down old depots and building new ones in this shop. It was really the first prefabrication of buildings that we had heard of, in about 1940. One crew would go to the small town where the new depot was to be located, and they would tear down the big, old existing depot and the cattle pens, and get the footing and block foundation ready for the new depot. Another crew worked in the shop and built the new depot in six pieces: the four walls and the two halves of the roof. Another crew would load these six pieces onto flat cars at our depot, and the railroad would ship it to the new site and put it on a sidetrack. Then a crew would go to that town and put it all together. They had to pour a lot of concrete for sidewalks, steps and platforms, and the railroad shipped in the best slingshot rock in the world for the concrete. There was a huge pile of this rock at our depot. I would ride to work with Dad and pick up coffee cans full of nice, round rocks of just the right size for my slingshot. I would put the cans in the truck for Dad to bring home. I would take a pocketful of rocks and my slingshot and walk on home by way of the bum jungle along the river below the railroad tracks. It was a good wood to look for birds and such.

* * *

We shot a few squirrels with the slingshots, but, because it was summer, we couldn't tell anyone since the season wasn't open. These weren't tame town squirrels either, as we got them in "Dummy" Myers' woods. We were very scared of "Dummy" Myers, and we weren't very nice to call him that. He was deaf and dumb. When he would catch us building a dam in his creek, he would scream horribly at us in the only way he could, and it literally scared us out of our wits. We would run off through the woods, and he would come down and tear out our dam. He had trouble toward the end as we got pretty good at dam building, putting in log foundations, etc. Much later, I was hunting squirrels in his woods, and I met him. He was a real nice guy like Dad had told me he was. We, Mr. Myers and I, conversed with a little pencil and note pad he carried. He asked who I was, and when I wrote my name, he knew who my Dad was, and he said I could hunt in his woods. That made him my friend. I did a better job from then on of not letting him see me, or so I thought, but maybe he didn't try so hard to catch me now that he knew who I was.

* * *

My beagle dog, "Jeep", treed an opossum in Mr. Myer's woods, and we knocked him out with our slingshots. We had to do it twice as the opossum played 'possum on us and came back to life. "Jeep" took the track again, and we did likewise with the slingshots. Since he was my first opossum, I took him home to show Dad, and would you believe it - that opossum came back to life in our basement, and I had to dig him out of our kindling pile! Of course, "Jeep" was in there telling me where to dig. Mom thought it was somethin' to have a hound in the house baying on a track! She put up with a lot from her family - what with muskrat hides drying in her fruit cellar, and a hickory bow soaking in the cistern so it could be bent around a mandrel, etc. etc.

* * *

One day we even tried to kill a big bull snake with our slingshots out in the middle of Bank's plowed field, but none of us would get close enough for a headshot, and our body hits just didn't do the job.

* * *

Even when I was in high school and working summers for Dad, I had a slingshot hanging in the garage with a coffee can of round rocks right under it. Dad and I came out of the house after eating lunch and headed for the truck to go back to work when we startled a blue jay. The jay squawked and flew up and lit on the neighbor's birdbath. I told Dad to wait a minute. I stepped into the garage, retrieved my slingshot and a rock, took aim and dumped that blue jay into the water. Dad was impressed, as it was about a 20-yard poke.

* * *

I liked to impress my Dad! He took me hunting, fishing and trapping, and he had lots of times to be impressed. When we would go fishing, he impressed me a lot of times. He would fish a minnow or chub very carefully around a stump, and invariably, he would finesse out a nice bass or catfish. I would copy him as best I could, but I wouldn't catch anything, except maybe a snag. He would tell me I wasn't holding my mouth right. I would hold my mouth in all different configurations, but it didn't help. I think Dad got some good out of it though, now that I think about it. He amazed me on a duck hunt, too, when he got two pintails with one shot. No, not just by accident. They came in low and slow over the decoys, and it was his shot. He aimed and aimed and aimed, and when he finally did shoot, I asked him what he was waiting for as they had almost gotten out of range. He said he was just waiting for them to get together!

THE TREE HOUSE

Chuck Gorman lived across the street from me. He was two years older, but we did lots of things together. One day, in early grade school time, we decided we would like to build a tree house. We went back behind his house to a row of trees between the houses and Bank's field, and found a big willow tree that had about five trunks that we thought would be just right for our purpose. We went back to his house, got some lumber, some nails and an old hammer and saw. The saw was so rusty it didn't have any teeth, just little bumps where the teeth should be. When we had it all carried to the site, we started by nailing 2x4 steps on oné trunk so we could get up into the tree. I was using the saw to try to cut off the 2x4 and I wore myself out. Chuck tried, too, and we finally gave up cutting anything with that saw.

We nailed 2x4s between the trunks for our floor joist, and put boards across them for our floor. The whole affair looked terrible, as the long 2x4s and floorboards stuck out all over when we couldn't cut them off. About then, the noon whistle blew, and we quit to go home for lunch. We left the hammer and saw on the floor of the tree house.

I told Dad all about our tree house and I asked him for some boards for the sides, as we didn't want people from the street to see us up in there. He gave me some, and I went to get Chuck to help me carry them. When we got to our tree and got up onto the floor, the hammer and saw were gone. We immediately thought of Sonny Barker who lived 4 or 5 houses down. We figured he probably heard us hammering and had spied on us. We walked down the fence to his place, and sure enough, he was out behind his big double garage/barn, and he was sawing away with Chuck's saw. His neighbor boy, who was younger, was using the hammer. When we walked up to them and told them they had our hammer and saw and we wanted them back, Barker gave us some argument. He claimed they were his, and he and the other boy had been playing with them all day. We told them they were Chuck's grandfather's, and we had to have them back. Chuck was standing in front of Sonny and I was standing in front of the neighbor boy. Eventually Barker said, "Here's your damn saw", and he hit Gorman on the leg with the saw blade. Since the teeth were not sharp, it only cut his pants and made a red mark on his thigh. The other boy, seeing Barker hit Chuck, felt that was the way he was supposed to give back the hammer, too. He reared back to hit me, but I was onto him and I hit him right on the nose with my fist.

Unfortunately, Sonny's older sister Vivian was looking out the back door of the house and she saw me hit the younger boy, but she hadn't seen her brother hit Gorman with the saw. She screamed and came out the door, down the porch step and came running after me. I took off for the back fence and dove through the hole by the corner post, and I started out across Bank's field. I didn't think she would go through the fence, as she was a big girl with a dress on. I was wrong. She hiked up her dress, ducked through that hole, and here she came running right after me. She was about ten years older that I was, and, with her long legs, she was about to catch me right away. As she reached for me, I ducked to the side and stuck out my leg, which she tripped over and she went sprawling. She lit in a big patch of sand burrs and those sharp little burrs stuck her summer dress right to her skin. She yowled and was in misery, but that was okay as the chase was over. I went on up the fence to the tree house, and after a while Chuck came along with the hammer and saw. We worked some more on the house, but I could only think of how much trouble I was in for hitting the younger boy. I didn't say anything to my parents that night or the next day, which was Sunday, and everything seemed like it was going to blow over. No one had apparently reported the incident to the boy's parents or to my parents, so I started to breathe easier.

The next day at school, I didn't have much to do with Sonny, who was in my class, but after school my sister, Arlene, corralled me and gave me what for! It seemed the two Barker girls, Vivian and Wanda, Sonny's sisters, jumped all over Arlene and told her what a bad boy I was for hitting this little boy for no reason, etc. etc. I related the whole story to her and told her that I did have a reason, as the boy was trying to hit me with a hammer. She listened to my explanation, and she must have kept it to herself or told the Barker girls what actually happened, because I never heard anymore about it.

    Within a couple of days, Sonny and I were playing together again, but it was weeks before Arlene and the Barker girls were on friendly terms.

Peck and Dolly's farmhouse where I spent many wonderful summers

OUT TO PECK'S

Dad had a younger brother named Roy, but everyone called him Peck because he had a barrel chest. His body looked like a barrel or peck with arms and legs and a head sticking out. He married a pretty little girl named Gladys, but everyone called her Dolly as she was like a little doll. Anyway, they were always referred to as Peck and Dolly. They had three children. Murlin was the oldest boy, Donald the middle boy, and Florence their daughter. Peck and Dolly were in love all their lives, and they hugged and kissed each other at each opportunity. This love was passed through the whole family, and it made a big impression on me, as my folks fought with each other. I always said I wanted to love my wife and family as Peck and Dolly did.

They lived on a farm south of Jesup, Iowa, about half-a-mile from the Shady Grove General Store. There was a rural Baptist Church across the road from the store. Their farmhouse was painted yellow, and it had two stories. There were no electric lights yet, as this part of Iowa had not been provided with rural electricity. Coal oil lamps were used for light, but it was pretty much - you went to bed early and got up with the sun. Water was pumped from two wells. One well was located on the edge of the barnyard, and it was connected to a windmill. There was a big concrete tank there that was kept full of water for the animals. The other well was in the kitchen, and it was connected to a pitcher pump. There was an outhouse at the end of a wooden plank path that provided the rest of the plumbing. The house consisted of a kitchen, a dining room, a living room and a bedroom downstairs, and there were bedrooms upstairs. There was an enclosed back porch off the kitchen, and there was also an open porch off the other side of the kitchen that could be accessed from the kitchen or the dining room. Southeast of the house was a big barn and a corncrib. A small garage south of the house completed the buildings. Later they would build a big chicken house. There was a large pasture east of the house and a small creek ran through it. There was another pasture west of the house, and there was a grove of big trees along its west side. The rest of the farm was fields for growing hay, oats, corn and sometimes wheat. None of the crops were for sale; they all were consumed on the farm. The corn went into the corncrib, the oats went into the oat bin in the barn, and the upstairs in the barn was for storage of the loose hay. The oat straw was made into a big stack in the barnyard where the cows would rub up against it to scratch themselves, and the straw itself was used for bedding for the animals. The only things they sold were the separated cream and the eggs.

Anyway, I tell you all of this because this is the place I got to spend my summers when I was in grade school. It was wonderful for me, as I was a townie. Cousin Don was about six years older than I was, but he took me under his wing, and I got to help him do all kinds of farm work. Peck and Dolly had a wonderful family, they all had chores to do, and they all got along famously. It was interesting for me in many ways. Cousin Murlin couldn't get along with the animals, and he was always getting into fixes with them. He eventually became a preacher. Cousin Don loved all the animals, and everyone and everything. Florence was the typical farm girl, learning to keep house, cook, gather the eggs etc.

I wasn't of much help at first. I was probably in the way more than anything, but I remember the first time I made myself useful. Peck had the Farmall tractor in the little orchard along the driveway, and he was attempting to pull up some small trees that had grown up. The trees were about eight feet tall. He would wrap a chain around them, hook the chain to the tractor and drive away. The trees would just bend over, and he would have to back up and try again. I was standing there, out of the way, watching, and after several attempts, I got the idea that I should hold the top of the now-limber tree so it was bent the other way. I did; it worked and Peck praised me at the time, and later he brought it up at the supper table. I was proud and pleased no end.

Peck had a hand-cranked corn sheller that he used to shell the corn for the hogs and the chickens. My first job was to bring the clean corncobs from the barn into the kitchen and put them in a box by the stove. They were used to start the fire in the kitchen stove first thing in the morning. Dolly had a big cooking stove with a water reservoir on the side, which kept the water warm. When we took baths on the back porch in a big washtub, she would bring in warm water and pour in into the tub behind your back, as you had to keep the rest of yourself covered by bending over so she couldn't see you.

* * *

As boys growing up, we had a little trouble with our personal hygiene. When we had to go tinkle in the middle of the night, Cousin Don and I didn't want to go all the way downstairs, through the house, out through the back porch and along the plank path to the outhouse. We got the idea we could tinkle through the window screen in our bedroom. We did this for some time until Uncle Peck took both of us out in the front yard, pointed up to the rusty screen window, and said, "No more". The urine had rusted the screen and the rust had stained the yellow house brown below our window. Another time, cousin Don told me that I was not supposed to use the slick pages in the catalogs in the outhouse to wipe myself. I asked him how he knew that I was, and he told me his mother told him. I was shocked, and I asked him how she knew. He said she did the laundry. As a townie, we had toilet paper, but in the outhouse there were three old catalogs. They were from Sears Roebuck, Montgomery Ward and Spiegel. You were supposed to use the softer paper for wiping and the slick, inked paper was what Uncle Peck used to make a torch to flame the underside of the toilet seat to get rid of the spiders and their webs. He said that the women didn't have to worry, but that the men's hangy-down-part was subject to getting bit by a black widow spider.

When in the woods one day, I used some leaves that made my backside break out, and it was painful to sit. I had a heck of a time sitting up to the table to eat. Don checked my bottom from time to time, and he would tell his mother what it looked like, and she would give him some salve for me to put on it until it finally got well. A lesson well learned.

* * *

They sent me to bible school at the Shady Grove Baptist Church, and they would have to stop everything to take me, and then go get me. One year, they got a pony from a neighbor and they said I could ride the pony to and from bible school. That seemed like a great idea, but it turned out not so great. The pony was very fat, and he was round where you sat on him. I was riding him bareback. The road to the church was mostly uphill, so it was mostly downhill on the way back. I would be able to stay on the pony all the way to the church by hanging onto his mane. However, on the way back he would trot down the hill and bounce me off into the ditch. He would then go on home by himself, and I would be left to walk. I was so mad at that pony, as he did this every day and it embarrassed me, and Don would tease me. I would cut across country through the grove, etc. so I got back home shortly after the pony did, but Don always knew I had fallen off.

The minister of the church was Rev. Erpelding, and it was a fun church. When we would have a potluck supper, they all loved to sing. The most fun was when they sang a Sunday school song, the B-I-B-L-E. In this song, the first line of each verse was a word that was spelled out, and the rest of the verse explains the word. Most folks only know two verses, but the men of this church could go on for 25 or 30 verses. Everyone would sing the verses they knew, and they would drop out as the men had learned or written new verses. They would continue until there were only one or two singing, and everyone learned new things. When the last man quit, they would all laugh and clap and congratulate him. Much fun. They spelled out big, long, complicated names from the Bible. I still remember some of those songs.

One weekend, we painted the church white. There were lots of volunteers, and everyone got a paintbrush and a can of paint. I was painting at the back of the church at a door that led into a storage area for firewood. I opened the door to paint the edge of it, and a bat flew out of the room. I hit the bat with my paintbrush as he went by, and he flew up and landed in a tree right next to the church. You could see him up there since he was painted white. Eventually, he fell out of the tree dead, and we all thought the paint had killed him.

*　*　*

I liked the fieldwork, but I didn't like the constant chores. You could get the fieldwork done and move on to something else, but you could never get rid of the chores. They were always there waiting for you, every morning and every evening. The cows had to be milked, the horses fed and the hogs slopped. Peck had about a dozen cows to milk, two big draft horses, and many pigs to feed. Dolly took care of the chickens, so I didn't get involved there except to help get the chicken feed to where she wanted it and to clean the chicken house.

They had a very smart farm dog named Sarge. He was a shepherd dog, and he would tree squirrels and watch the tree to see if the squirrel would jump to another tree. He would always be barking at the tree the squirrel was in. When we went coon hunting at night, Don always took Sarge although he had a black and tan coonhound that was a silent trailer. That hound would bark treed, but he wouldn't stay at the tree as you came up. He would go off looking for another coon to track. We never knew which tree the coon was in. Sarge would get there before we did, and he would tell us where the coon was.

It was funny, too, that Sarge couldn't kill a mouse because he had a bad overbite. His teeth didn't match up by about an inch, and he would bite and bite, but the mouse would run away when he spit him out. Sarge also always knew where the cows were, and Don could just speak to him and say, "Go get the cows, Sarge," and off he would go. In a short while, the cows would all be up at the tank getting a drink of water. Then they would go down to the barn, into the basement of the barn, and I would get to go along in front of them and close the stanchions on their necks. They always knew which stanchion was theirs and they went to the right place. Normally, I didn't have to wait on them, but one time, one was missing. I went out the barn door and around the corner to a little alcove between the barn and the corncrib, and there she was. She was standing there with the bull. They both looked at me, and then the bull reared up, mounted her, and bred her right in front of me. When he finished, she went on down around the corner and into the barn where she knew she belonged. When Don saw her as he was milking, she had her back arched, and he said she must have bulled. I said "Yes" and he asked me if I saw it. I told him how it all happened. He was pleased that I had seen it happen. Some of my education, I guess.

* * *

They milked all the cows by hand, sitting on little milking stools and holding the milk bucket between their knees. My hands weren't strong enough to milk, so they would send me to feed the horses. The cows were in the basement of the barn, and the horses were on the first floor. I was to go to the corncrib, get six ears of corn for each horse and put the corn in the manger box in front of the horse. I could only carry six ears at a time, and I would be approaching the horses from the rear. They were very big. I was scared of them, and they knew it. They wouldn't move their feet, but as I tried to get past them to put the corn in the box, they would lean to the side and cut me off between the horse and the wall. I would back up and try to go around the other side, and they would do the same thing. Eventually, I would get them fed one at a time, but they both would go through the leaning bit on me. Most of the time I had to go back to the corncrib and into the barn to be in front of the horses. I told Peck about it and he laughed and said to just put my hand on their hip and tell them to move over. I never could do that as I was too short to reach their hip, and my arms were full of ears of corn anyway.

* * *

The barn was an interesting place. Up between the floor joists on the wall in the milking parlor there was an old radio. You couldn't see it due to all the cobwebs that covered it, but you could see a little red glow in there, as the radio did not have a cover over the tubes. The radio came on when you turned the lights on, and it was always tuned to the same station. They had a couple of cats that would sit and wait for Peck or Don to squirt milk into their mouths right from the cow's teat.

After I let the cows into the barn and shut them into their stanchions, my next job was to let the calves out of their pen so they could go find their mamas and get their supper. One day I had left the barn door open - my mistake - and a big calf didn't go to her mama. She went out the barn door with me right after her. She took off up the barnyard, and I finally caught her by the tail. She looked back and kicked me with both hind feet right in my face. It knocked me out cold. Don came looking for me and found me just as I was coming to.

I had landed in some fresh cow pies, and I had two hoof prints on my face, so everyone knew what had happened.

One cow was named Red, as she was reddish in color. We had taken to riding her when she was a big heifer, and she got smart and would rub us off at the board fence if she couldn't buck us off. Anyway, she was always devilish and didn't like to be milked. One night, when Don was trying to milk her, she kept swishing him with her tail. He would take the end of her tail and pinch it between his leg and hers, but she was able to jerk it out, and he got switched right in the eyes. He went and got a piece of binder twine and tied her tail up to a nail in the floor joist up above her back. She didn't like it when she couldn't switch, and she kicked out with her right leg and knocked the milk bucket out of Don's knees. He went and got some kickers, two metal cuffs held together by a chain. They were usually to be fastened to both of a cow's legs to keep her from kicking, but Don fastened one end to her leg and the other to the side of the pen she was in. He went back to milking, but when she couldn't kick with that leg; she kicked out with her other hind leg and knocked him down. He spilled his bucket of milk. He got upset with her about then, and he got another pair of kickers and fastened her other leg to the other side of the pen. About then Peck came along, and Don had a heck of a time trying to tell his dad he was just trying to milk that cow.

* * *

If we found a bull snake when we were out in the fields shocking oats, or whatever, Peck would send me back to the barn carrying that snake, so I could put it in the oat bin to catch rats. I didn't like snakes, and as I carried them by the tail, they would try to climb up themselves. I would shake them back down. Peck said I shouldn't do that, as I could break their neck. He wanted me to carry them in my arms, but I didn't want to get that close to them.

There were lots of rats in the corncrib. We kept a single shot 22 rifle in there, and it was always loaded. We would check the corncrib, and if we found a rat out in the open, we would shoot it. Most of the time the rats only came out at night. Don and I would sneak up to the corncrib at night with flashlights, and we would try to shoot them then, but at the first shot, they would all dash back into the corn. One day, when I was sent back to the house to get some water, I checked the corncrib, and a big rat ran and jumped up into the corn about two feet off the floor. He was in the corn, but his tail was hanging out. I sneaked up and grabbed him by the tail and started yelling for someone to come help me. I yelled and yelled. I was hanging on tight to his tail, and the rat was hanging onto the corn. Dolly finally heard me and came running as she thought that I was hurt or trapped or something. I told her to bring me the rifle, and when she did, I held the rat's tail by one hand and shot him with the other. She went back to the house, probably muttering something about "dumb kid", because I had scared her.

* * *

When I first went out to Peck's, he was making hay using horses to mow, rake, and haul the hay to the barn and to pull the hay up into the barn. I got to drive the horses on the hayrack while the men were loading the rack with the hay. I drove the rack to the barn, too, and one day I tipped the whole load over as I was trying to steer the horses and wagon through the gate and into the narrow lane. I was embarrassed, but the men quickly reloaded the wagon after they got it back on its wheels.

When they mowed and raked the hay, there was no place for a second person to ride as each just had one metal seat. Later, Peck cut the tongue off the mower and connected it to the Case tractor. I could ride on the tractor with him, and when Don and I were mowing, we would chase down and catch the half-grown rabbits that ran out of the hay on the last few passes before the hay was all cut. We would clean the rabbits, and Dolly would cook them for supper.

The hay was first raked with a buck rake that you lifted up to dump the hay for later picking it up with hayforks. Then it was loaded onto the hayracks or wagons. Later Peck got a windrow rake and a mechanical loader that picked the hay up in the windrows and elevated it up into the hayrack where it was mowed around to distribute the load. I would drive the horses and straddle the windrows so the loader could pick it up. When I didn't allow enough sweep on the corners, Don, who was up on the rack distributing the load, would give me a sign, like he smelled something bad, as we would have to go back later and get the hay that was missed.

When the hayrack was loaded, it was driven to the barn and parked on the north end under the projection of the roof that held the track that the pulley and hayfork would ride on, into the barn. Don would position the hayfork into the hay on the hayrack and he would yell, "Stuck". I would be on the other end of the barn to connect the hay rope onto the double tree, and drive the horses out into the barnyard to pull the hay up into the barn. I had lots of trouble with this. One day Dolly had invited two little girls to come out to the farm, and they were up in the haymow at a window up above my head. They started clucking to the horses, which would make them start to go, and I would yell for them to whoa, but it was too late. The rope was just long enough to reach the double tree if the horses were positioned close to the barn. I wasn't big enough or strong enough to back the horses and pull the heavy doubletree back, so I had to drive them in a circle to reposition them next to the barn again. Don would be yelling, "Stuck, stuck!" When I didn't go, he felt I hadn't heard him. I kept threatening those little girls, but I never got them to stop clucking to the horses. I was glad when they left.

* * *

Another time the horses ran away with me. Peck had purchased a new bigger fork so Don could get a bigger bite when he stuck the fork into the hay on the wagon. He got a very big bite and the horses were really struggling to pull it up to the track. When the hay reached the track, the load was too big to go into the barn. The horses were stopped in their tracks while holding this big load, and they panicked and took off sideways. I saw the rope coming at me about chest high, and I ducked and dropped the reins. Some of the hay fell off the fork, and the rest went into the barn. The horses stopped running when the load was off and they came to the end of the rope. Peck and Bill Tunks, the neighbor, came to the window to see what had happened, but I had reached the horses and was driving them back where they were supposed to be. Another time Don stuck the fork so deep the tines went into the wooden floor of the wagon, and the horses lifted the whole end of the wagon. Fortunately, the fork split the floorboards and the wagon dropped back down so I didn't have runaway horses again.

When we all went to help Bill Tunks with his hay, I had to drive his mules. Ugh! I was very apprehensive, but I managed to get through it. Bill was a colorful guy. When he was plowing corn with his mules, they would reach out, and bite off a leaf of corn. Bill would yell at them so loud we could hear it clear over at our farm. I went with Bill and Uncle Peck to a farm sale once, and Bill bought a farm implement for several hundred dollars. He paid cash. He pulled up his shirt where he had a white sock pinned to his long underwear. This was summer, but he always wore long underwear. Anyway, he had a big roll of bills in the sock, and he counted out the money right in front of all of us. Peck cautioned Bill on the way home that he shouldn't flash that much money around, but all Bill said was he didn't trust banks.

* * *

When the hay was all put up, the next big field job was to harvest the oats. Peck had a bailer that would cut the oats and tie them in bundles with binder twine. We would all go to the field and pick up the bundles and make a shock out of them. There were at least seven bundles to a shock, two in the middle, two more bundles on each end, and one spread out across the top to shed the rain.

When it was our turn to use the big threshing machine, they would pull it to Peck's farm and hook it up to the Case tractor with a big belt, as it was belt-driven. Then all the neighbors would come to help get the oats in. One neighbor had a matched set of horses and a fancy harness rig. The harness had strings hanging down all around it for show and to shoo away the flies. When he came up Peck's lane, everyone turned to watch as the neighbor was proud of his horses, and you could tell by the prancing that the horses were proud, too. Anyway, everyone drove their wagons to the field, and with pitchforks, they loaded the oat bundles on the wagons and hauled them to the threshing machine. There the oats were separated from the stalks, and the stalks were blown into a straw stack. Of course, the oats went into the oat bin in the barn by way of a wagon that was parked next to the threshing machine. At noon, we would all quit for lunch. We would be served the biggest meal I had ever seen. The farmers' wives would come and bring dishes to eat, and they helped Dolly set up big long tables out in the yard. Since I was helping drive the horses, etc. I got to eat with the men. They would all make fun of us kids but they would let us wash up with them, using a pitcher of water and a washbasin. After lunch, it was back to the field and everyone worked hard to get it all done in one day or two, at the outside. Of course, the weather was always good on the day that they picked to thrash.

* * *

A couple of years Peck planted a small patch of wheat so Dolly could bake, using wheat they raised on their own farm. It was harvested in the same way as the oats, but I didn't like shocking the wheat as the heads had long stiff bristles that made your arms itch.

* * *

I learned to drive on the Case tractor, which had huge big lugged rear wheels. It had a hand clutch, and when you wanted to go, you pulled the clutch handle back and you went forward. When you wanted to stop, you pushed the handle in and the tractor was so heavy it stopped. When I first was allowed to drive the Farmall tractor, Don and I were spreading manure and pulling the old manure spreader. He got off to open the gate, and he let me drive the tractor and spreader into the barnyard. He yelled for me to pull the clevis pin and unhook the spreader, but when I did that, the tractor started rolling. I climbed up in the seat and started steering, but it didn't stop when I put in the clutch. Don kept yelling for me to put on the brake, but I didn't know where the brake was. I ran it into the gate and bent the top bar of the gate. Don then showed me the brake and how you could get that tractor to turn on a dime. The brake for each wheel had been extended right up to each side of the steering wheel.

George, Dale and Don – WW2

While the hay and oats were growing, the corn needed plowing to remove the weeds. When Don was in the army, I went out to help Peck, and he put me to plowing corn. The corn was high, and it came way up on the Farmall tractor. I didn't do well at all. I thought I was supposed to be a good enough driver to turn the tractor at the end of the two rows I was plowing, skip two rows, and be lined up to go back across the field plowing the next two rows. I didn't pick up the plows when I did that, and I would plow out several hills of corn every time. I would get off the tractor and try to replant the corn, which I could tell wasn't going to work. I think a neighbor called Peck and told him he better let someone else plow his corn. Once when I was halfway across the field, listening to the drone of the tractor, I fell asleep and woke up and straightened out the tractor and kept going. Cousin Maynard Renfrow was recruited to finish the corn plowing, and at the dinner table he questioned who had switched rows in the middle of the field. I didn't know I had, and Peck knew he hadn't. Maynard said that I hadn't plowed out any corn so all was okay.

We liked to fish, so Cousin Don and I went over into Bill Tunks' pasture to seine minnows to use for bait. The creek that ran through Bill's pasture was twice as big as the creek in our pasture, and there were a lot more minnows there. When we got to the creek, there was a herd of Bill's cows over on a hill in the same field, and there was a big bull with them. All the time we were seining, the bull was up there with the cows, and he was bellowing and pawing the ground. He would even pick up dirt and throw it over his back. We didn't pay him much attention, as he wasn't very close. When we got all the bait we wanted, Don picked up the two milk pails full of water and minnows. I picked up the wet seine, and we headed out of the pasture. The bull decided if he was going to carry out his threat, he had to do it now, and he came charging down the hill at us. We ran to the closest fence, which was at a cornfield. I threw the seine over and climbed the fence. When I looked back, that bull was coming so fast and he was so big that I knew that fence was not going to stop him. I took off through the corn, running across the rows. I found that I could run much faster going with the rows, and I ran and ran. I finally got tired, but I kept going until I came to a road. I started walking down the road looking for the farm, but I was lost.

When Don got back home with the minnows and the seine, he told his mother about me being lost, as he had yelled and yelled to try to find me, but I hadn't responded. Dolly got in the car and drove the road. When she got to the Shady Grove General Store, she went in and asked if anyone had seen a little boy. One woman said she had, and told Dolly where to go look. When she found me walking down the road, I was going the wrong way, getting farther from the farm at every step.

This was my first experience with a bull, and it made a big impression on me. For years I had a recurring dream at night that a bull with wide horns was in the house, and he was coming up the stairs to get me. His horns were so wide he couldn't get up the stairs without turning his head sideways. He always made a lot of noise, and I couldn't understand why someone didn't come rescue me. When the bull finally got into my bedroom, Dad would come through the door right behind him. The bull would turn on Dad and stick his horns into the wall on either side of Dad, trapping him. About then I would wake up.

There was a time that Peck had a lot of trouble with bulls. One was killed in the pasture when he was struck by lightning. Another mean one would charge you at every opportunity. Peck had bought some blinders that he had strapped to the bull's head so that he couldn't see if he put his head down to charge. The bull wore all the padding off the blinders, and we had to get him in the barn so we could take them off him, as he had rubbed all his hair off and he was bleeding. We were all trying to herd the bull toward the pasture fence, and I was on the outside trying to get ahead of him to turn him. He had his head up running, saw me beside him, and put his head down and swung it toward me. I let him have it with an axe handle rat club that I was carrying. We finally got him corralled, got the blinders off him, and treated his wounds.

** * *

Once a bull had Cousin Murlin up against the corncrib, and he was raising Murlin up and down with his head. He wasn't hurting him, but he was scaring Murlin to death. He was raising him up and down the siding, bump, bump, bump. Don heard Murlin yelling, and he came to help. Don went into the barn and grabbed a hayfork, ran back out and stuck that fork into the bull's rear end. When the bull turned to look at Don, Murlin was able to duck into the corncrib through the hog door. The bull ran away with the fork sticking out of his rear end. Don knew he had to retrieve that fork, as his dad would be most displeased to see it sticking out of the bull. Every time Don got the bull cornered and tried to pull the fork out, it wouldn't come, as the tines were curved and he was pulling straight back. He finally realized the problem, and the next time he got a hold of the fork, he pulled upwards and was able to remove it.

One bull would sometimes trap Dolly in the pasture for hours. Peck had dragged a brooder house out into the pasture east of the house, and had built a barbed wire fence around it to keep the bull from attacking the house. Dolly had her pullets in this house, so she had to feed and tend them each day. She would always wait until the bull was in the other end of the pasture before she went out to do this, but when she was done and ready to go back to the house to cook dinner, the bull was always waiting for her between the gate and the brooder house. She would have to yell and yell to call for Sarge, the farm dog, to come rescue her. Since the dog was most often out in the field with us, it sometimes took a long time for the dog to hear her. The dog would chase the bull away, but this all happened way too often to satisfy her.

Another time when Murlin went out to push the cows down into the barn for milking, he met the bull between the straw stack and the fence. The bull immediately charged and pushed Murlin right through the fence. The bull had Murlin down on the ground, and he was mauling him. Of course, Murlin was yelling and that brought his Dad. Peck assessed the situation and decided he was going to have to throw the bull. He rolled under the bull and reached up for the ring that was in the bull's nose. He couldn't reach high enough to get the ring, but he got hold of the chain that was fastened to the ring. Unfortunately, the bull had the barbed wire from the fence tangled in the chain, and when the bull reared his head back, he pulled the barbed wire through Peck's hands, and it cut him up really bad. Peck just had to endure the pain and go ahead and get the ring in his fingers and twist as hard as he could. It finally worked and Peck did manage to throw the bull, and he and Murlin escaped.

Peck went to the house to have Dolly look at his hands. It was decided he needed stitches, so they went to town. Peck came back with his hands all bandaged up. Peck decided he had had enough of that bull, so he told Murlin to go get the tractor and the wagon as they were going to load the bull up and get rid of him. Murlin went out and cranked up the tractor, but the tractor backfired on him and the crank handle broke Murlin's arm. Now, with Murlin's arm in a sling and Peck's hands bandaged up, there was no one to milk the cows and do the chores. They had to rely on friends and neighbors.

* * *

Once when we were out shocking oats, Peck told me to go back to the house and get some cold water for them to drink, and to drive the Ford car back out to the field so we could all ride in for lunch. Well, that was big doings for me, as I had never driven the Ford or any other car. I got the water, backed the Ford out of the garage, and drove it up to the gate into the barnyard. There was a little slope, and I didn't know about the emergency brake, so I ended up killing the engine when I stopped. I opened the gate, drove the car through, and killed the engine again when I went back to close the gate. When I tried to start the car, I flooded it, and I couldn't get it started again. I walked back out to the field carrying the water, and I left that black Ford car in the barnyard, which turned out to be a big mistake. The big black bull came into the barnyard to get a drink at the water tank, and he took issue with the black car. He bent the running board up against the driver's side door, got his head under the car and was raising the car up to almost tipping it over. Dolly saw all this and tried to shoo the bull away, but the bull wasn't paying her any attention. She kept yelling for Sarge, the farm dog, as he could drive the bull away. Sarge was out in the field with us, but he apparently heard her calling as he came in and chased the bull away. Dolly had to open the gate, climb into the car through the passenger side and drive the car out of the barnyard.

* * *

Peck liked to eat fish, and he would let us go fishing when we got the fieldwork done. Don and I, and maybe the neighbor boy, would fish for smallmouth bass in Bear Creek and Lime Creek, and we loved to go to the Old Glory Quarry to fish for bluegills and largemouth bass. The quarry was large, but it wasn't active anymore, as the big hole had filled with water. The water was very clear, and you could see all the fish that were in shallow water. The deep water was very blue. Many folks came to swim in the quarry, and we did, too, but we always fished. I didn't like the swimming, as the little bluegills would bite me when I was just standing around in the clear water. They liked to bite me on my nipples, and it hurt.

We would fish for big bluegills using worms for bait and casting out into the deep water. It was slow going, as we couldn't tell if we were in a good spot. We could always see nice two-pound bass swimming around, but they could see us, too, and they wouldn't bite. We tried everything we could think of to catch them. We brought minnows and small crawdads, but we would catch very few bass and usually none. One day we had caught a huge soft-shelled crawdad, and we kept him in with the minnows. When we were picking up our stuff to go home, Don said, "I wonder if there is anything in here big enough to take this". He put the five-inch-long crawdad on his hook and cast it out into the water. It didn't sink two feet when a big bass came up from the bottom and nailed it. There were two or three other bass chasing the one that had the crawdad as they could see it sticking out of his mouth. I quickly put on a big minnow and cast out while Don was playing his fish. I hooked one of the bass, and we each caught a nice fish during the feeding frenzy brought on by the soft crawdad.

* * *

One summer Peck was recovering from an illness, and he decided to drive up to Minnesota to fish. He asked me if I wanted to go along, and I jumped at the chance. He had obtained a panel truck, and he had a mattress and blankets in the back for us to sleep on. We would try to park at rural schoolhouses each night, as they would have a pump for water and an outhouse. The mosquitoes were so bad that we would stop early so we could cook supper in the daylight. When night came, we would unload the truck and pile all our gear out on the ground. Then we would jump in the back of the truck, shut the door and prepare to kill mosquitoes. We would lie on our backs and shine our flashlights onto the ceiling and walls and smash the mosquitoes with our fingers. We would count them out loud, and we killed hundreds. When we got them sufficiently thinned out, we would get undressed and under our blankets where the others couldn't find us. We rented a cabin at a lake, and it was full of mosquitoes, too. Peck built a fire in the fireplace, and he had me pulling up long green grass from around the building to put on the fire to make smoke to chase the mosquitoes out. It got so smoky in there I couldn't see Peck, and I couldn't tell that it chased any mosquitoes out either.

When we were eating at a restaurant, the waitress asked us how we were doing, and we told her we weren't catching any fish. She told us how to get to a hidden lake that was full of fish. She said she was sure we would catch all we wanted. We drove down this little rural road and came right to a small lake that was full of reeds. An old man was there to rent boats, so we got in a boat and started trolling. We caught lots of northern pike, but they were all small, what folks called hammer handles. When we got back to the dock, the man wanted to see our fish, and I told him we threw them all back because we wanted to catch big ones, boat oars, etc. He got upset with me and said, "I, I, I'll call the sheriff". Peck asked me to go to the truck and get out the stuff for lunch while he talked to the man. It turned out that the man said there were too many northerns in this lake, and you had to keep everything you caught. Since there was a three-fish-limit on northerns, we should have six fish. We went back out in the boat, caught our six fish and left.

* * *

On another trip like that, Murlin went along. When we got to a lake we tried to start Dad's little five-horse motor we had brought along. The motor was frozen solid; it wouldn't turn over. We had not stored it properly and the cylinders were stuck to the block with varnish from the dried gasoline. As we drove to the next lake, Murlin was in the back seat taking the motor apart. He had a devil of a time as he didn't have any place to store all the parts. When he got the top of the block off, he hit the cylinder heads with a hammer to loosen them, and he got things to move. When he put it all back together, he had a handful of parts left over. The motor would run, but it sounded like a kid shaking rocks in a can. Dad bought a new motor.

* * *

One year they had a real tragedy. The barn burned down. No one knew for sure what happened, but Peck had some brood sows in the basement. He was constantly checking them so he could help with the birth of the little pigs and keep the sow from rolling over on them, etc. He always checked them before going to bed, and sometimes he would sit with them for a while and he would smoke his pipe while he waited. He might not have gotten the match out all the way, and there was straw bedding.

When a neighbor saw it and contacted them in the middle of the night, the barn was fully engulfed in flames. When Peck got to the door, the nails in the door were glowing red. They lost all the animals, all the cows, two big draft horses, the brood sows and all the dogs. They had the coonhounds and the farm dog shut in the barn to keep them warm. Peck got up on the roof of the corncrib to wet it down, and he managed to save it even though the heat melted the rubber boots he had on. When we heard about it back in Manchester, and got out there, the oats were still smoldering and had to be stirred and watered to get the last of the fire out. The big cupola that was up on the roof was a melted piece of tin that you couldn't recognize.

The barn was eventually built back. The basement was the same with the stanchions and pens, but it was only one story above that. They didn't need the big haymow as all the hay was bailed by then.

* * *

There was a big orchard out at Peck's. They had lots of apple trees, a few pear trees, a big cherry tree, mulberry tree, blackberry and black raspberry bushes, plus a big strawberry patch. We were always fighting the birds when the cherry tree was full of cherries. The robins and other birds were always beating us to the cherries. One year we covered the whole tree with blue cheesecloth but it didn't work, as the birds either found a hole or flew up underneath and still got at the cherries. I could see why; they were very good to eat.

We would all be invited out to pick the blackberries when they were ripe. Peck loved ice cream, and Dolly would always have him making ice cream while we were picking the berries. He would be turning the crank on the big old wooden ice cream maker as we left for the berry patch, so we could have ice cream and blackberries when we got back with our buckets full. I didn't ever have many in my bucket, as I would eat all the big ones. Anyway, one day when we got back to the house, Peck was still turning the crank on the ice cream maker and it should have been done a long time ago. It turned out he was embarrassed about it. He always got to eat the ice cream off the dasher and it was so good he got a bowl, had a bowl full and another, and ate the whole gallon. Dolly was upset with him, so he was put to cranking on a second gallon for the rest of us to eat with our blackberries. We always took berries home with us for our cereal and to put in pies, cobbler, etc.

* * *

The 4th of July was Grandpa George Washington Hansel's birthday. Everyone was to come to his birthday party. It was a family reunion. Dolly always brought fried chicken, and she had 4 big containers that kept the chicken hot. Of interest to me was how she prepared the chickens. Since she raised them, she couldn't kill them, so that was Peck's job. She would get up early, and when it was still dark, she would go to the chicken house, and using a flashlight and a wire with a hook on it, she would hook the chicken's legs, tie their feet together and carry them all down to the house before we even got up. Then she would cook breakfast. While we were eating, she would be out in the yard laying the chickens out in two rows about a foot apart. Each bird was a little ahead of the one in the next row. When Peck came out to go milk the cows, he would step on a chicken's head and pull on the legs and thereby pull its head off. She would have them all laid out just right so each step was a different chicken, and he would just walk down the rows with each step on the next chicken's head. It was a sight to behold as the chickens would be jumping all around and even up against the yellow house, bleeding, Dolly would do all the rest of the preparing, i.e. the scalding, picking, dressing and then cooking so we could go to the reunion.

* * *

Peck changed all his wagon wheels to automobile tires, and he bought used tires to put on them. They were always going flat, so he had all the equipment to take the tire off the rim and to patch the tubes. He used a hot patch method in the garage, which was really neat. It made a whole lot nicer job of it than we could do at our house with glue and the rubber patch, where you peeled the paper off and stuck it on the tube. When I was in college and had a '50 Chevy, Peck gave me a whole trunk full of tires and tubes and old leaf springs to use as tire irons. I usually had at least one flat every time I came home from college, but I was ready to fix it wherever I was, thanks to Peck.

In later years, Peck and Dolly moved to Waterloo, Iowa, where Dolly opened a doll shop. Peck helped out, putting arms, legs and heads on damaged dolls. They had fun with it for a while. Cousin Maynard Renfrow and his family ran the farm for a while, and he enjoyed it as he always had when we worked with cousin Don.

I remember riding way up on top of a full hay rack with Don driving the horses and singing with him:

Tweedle-o twill – puffin on corn silk. Tweedle-o twill – whittling away.
Settin' here wishin' that we was a fishin' In Old Glory Quarry – Tweedle–o twill
Tweedle-o-twill – bobbin' and weavin'. Tweedle-o twill ridin' this hay rack Old Dixie is strainin' – but since it ain't rainin' We gotta make hay – Tweedle-o twill.
Tweedle-o twill – the folks are all gone now. Tweedle-o twill only memories remain.
We can sit and ponder – When we'll meet again up yonder. Over the hill – Tweedle-o twill.

My favorite cousin, Don Hansel

COUSIN DON

I couldn't write about Peck without talking about Don. He was a treasure. Don was born on January 9, 1926, so he was 6 years older than I was, but he was perfect for me at that time. He loved all the animals, and he taught me so much about hunting, fishing and trapping. He gave me my first rifle, my first books on trapping and taught me to use lure (scent) to catch muskrats, etc. He was a delight to be around. He was always a leader, but he led by deeds. He could do everything better than anyone else because he practiced until he could. He was a fast learner, and he was a strong, healthy farm boy. He only had one eye that worked. The other one had a pupil that was triangular in the shape of the blade of a scissors, due to a sibling dispute.

One of the fun things Don did was to give people nicknames. Some of them stuck, too. Cousin Chuck Renfrow had curly hair, so of course, he was Curly. I still call him Curly on occasion. When Don heard that my Grandfather on my mother's side was named Gustav Engel, my nickname was "Gus". I was "Gus" all the way through grade school and high school, and I am still "Gus" to all those classmates and folks in my hometown.

Don also coined new words and sayings. If you were lazy or didn't want to do something, he said you had asthma. One of his best words was "frune." It meant, a lot. Two was a couple, three was a few, and "frune" was many. It was and is a fun word.

* * *

We had boats in the stock tank, and we would skip them from one end to the other and hope they would turn at the end and splash the other fellow. One time we had gone to the windmill at the tank to get a pail of well water to rinse the milk separator. Don had drawn the cold water, and we stopped to skip the boats. He was lucky and his boat turned just right, and it splashed me. I knew I wasn't going to be so lucky, so I picked up my boat and threw it the length of the tank so it landed in the water right in front of him, and it splashed him good.

He couldn't let that illegal move go unpunished, so he took after me with that full pail of cold water. I ran all the way to the house, went across the yard, and I was going out through the front gate when he finally got close enough to douse me with the bucket of water. It was so cold that it took my breath away, and I just stood there and gasped for a while. He calmly went back to the tank, drew another bucket of water from the well and proceeded to the barn to wash the separator. I met him there with my wet clothes, and we laughed about it, as he really had gotten back at me.

* * *

The back 40 acres were used as a pasture for the cows or for heifers, but there was no creek for them to get water. There was a round metal tank there and a pump. We would walk all the way back there in the middle of the day and pump more water in the tank to make up for whatever the stock drank or that had evaporated. There were three big willow trees growing there, due to the excess water. The trees were thick, but they weren't very tall. Anyway, there were always crows there, and when we came over the hill, the crows would take to cawing and carrying on because we were disturbing them. All the time we were pumping water, they were right above us in those willow trees. We were annoyed by them being so brash, so we decided to bring a shotgun and shoot them. Don had a single barrel 12-gauge shotgun, so we loaded it and come over the hill carrying it. The crows immediately left and flew over to the big cottonwood trees in the grove. The next day we didn't bring the gun, and the crows were all over us again. We decided they knew what a gun was, so the next day we took the gun apart. Don carried the stock, and I stuck the barrel down my pant leg. We came over the hill carrying a hidden gun. The crows left again for the grove. We tried for a week to fool those crows, and everything we tried didn't work. We thought that crows had to be the smartest birds around. Since the crows were always making so much noise cawing, we took to trying to imitate them, and we got pretty good at it. We finally did succeed in shooting a few. We would go to the big cottonwood trees in the grove when they weren't there, and we would hide and call them in, cawing with our voices. It worked and we got our revenge.

Cousin Don

* * *

Sometimes we would go fishing on the Cedar River at night. We would get the chores done a little early and load everything in Don's car. He had a black Ford coupe with a rumble seat in the back. We always took neighbor boys along, too. To prepare for this fishing trip, we would need lots of bait as we were going to be fishing for catfish using trot lines with lots of hooks. Don liked to use stink bait for catfish, and we made it one time out of freshwater clams we got out of the river. We opened the clams and cut up the mussel in small bait size pieces. We then put the pieces in a gallon glass jug and buried it in the ground for a week. When we used it, the smell was so bad that you had to turn your head away so you wouldn't breathe it. Your fingers would smell so bad because the juice would soak into your pores and you couldn't wash it off. Ugh!

We would build a fire, and we would sleep under Dad's long narrow canvas. We would put the canvas down, put our blankets on it and throw the other end of the canvas over us to keep us warm and out of the wind or rain. We would get up two or three times in the night to go check the trotlines and to re-bait, etc. Howard Hartsberg usually went along. He was a neighbor boy that lived several farms to the southeast of Peck's. One night the wind came up. Howard had gotten his shoes wet and when he took them off to go to bed, he put them downwind of the fire so they could dry out. During the night, when we got up to tend the trot lines, someone would always put more wood on the fire before we went back to bed. When we got up in the morning, Howard couldn't find his shoes. It seemed the fire had moved during the night. The wind had blown, and everyone who tended the fire put the wood where the flame was. The fire had moved downwind about three feet. By stirring the ashes, we found the rubber heels of Howard's shoes. He had to go home in his stocking feet, and he said his dad was going to kill him for burning up his shoes.

We would have to get up early in the morning to tend the trotlines, take off the fish, and then wrap the trotlines around a board to carry them home. The hooks on the dropper lines were always stuck into the end of the board so they wouldn't tangle or get caught in something or someone. This was all done very quickly as we all had to get home to do the chores. One night I was holding the 6-volt lantern so the guys could see to bait the hooks, and I set it on the ground. The lantern got knocked into the river, and it was still on. We could see it way down there in a deep hole. As we were all looking at the problem, Don took off his clothes, jumped into the river and dove down with his eyes open, picked up the lantern and retrieved it for us. Nothing to it. The water was about eight feet deep, and I don't think anyone else would have gone after it.

* * *

Don had a knack of making everything fun. One time after the corn was planted and the hay wasn't ready yet, Peck and Dolly decided to plant a big garden. They always had a garden west of the house and north of the strawberry patch, but they wanted a really big garden. Peck plowed up a big garden right in part of a cornfield along the pasture east of the barn. They planted all the usual vegetables, plus watermelons, pumpkins etc. The problem was, before they went back to the garden, the corn needed plowing, the hay needed cutting, and the oats were getting ripe. All that fieldwork was done before they thought about the garden again. Well, the weeds had taken over the garden, and it looked like it was all weeds and no vegetables. Peck asked us boys if we wouldn't like to hoe the garden. We hadn't seen it, so we didn't object. We took hoes and headed for the new garden. When we got there, we were flabbergasted. We couldn't see anything but weeds, and they were so big we couldn't touch them with a hoe. It was very hot and soon dusty, and we were griping big time. We came back for lunch, and you never heard so much moaning from three guys. We thought that Peck should give up on the garden and just let it go. There were all kinds of weeds, like big horseweeds six or seven feet tall. There were big clumps of weeds two feet in diameter and a foot high. It was impossible.

Well, Don came up with a plan. We were going to declare war on the weeds. They had attacked our garden, and it was our job to repel the attack and defeat the weed army. He said the big clumps of weeds were machine gun nests, and the big horseweeds were big gun emplacements. The smaller weeds were soldiers like us, and we could handle them, but we might need reinforcements to handle the machine gun nests and the big gun emplacements. Well, we attacked and started to thin out the enemy. In order to see what we were doing, we had to carry all the chopped-out weeds to the end of the row by the fence and pile them up. We would try to attack the machine gun nests, and if we could, we would wipe them out, but we always called for reinforcements to handle the big horseweeds. We each had two rows, and the one assigned the row would attack the gun emplacement from the front while the other two guys came in from each side. We would all chop until the big weed toppled over. Since we were helping each other with the big weeds, we looked forward to finding the next one in whatever row it was in. Now it took several days to clean out this garden, but you never heard another gripe. Just the opposite. We couldn't wait to get back at it. Even though it was hot, dusty, hard work, it was fun. We couldn't believe it when we got done. We sat on that huge pile of weeds and laughed and laughed. What had been drudgery had ended up fun, courtesy of Don.

* * *

Don and Maynard took me along squirrel hunting one time. They each had shot a couple of squirrels, and they wanted me to shoot one. I didn't have my glasses as yet, and I couldn't see anything that was very far away. Sarge, the dog, treed another squirrel, and they could see him up in the tree. They kept trying to get me to see him. Finally, they said he was in the second crotch on the right side of the tree. They gave me Maynard's 20 gauge double barrel shotgun and told me to aim at that crotch and shoot up there. I did, and I guess I missed, but shooting the gun straight up in the air about broke my shoulder. It didn't knock me down, but I was weaving around and rubbing my shoulder. Maynard took the gun, reloaded it and found that I had fired both barrels at the same time. I had put my fingers on both triggers. No wonder I was sore!

* * *

I went along one winter when Don had some traps out, and he caught a mink in a little spring that didn't freeze. Everything else was snow and ice. This was the first mink I had ever seen, and Don thanked God for letting him catch him. This was new to me, too, and I was impressed. He let me carry the mink home, and I petted him all the way. Don said it was a "cotton" mink and wasn't worth as much as his others, but I didn't know what he was talking about. That meant his fur was white underneath when you blew the guard hairs away.

* * *

Don saw a fresh mound of earth in the middle of a pasture on a rise, and it seemed to him a perfect place to catch a fox. He put a number-two jump trap in the fresh earth, and covering the pan with waxed paper, he sifted dirt over the trap. He felt he did a good job and that he would catch himself a fox. The next day he checked the set, and the trap was gone. He had staked it down, but something must have gotten caught and took his trap away. He looked everywhere to no avail. Much later, he saw fresh digging at the site, and he went up to investigate. What do you know! He had caught a badger, and it had dug down into its burrow and that was why Don couldn't find his trap. That was the only badger that he or I or anyone else I knew ever caught.

* * *

One time when we had gone off in Don's Ford coupe, and we were coming back in the night, the gas line broke, and the car wouldn't run. Don siphoned gas out of the gas tank, and he had me ride on the fender with the side hood up. I had a coffee can full of gas, and he had the top of the carburetor off so I could pour gas into it when he needed me to. He would tap on the windshield, and I would slop some gas in. He would gun the car up the hill and coast down the other side, and tap on the glass again. I would pour some more in the carburetor. We got home that way, and it was fun, too.

* * *

Don devised a ball game that he and the neighbors could play. It was fast pitch softball. The garage was home plate, and you stood in front of the closed garage door to bat. Someone pitched to you, whirling his arm around to make the ball come in as fast as possible. If you could hit the ball, a grounder was a first base hit, but there were no bases. If you could hit the ball hard enough to hit the corncrib wall, it was a double. The roof of the corncrib was a triple, as was the barn wall. Over the corncrib was a home run, as was the roof of the barn. You could play this game with only two players, the pitcher and the batter, but it was better if you had a fielder to throw the balls back. Don was the best pitcher, and he threw the ball into the home plate so fast I was scared to death when he wanted me to try to hit it. He saw how scared I was, and from then on, I was the fielder, which I liked much better.

* * *

When Don was in the Army, he took up boxing. They taught him how, and he became good at it. He won his matches for his unit when they would have competition-boxing matches with other units. He had a cigar box full of metals and ribbons.

Not long after he came back from the Army, he had some pain, and they found he had colon cancer. They opened him up and took about six feet of this intestine out and sewed him back up. He began to feel better and was healing up. He wanted to go fishing, and he asked me to go along to Minnesota. I was in high school, and my coach and his wife, Mr. and Mrs. Kinch, had been to a lake in Wisconsin when the fishing was so good, they caught Northern Pike on every cast. The pike ate the paint off the daredevil spoons they were using, and their arms got so tired they had to quit fishing. I told Don about it and he thought we ought to go there. We did, and when we got to the resort, we rented a cabin and a boat. At the office, the owner's daughter, who was about our age, was trying to teach a pet crow to talk. The crow would come to her and sit on her shoulder and make noises, but we couldn't recognize any words. The funny thing was, we were very interested in the girl and her crow, but we never saw either of them again. I think her Dad felt we would be a bad influence on her.

As we were moving into our cabin, there was a group of fishermen loading their car to go home. They were packing lots of cleaned fish in dry ice in the trunk of their car. We felt we were in the right place at the right time. Well, we fished and fished, but we couldn't catch a fish. We even fished in a rainstorm, but all we caught were two big bullheads. We did learn to play the harmonica as we both had bought one and had the beginner's instructions. Three Blind Mice was the first song, and we covered all the other holes with our fingers, and we would blow, draw, and blow as instructed. We finally asked the owner about the fishing and told him about our coach. He told us they were there at the right time, and this wasn't it. When we asked him about all the fish the other fellows were loading into their car, he told us they were all catfish that the men had caught on trotlines. It was all a bust, no girl, no crow and no fish.

When we got home, Don was feeling good, and he and a neighbor tried to play the fast pitch softball game. When Don was pitching, he pulled something, and he knew it was bad. They performed surgery on him again, and he was full of cancer. They closed him up and sent him home to die. It took him a long time. Peck got him a hospital bed so he could be as comfortable as possible. At Christmas time, he said he wanted a chromatic harmonica or he was going to have venison to eat, i.e. one of Santa's reindeer. He got it, but he never played it, as he was too sick by then. Being a strong lad with a strong heart, the cancer ate away at him until he was nothing but a skeleton with skin on it. Dolly nursed him as best she could, but he was a terrible sight. He had no meat on him at all, and he couldn't talk etc. He finally, mercifully, died on the 24th of April 1951, at the age of 25. Everyone was devastated that such a wonderful boy with a cheery disposition had to die at such a young age. I was in college, but I wasn't interested in it anymore. The folks let me quit for a semester, and I helped brother Dale build a house in Estherville, Iowa. I still cry every time I think about it. He was a wonderful boy and special young man.

WILLIE

Let me tell you about Willie the coon. My cousin Don loved hunting, fishing and trapping, but due to the chores and farming, he was hampered as to when he could find the time to go. Well, the nights were free from farm work, so he took to coon hunting. Don lived on a farm, and he had coon hounds. Several of the neighbors' boys had dogs, too, and they loved to listen to the music of those hounds running coons at night. When I was a squirt, I'd go along sometimes, and they would build a fire and lay around it, with one fellow's legs being the pillow for the next guy, etc. Each knew the voice of his dogs, but I couldn't tell one from the other. We always had something to eat and drink so we had a picnic around the fire, too. They would identify each hound by its voice, and argue over whose dog was doing the best job.

One night they rescued a young raccoon that was about to be killed by the dogs and brought it home and asked if I wanted to keep it. Well - you betcha! I was just the right age and very interested in all wildlife. Don named him Willie, and I took him home.

Dad built a fancy vertical cage for him with a long trough for water, and a tree to climb that led to an insulated box in the top filled with straw. Willie loved his new home. With his quick little hands, he fished for minnows and crawdads that I put in his water trough from our fishing bait tank. The neighborhood kids got a big kick out of his antics, like shaking his leg when he pulled out his front paw with a crawdad attached, pinching his finger. Willie quickly learned which foods he could wash and which ones he couldn't. He never again dipped a cookie in the trough after the first time, when he melted a gingersnap.

He knew his enemies, and when dogs would come around, he would quickly climb his tree and disappear into his house. He was also afraid of car lights, and when I had him loose in the yard at night, he would run to me every time a car approached, and he would climb me like a tree. His claws were sharp, too! He would sit on my shoulder until the car had passed and then down he'd come to wander around the yard again.

Willie grew up, and we started talking about turning him loose back into the wilds. We felt he was pretty well ready, but we were concerned that he might be too tame. We took him back to the farm, and Don and I decided to lay a trail through the woods by leading Willie on a leash and putting him in a tree. We then let the dogs follow the trail and tree him, thinking that would convince Willie to stay clear of dogs and people. Well, one of the more athletic dogs jumped up and bit Willie, and he decided none of us were worth sticking around for. That night he got out of his temporary chicken wire cage and left the farm.

Cousin Don and I went looking for him and we found coon tracks under the bridge where the creek entered the pasture. We decided that each of us would set one trap and see who was the best trapper. Don had read an article describing how to modify a steel trap that would allow the trigger to trip when the pan was raised, as well as when the animal stepped on the pan. His scheme was to tie a big crawdad on the pan, and when Willie came along, he would grab that crawdad and be caught. For my set, I planned to build a driftwood fence across the creek under the bridge, leaving just a small opening, which would contain my trap. Any coon coming down the creek would be funneled right into it.

We wrapped the jaws of the traps, since we didn't want to hurt Willie, and that afternoon we set the traps. Don placed his above the bridge, and I went just below it. There were all sorts of vines growing all over the bridge abutments and hanging down from the superstructure. When I set the trap, there was nothing to fasten it to, so I hung a long wire from the bridge down to the water.

The next morning, during milking, Don suggested that I go down and check our traps. I was proud to go and was surprised he would send me alone, but I guessed he knew I would come a-running if we had caught anything.

When I reached the bridge, it didn't look like the same place. The driftwood fence I had built was all gone, and all the vines which covered the concrete walls and hung down from the bridge were gone - I mean, completely all cleared out! I couldn't believe it. I walked up and stood on a little sand bar in the center of the creek as I looked around at the denuded scene.

I finally got the idea to look for my trap, and I started following the wire with my eyes. It led to the right concrete abutment and into an eroded hole under it. When my eyes met the eyes of the big old boar coon that my trap had caught, he came out from under there like a freight train, and he headed straight for my throat. I backpedaled as fast as I could, but my feet got tripped up, and I sat down in the middle of the creek. That coon came to the end of the wire about two feet from my face. That was one mad animal, and I was one scared little boy.

We eventually got that coon into Willie's temporary cage and got the trap off his foot. We gave up looking for Willie.

Me and Willie the coon

SKUNK STORIES

My first encounter with a skunk was a spotted skunk which we called a civet cat. This was a small black animal with white spots or short irregular stripes. I was a young lad and my brother, who was twelve years older and my dad were both trappers. There were traps hanging in the loft over the garage. I had a single shot Steven's "Little Scout" rifle that my cousin Don had given me, and I was a hunter and fisherman.

While walking along the railroad tracks to get out of town to go hunting, I noticed a little trail along a fence near the "Dry Run". This was a wet weather creek that flowed under a timber trestle bridge east of the town of Manchester, Iowa, where we lived. This trail ran along through the grass and ended at a hole in the bank, which obviously was some animal's home. I decided to return with a steel trap to see what lived in the hole.

After setting the trap and returning the next day, I learned that a civet cat lived there, as he was now in my trap, alive. I could not get close to him without getting a dose of his foul-smelling musk, so I decided to shoot him with my rifle so that I could retrieve my trap. When I shot him, he stunk up the place good before he died, and I decided to come back later to retrieve the trap. I came back several times and much later, weeks later, I finally brought the trap home. I washed and washed the trap, but I couldn't get rid of the smell. I finally hung the trap back up with the others over the garage, and as I did, I saw a small green object shining up by the roof. I got a stepladder and retrieved a little green jack knife with the blade open that had been stuck in the rafter. Would you believe that knife smelled of skunk? This was strange!!

When I told my dad about it, he said that my cousin Mary Adele had given the cute little knife to my brother Dale. Big brother had skinned a skunk with it years before, and he could not get the smell out of the knife, so he had stuck it up in the rafter to let time take care of it. Well, I stuck it back up there to give it some more time.

Eventually, I took it down and carried it, but I lost it at the sale barns. I was sitting up in the bleachers fiddling with the knife when I dropped it. The bleachers were over the hog pens, so that was the end of that!

I almost got into trouble that day, too. While in the bleachers waiting for my buddies, the auctioneer was trying to sell three ponies. When the guys walked in, I waved at them and kept waving so they could see me. The man next to me told me to quit waving, as I had raised the price of the ponies twice, and I was now set to buy them.

* * *

My second meeting with a spotted skunk, or civet cat, was on a sunny afternoon when the snow was melting, and I was going rabbit hunting. As I left home on South Brewer Street in Manchester, I crossed the vacant lot east of the house and was going past Blair's barn when I saw something moving along the concrete foundation. A civet cat was walking in the grass next to the foundation where the sun had melted the snow. He wasn't paying any attention, and I was able to get quite close to him without him taking notice. When I was about twenty feet away, I decided to shoot him to try to break his backbone, to test the theory that a skunk cannot "shoot" if his back is broken. At my shot, the civet cat died instantly, and he did not stink. It worked!!! I was going to take him home and skin him, but he was a very skinny, poor animal with the mange, so I buried him under some broken concrete rip rap so no other animal could catch the mange from him. But, I had learned that a well-placed bullet could prevent a skunk from shooting back.

A few years later, while hunting with our very smart beagle dog, Jeep, I heard the dog baying like he was treed over in the scrub oaks, a cut-over area of oak trees where oak brush had grown up from the stumps. When I hurried over there, I found the dog barking at a big striped skunk that apparently had come out of hibernation on this warm, sunny day, and was out walking in the snow. The dog would retreat every time the skunk would turn his rear end toward him, and as the skunk would start off again, the dog would circle around and approach him from the front and stop him with his barking. I watched this occur three or four times, and then I got an idea. This was a big beautiful skunk that was mostly black with two short white stripes. He would make a great fur hat!

I decided to shoot him in the back, so he wouldn't stink, and take him home to skin him. When the rifle cracked, he only stunk for a very brief moment, and the dog left to look for something else. I picked up the skunk, and when I got home, I took him right into the garage. There was a pot-bellied stove in the garage that I stoked up with kindling and started a fire to warm the place up. When it got warmer, I took off my coat, hung the skunk from the ceiling with a wire and proceeded to skin him. Mind you, he did not smell - to me.

When I was about half done, the small garage door opened and my mother came in and then jumped back out and yelled, "What are you doing in there?" I yelled back, "I'm skinning a skunk." There was some laughing, and finally the big garage door opened, and in came all sorts of folks My cousin Maynard Renfrow had come home on furlough from the Air Force, and he had to catch the train back to his base. His folks' car wouldn't start, and they had walked down the four doors so Mom could drive them to the depot. Maynard threw his B-4 bag in the trunk, and off they went. I closed the garage door and went back to my skinning.

Mom said when they got to the depot, they couldn't smell the skunk, but when they walked in, the other people in the depot could. It appears that skunk smell is so strong that it overwhelms our olfactory nerves, and we can no longer detect it. However, the smell is there to others until their noses are overwhelmed, too. I always wondered if Maynard's clothes smelled when he got back to his base.

I stretched and dried the skunk skin and stitched it to a wool hat I had. It was one sharp hat with the skunk's face in the front, two white stripes on top and the black tail hanging down the back. Unfortunately, I didn't know how to tan the hide, and every time I took it outside, the humidity softened the skin, and before long, the smell of the rotting hide was worse than the smell of the skunk, and I had to chuck the whole thing. It was sharp while it lasted, though.

That black shiny fur with the white stripes made me the envy of the other kids - if they didn't get too close so they could smell it!

* * *

Another time, when I was in grade school, I went fishing at Crow Wing Lakes in Minnesota with my sister Arlene and her husband. They had rented a cabin at a resort on one of the lakes, and I stayed up one night getting my tackle box in order for the next day's fishing. I had only one light on over the table and something moved out in the center of the room! Thinking it was a mouse, I jumped up to try to "get" him. Would you believe it was a huge spider - the largest I had ever seen. Spiders and snakes were the two species I was most frightened of, and I always made my best effort to try to kill them before they got me.

When I pursued this 4-inch diameter (legs) spider, he ran out of the light and underneath the table. I shined my flashlight under there, and two lights shined back at me. The two lights were the flashlights reflection off the spider's eyes, and he had just earned more respect from me, as they seemed to be about a half inch apart. I got the broom that we used to sweep out the place and attacked the spider. Every time I would try to mush him with the broom, his body would go between the broom straws and when I picked up the broom, off he would go again.

I had a canvas hunting coat that I was using as a fishing vest to carry some of my tackle in and to keep the wind off me out on the lake. It was lying on the floor, and the spider came out from one of my worryings with the broom and ran under the coat. I had him now! I systematically stepped on every inch of that coat in order to smash that spider. When I was sure he was dead, I slowly started to turn the coat over for confirmation. This was all done very carefully, as he might not be dead, and I didn't want him jumping up on me! To shorten a long story, I never did find the spider, and I was now afraid to wear the coat, should he be hiding in a sleeve or a pocket.

* * *

All of this is mentioned in passing to get to the next skunk story. The next night we were all kept awake in that log cabin by a mysterious thumping noise coming from under the floor. It was an intermittent sound, but when you could hear it, you could almost feel it - thump - thump – thump, kind of a soft sound as if someone was trying to wake us up, then it would stop for a while. This went on for a long time, and it would move from one place to another. It was eerie and very disconcerting, to say the least.

In the morning at breakfast we all talked about it, and we got the idea to look under the cabin. When we shined the flashlight under there, we found a skunk, with his head in an olive bottle. He couldn't get it out, and when he walked along the side of the cabin's foundation log, his head would sway from side to side and the bottle would hit the log - thump - thump -thump! Wheeeeooo! We had lost sleep, but so far we hadn't had to put up with skunk smell. We reported the skunk to the resort management, and they sent two fellows to round him up. They escorted the skunk out from under the cabin and out of the camp to the garbage dump. They dispatched him there, but he still stunk up that place and the camp, when the wind was from that direction.

* * *

When I got out of the Army in 1958, I took a job as a sanitary engineer in Milwaukee, Wisconsin. That first fall, Shirley and I went pheasant hunting with a draftsman from work, and his wife. The girls mostly stayed in the car while we hunted with our beagle dog "Rummy" that we had bought in Kansas and raised from a puppy. The vegetation was very heavy, and we couldn't get the birds to fly, but, if you stayed with the dog, he would get them up. I had gotten a couple of roosters by staying right behind Rummy.

We came to a low swampy area, and I was standing among big bogs, when something moved under my feet. I stepped back and looked down, and two big skunks were under my feet. They had been in a ball in hibernation, and I had been standing right on top of them. I jumped back about 10 yards, and they separated about 10 feet.

The dog showed up on the other side of the skunks. I only smelled skunk for a few seconds, but I was afraid the dog would get sprayed. He stopped, looked at the two skunks, and then at me. I didn't call him, but he quickly ran between the skunks to me. I was most happy that neither of us had been sprayed, and we started for the car.

As the dog and I were coming up the road, the girls started to complain about skunk smell, and I yelled that I had seen two skunks, but that we hadn't gotten sprayed. They informed me, that was what I thought. They thought differently! I put the dog in the trunk of the car with my pants, and I put on my chest waders to drive home in. I tied my boots, that had stood on the skunks, to the hood ornament, and we started for home. We couldn't smell skunk any more, but when we stopped at a drive-in for lunch, we were informed by the girl who came out to wait on us, that my boots or something, stunk of skunk.

I was wearing a pair of cushioned-sole army socks at the time, and we never did get the smell out of those socks! When they were dry, you couldn't smell them, but when my wife would wash them, you could smell skunk when you opened the lid of the washing machine. You never knew which pair smelled, but you knew they were in the wash. I just wore these socks for hunting, so they lasted many years, as I had several pair of them. We estimated I had them for ten years, and the smell was always on top of the water in the washing machine when they were in the wash. We would have thrown them away earlier, but you just couldn't tell which pair was the smelly pair when they were dry. We never thought of getting them wet and sniffing them.

TRAPPING

When I was about fourteen, I ran a trap line on the backwater as my brother, father and grandfather had done before me. Of course, one had to adequately prepare, and I had boiled my traps in chopped-up soft maple bark and leaves to dye them a deep black color for camouflage, then dipped them in melted beeswax to take any odor away.

Two things were essential on any successful trap line. One was placing the trap so an animal would step in it, and the other was hiding the trap to keep an unscrupulous trapper from finding it. When you found a good place for a "set", you entered the water a little way down the bank and approached by water so as to leave no scent to shy the animal away, and no tracks for the unscrupulous to follow.

Well, this one day it had snowed a little, and I left tracks. Even though I approached each "set" by water, it allowed someone to follow behind me. The next day I found myself short fourteen traps. I could see the man tracks that had followed my trail, and he went into the water every place I did, and although he didn't find all of my traps, he got most of them. Fortunately, it was a weekend, and I didn't have school, so I followed his tracks. He continued around the backwater and went up the river. He waded across the river at the mouth of Coffin's Creek and continued up the creek where he started setting my traps. Well, I just "collected" them back, and I got all of mine and one dozen shiny brand new ones of his. Since I had no use for his traps, I stashed them under a log and came on home. Of course, I told my Dad about it, and we had a laugh since I had gotten even with the thievin' galoot, whoever he was.

A couple of days later, Dad answered the door, and came and got me where I was tending hides in the basement. He said there was someone who wanted to talk to me. It turned out to be Fred Hilsenbeck, a man who worked for Dad on occasion as a mason or a plasterer. I had known him all my life as a fun fellow. He always called me "Pod" since that was what I had called him before I learned to say his name. He said, "Pod, you got my traps", and I blurted out, "Well, you got mine first!" He said, "Hell, Pod, I didn't know they was yours," and I said, "Would it have made any difference?" etc., etc. Eventually I told him where he could find his traps, and we parted friendly.

I always liked Hilsey. Dad said he was a mighty good trapper, and when they would go coon hunting, Hilsey would wade the creeks to see if anyone was trapping. If so, he would move a trap ever so little or place a stick just right to make a mink step on the pan. Of course, if the trap caught anything the next night, Hilsey figured that one was his, and then he'd set the trap back so the other fellow could catch himself one.

* * *

Charlie Arnold, Maynard's father in law, had a problem with beavers cutting down his trees along Honey Creek and he got a permit to trap them as at the time there was no open season on beaver. Charlie tried to trap them for several weeks to no avail as his traps were too small, and they wouldn't hold a beaver. Maynard asked Charlie if I could try, and when he said okay, Maynard asked me if I would be interested. You bet! I had of course, never caught a beaver, but I took some number two fox traps and Maynard helped me make a set in a caved-in beaver run. Maynard lowered me into the hole holding me by my feet, and I set two or three traps and wired them to a pole up on top of the bank.

I caught a beaver that night, but the next morning I couldn't get him up through the hole alive, so I had to shoot him with the 22 rifle I carried. I skinned him and stretched him round, nailed to Charlie's barn. I caught a couple more, but Charlie claimed I was taking them out of his traps and he never paid me for my trouble.

* * *

Around that same time, I had a really frightening experience. I had set a trap on a tree that had blown down across the creek as a natural bridge. The first night I caught an opossum, the second night a raccoon, and the last night I had no trap. It turned out that several kids crossed the creek on that downed tree and the last one stepped in my trap. It held him fast and if he had fallen off the tree he would have drowned as the current would have pulled him under the log. His buddies came to his aid and unwired the trap and got him to bank and got the trap off with a lot of difficulty as they were strong traps. It cut his leather shoe toe and ruined the shoes. His brother gave me the trap back and showed me the shoe. I had caught a boy in a number two fox trap and it scared me to death because of what might have been.

* * *

In about the sixth or seventh grade, I was becoming a little bit proficient at trapping. At least my success was sufficient to be noticed. One of my buddies, Skeeter Barker, decided he wanted to try trapping, too, so he set a trap about two blocks from his house near the river bank. There was a big pile of broken concrete rubble that had been dumped there to keep the bank from eroding at that spot, and there was a hole at the top that some animal had been going in and out of, according to Skeeter.

He came up to me in school and said, "Hansel, what do you do if you catch a skunk?" When I asked him about the situation, I learned he had set the trap in the hole and had wired the ring of the trap chain to a long pole he found there. Perfect! I had read that if a skunk did not have his hind feet on the ground, he could not control his musk glands, i.e. he could not squirt. I was always reading everything I could find about hunting and trapping. According to this article, if the skunk was caught by the front foot, you could carefully raise him off the ground and carry him to the water lower him into the river and drown him, all without the skunk activating his artillery.

I related all this to Barker and he was to try it that night after school. He did not come to school the next day. When he did the following day, he still smelled a little like skunk. He had been bathed a number of times in tomato juice to try to make him a little more presentable.

He said all went well, to a point. He had slowly approached the trapped skunk and was able to get him out of the hole on the other end of the long pole, all without any smell. He had a hard time lifting the skunk up off the ground, but he finally managed it and started down the broken rubble to get to the river, while holding the skunk up over his head. When he was about halfway down the bank, his foot slipped on the sloping concrete rubble, and he fell down and dropped the whole thing. The butt of the pole slid down the bank into the river, and that brought the trapped skunk on the other end right to Barker. The skunk now had his hind feet on the ground, and he was aware of his tormentor. Everything was in order for a good counter attack. Skeeter got both barrels, fired at close range. His folks buried his clothes and never dug them up.

DUCK BLINDS I HAVE KNOWN

When I was in grade school, I hunted ducks with Bob Davis, a jeweler who worked for Walter Rossman in his jewelry store. We had a duck blind on a little island out in the middle of the backwater that was formed by the Marion Street Dam. One morning I had invited Chuck Martensen to hunt with us, and as we were waiting for the ducks to appear, we noted that each of us was hunting with a Winchester Model 12 shotgun. The interesting thing was that they were all different gauges: a 12 gauge, a 16 and a 20 gauge gun. I was the youngest, and I had the 12 gauge, the biggest gun. It was my brother's gun, and he was away in the Air Force. Chuck Martensen had the 16 gauge and Bob Davis, the man among us, was using the 20 gauge.

That summer Dad got the job of remodeling the library, including putting down a new tile floor and redoing the roof. The roof had large eaves with wide copper gutters that had deteriorated, and they were to be torn out and replaced with standard gutters.

The old lumber that was torn out would make a good duck blind, and I talked Dad into letting me have it for that purpose. What he didn't haul to Terrill Park for me in his truck, I hauled in a coaster wagon and ferried it out to the island in our boat. I built a dandy blind. I dug the posts in with a posthole digger and put up a 2x4 frame and covered it with boards. All of it was from the very used lumber from the library, so it was a dark brown, camouflaged color. The back wall extended up above the front and sides, and it ended at a sloped half roof over the bench seat. The seat was split in the middle, and a space was left for Bob's little oil stove that would be between us. The blind also had a shooting bench. The sides of the blind were just about head high, so you could watch the ducks, and then you would step up on a bench that ran across the front of the blind which would put you up above the brush so you could swing your gun and shoot. I covered it all with tarpaper to keep out the wind and rain and dug a little boat slip on the other end of the island. It was a perfect set-up.

During the rest of the summer the bushes grew in around it, and by fall, you couldn't even see it.

Come opening day of the duck season, Bob and I found the two Stephenson brothers in the blind, and would you believe, they claimed they had built it!! Well, Bob and I were out in the blind the next few mornings way before daylight, and we always beat them to the blind. They took to sitting out in front of our decoys in their boat so as to discourage us and the ducks. After a few days of this, when we didn't discourage, they resorted to more drastic measures. When we arrived at the blind, we found it completed denuded. They had brought out their saws and brush hooks, and had systematically cut all the trees and brush on the island and thrown it all out in the water. The blind was now a little shack sitting out all by itself on a bare island. Bob and I fished as much of the brush out of the water as we could and covered the blind and the boat hide, but needless to say, it wasn't nearly as good.

The blind was now out where everyone could see it, and that winter the ice skaters used it as a warm-up shack. That worked well, I guess, until they took to building fires in it, and eventually burned it down. I have built lots of duck blinds in my day, but that one was the best. We had poor luck hunting out of it though, as the ducks could see it and us.

***

When I went to college, Jim Malven and Bert Retz, two of my hunting buddies, decided to build a blind on the same island. Since the vegetation was now low, they decided to build a waterproof blind and dig it in like a sink box. They built the blind at home, and they worked like beavers on it. It got heavy. It was a wedge-shaped affair with a dandy hinged roof that could be tilted either way to form a half roof. Depending on the wind, they could open it to either the North or South. They waterproofed it with tar, and now it was time to get it out to the island. Somehow they got it hauled to the park and to the water's edge. As it was too heavy to put in the boat, they managed to float it out to the island towing it with the boat. In any case, they proceeded to dig a pit in the island to set it in. The island was only about a foot above the water, so they were soon standing in the water and trying to shovel mud from the bottom of the hole. The sandy soil would slide off their shovels, and it was a futile task. They had to give up the idea of digging it in. When they put the blind into the hole, it leaked, and since they didn't want to stand in water or on ice, they pulled the blind out of the hole and filled the hole back in. Then they set the blind back on the filled-in spot and covered it with brush. Another idea gone wrong.

* * *

During the period when the three of us were in high school, we had competition from the Goodmans who had a blind out on another island to our left front. Jim Goodman was our high school principal, and, as he was new to the area, he had asked me about duck hunting, and I had told him about the backwater off Terrill Park.

We had an agreement with them, not to shoot at the ducks in the air, but to let the ducks decide where they wanted to land. This gave each of us a chance, and one blind didn't shoot too early and scare the ducks away from the other blind. Of course, both blinds were trying to work the ducks. Our blind was in a little better location, and we had an ace in the hole. Bert had bought a dozen brand-new molded plastic mallard Victor decoys that were very realistic, compared to the cork decoys I was using that my Dad had made. We would set Bert's new decoys in a group off to one side by themselves, and invariably the ducks would light in those decoys. Needless to say, we got the most shooting.

One morning when Bert and I were hunting, we had knocked down a couple of ducks, and Bert was about to go out in the boat to retrieve them when we saw a huge flock of ducks way up high over the river, heading south. I called to them, but they didn't even acknowledge we were there. It was just too big a flock to come into our little backwater, so we forgot them and Bert left to get the downed ducks. I was standing up in the blind and talking to Bert who was out in the boat to the right of the decoys, when I heard a strange sound.

I looked up, and that big flock of mallard ducks had come down, and they were right over me! The sound from their wings was like a roar. They were so thick you couldn't have thrown a football up through them without hitting one. The sky was literally black with ducks. I just stood there looking at them, and it never occurred to me to shoot. Bert was twice as far away from the ducks as I was, and he up and shot one time, and two ducks dropped out. He didn't shoot again as we were just awed by so many ducks.

* * *

When I was in the army at Fort Riley, Kansas, I built a duck blind on a sand bar out in the middle of the river east of Ogden, Kansas. I went hunting early one Saturday morning, but I had to work in the Polio Clinic later that morning, and I planned to come back that afternoon and hunt. I decided to leave my two dozen cork decoys that I had made, sacked up and in the blind. I also had a dozen semi-silhouette Canadian goose decoys that I had made out of tin, that I left in the blind. When I came back that afternoon, I found 5 feet of water over the sand bar and my blind and decoys all gone. I looked for the decoys in their sack as they would float, but I didn't find them down river. The metal goose decoys must have been covered with a new layer of sand as I didn't find them either. I learned a valuable lesson though. It hadn't rained around there, but it had way upstream, and that wide flat river carried a lot of water from somewhere.

* * *

You couldn't by law build a permanent duck blind on J. Percy Priest Lake where I lived in Tennessee. The Corps of Engineers dropped the water 10 feet in the winter to store winter and spring flood waters, so it was hard to hunt ducks as the vegetation was fifty feet from the water. Most folks illegally cut cedar trees and piled them up near the water and sat in them, but I came up with another idea. I wanted to hunt on a little island, and it had a sand beach now that the water was down. My neighbor had gotten a new air conditioner that summer, and I saved the metal housing from his old one to go with the housing from mine that I had salvaged. I built a slope-sided blind that would seat two, and I had discarded bucket car seats in it. I shoveled out the sand and piled it around the base of the blind. It looked pretty good after we painted it sand color. Nevertheless, it didn't work because someone decided it was a permanent blind, and they worked hard and apparently tore it apart and threw it out in the water. I would have taken it down – honest!

Dad, me, Jeep and pheasants

MEMORIES OF MY DAD

My Dad, Walter N. Hansel, was born in Manchester, Iowa, on May 5, 1899. He had many stories to tell and I want to relate to you just a few that I can remember. Walter was the second son of George Washington and Emma (Moser) Hansel. Dad had three brothers - Carl, Roy and Art, and two sisters, Gladys and Mildred. They lived in the north end of Manchester in a house that George W. had built. The house was located a block west of Franklin Street, the main N/S street in the town, and right beside the M&O Railroad tracks. The M&O, Manchester and Oneida, was a small spur track that ran infrequently between the two towns. The house was also located just north of the backwater formed by the Marion Street dam, which dammed up the Maquoketa River that ran through the town.

Grandpa George was a carpenter, and when the house was being built, he made all the crown molding, chair rails and baseboards, etc. by hand with wood block planes. He wanted quarter-sawn oak, and he took the sawyer into the woods where they picked out the trees that would be sawn up into lumber. The sawyer was to cut down the trees, and Grandpa questioned him about the way to quarter saw the boards. The sawyer assured him that he knew what Grandpa wanted, and he would be notified when the lumber was ready. When Grandpa came to pick up the lumber in his wagon to haul it to the shop, he rejected the whole lot. Back to the woods they went to pick out new trees to be cut. This time Grandpa drew the man pictures and schooled him on how to quarter saw the logs to get the very best grain. All the woodwork in the house and the doors were stained and varnished, as Grandpa loved the beauty of wood.

The outside of the house was painted white, and there was a nice front porch with a swing and a railing in front of it. Great Grandpa John (Green County) Hansel would sit in the swing and swing back and forth for hours during the day when the younger men were all working. He chewed tobacco, and when he would have to spit, he would swing up and attempt to spit out over the railing. He would sometimes miss, and when Grandma came out to check on him, she would see that big, brown, juicy stain all over the white railing, and she would say, "Oh, Green County, you missed again." He would say, "By Gawd, I never," and he would rock forward and wipe the stain off on the sleeve of his nice white shirt, which, of course, she was going to have to wash.

* * *

I don't know much about Dad's younger life, but he told me a few stories of his growing up. When he was a boy, he and other kids earned money unloading bulk cement from railroad cars when they were paving Highway 20 through Manchester. The cement was shipped loose, in boxcars. The cement would be hauled to the site where they were mixing the concrete. The loose cement was hard to handle, and they hired kids to climb up into the boxcars and shovel the cement towards the door, and then out into wagons, but there were problems. The loose cement was very dusty when disturbed, and it would not hold up your weight, so you would sink down - up to your knees. It was very difficult to breathe, and you developed weeping sores on your legs. The man in charge would inspect each boy's legs every morning, and if you had sores, he would not let you work until they had healed. It was a good-paying job for kids, but tough work.

* * *

Dad said that one time, on Halloween night, he and his brothers and some neighbor boys took a wagon apart and reassembled it, up on top of Grandpa's garage. They worked very hard, and it took them practically all night, as the wheels and box were very heavy. They were tired the next day, and, of course, knew nothing about how the wagon got up there. Grandpa and some neighbor men disassembled the wagon and got it down. The men were all laughing and joking about it, and they wouldn't let the boys help take it down, as they might get hurt.

* * *

When Dad was in high school, he loved to play football. The ends on the football team were the only ones to catch passes, and they would practice during the noon hour by having Dad try to knock them down. The ruse was for Dad to throw passes to them as hard as he could, and just high enough that they had to stretch way up or jump to reach the ball. If they had to reach high enough, and the pass was strong enough, they would be off balance and fall down. Dad said it was good practice.

When Dad was running the ball, he took to trying to jump over tacklers. Since the coach always taught tacklers to "hit 'em low," Dad figured he could jump up as he was about to get tackled and make them miss. He had some success with it until he tried to run between two big linemen. When he tried to jump over them, they just stood there, and he landed with one knee on each of their shoulders. They reached up, grabbed Dad and threw him to the ground backwards. He lit on his back with the wind knocked out of him. He was so stunned he decided that maybe the jumping wasn't such a good idea.

* * *

During the year 1919, young Walter took a job stringing wire for the REA (Rural Electric Administration) out near Sutherland, Iowa. He and several other boys walked up to a farmhouse to get a drink of water. There they met the Engel girls, and since the girls were home alone, the boys felt they had to show off for them. The boys took to riding back and forth on the sliding barn door until they overdid it, and the door fell off the track. The other boys left, but young Walter, coming from a "fix-it" family, stayed, and with great effort, put the door back on the track. The girls were glad he did, too, as their dad, Gustav, would have 'kilt those kits' had he found the door off.

Later Walter and another fellow came back and asked to take the two oldest girls to a dance. Alma, the younger girl, didn't want to go as she wasn't interested in men, but if she didn't go, Hilda, the oldest, wouldn't get to go, so Alma got talked into it. Walter took a shine to Alma, 'the cute one', and kept coming back to see her. Alma's mother tried to push him off onto Hilda, the oldest girl, but Walt said if he couldn't see the one he came to see, he wouldn't come at all. Eventually, Alma and Walt got married and lived a long and productive life together.

※ ※ ※

In Manchester, one beautiful spring day, the young men were goofing off. It was a Sunday, and they were reminiscing on how, on a day like today, as kids, they would have run for the river and gone skinny-dipping for the first time of the year. "Well," they said, "why not now?" So off they went, running for the old swimming hole, which was below a high bank on the river where they would dive off. Well, it was, "Last one in is a rotten egg," and Dad was leading the pack. He shed his clothes and dove off into the water, which was a little murky due to the spring rains. What they didn't know was that during the lapsed time, the river had changed, and it was now shallow below the high bank. Dad hit the bottom big time, and drove his head into the gravel and mud. The other fellows had to wade out and physically pull his head out of the bottom. He came home with his face all bloody, and it scared Mom to death. He healed up all right, but some 20-plus years later, when he had back problems and went to Mayo Clinic and had his vertebrae fused together, it was felt the problem might have stemmed from that dive into the river. During the operation, they cut the nerves to his leg, and he had no feeling in some spots on the leg. Also, when he straightened his foot out to put on a boot, his leg would cramp up until he could work it out.

To recuperate after the surgery, he and a painter friend, Herb Mueller, who had just had the calluses carved off his feet, took an extended vacation. The back of the pickup had a box on it that Dad had built, and it served them well as sleeping quarters. They threw a bedsprings and mattress in the back and took off for Florida. Then they went across the southern U.S. to California, up through California to Washington, and back across northern U.S. to Iowa. Dad was sitting on a rubber donut cushion, and Herb wouldn't get out of the truck as he couldn't walk because his feet hurt, so they saw the U.S.A. from the truck. They got stuck in the mud one evening and just crawled across the top of the truck and went to bed. They were awakened the next morning by a wrecker driver who asked if they would like to be pulled out. Why, sure. Dad put on his clothes, climbed out and back into the cab of the pickup and got pulled out. Another fellow who was stuck up ahead of them had walked to town to get help. Dad said his feet never touched the ground on that whole ordeal.

As a boy and a young man, Dad loved to hunt, fish and trap. He owned some excellent hounds, and he entered his dogs in many field trials where they often won. He also put on field trials to show off his dogs and to keep them in shape. He hunted fox with his hounds, and one day, up at Backbone State Park, he shot a wolf, and the dogs caught another young wolf. He tried to raise the young wolf, but it would not respond to anything. It would not move or eat, and he had to pour water down its throat to get it to drink. He watched it at night, hoping it would get up and move around, but it never moved, and it eventually died of fright or a broken heart. Dad said he never saw a wilder look than in that wolf's eyes.

Another thing Dad did as a young man was to catch squirrels, keeping both fox and grey squirrels in pens, trying to train them. He had made a small box-like trap that he could belt onto a tree at a hole that a squirrel had gone in. The squirrel would come out of the hole, go into the trap and then couldn't get back out. Dad said it was fun working with the squirrels, and he learned a lot about them. One thing that was very interesting was that you didn't mix the two kinds of squirrels. One time he had two fox squirrels in a large pen with a tree in it for them to climb around in. He had caught a grey squirrel, and using his heavy leather gloves, he put the grey squirrel in with the fox squirrels. Before he could make a move to stop him, the grey squirrel jumped from one fox squirrel to the other and killed them by biting them in the back of the head as Dad watched. That was the end of that project.

When I was about 5 years old, my dad and brother Dale went duck hunting up at Kelley Springs, north of town. They looked down the river from the car, way up on the road above the springs, and saw a flock of geese sitting on the river below them. They got out of the car, loaded their shotguns with the biggest shot they had and proceeded to sneak the geese. The only way they could find to get down the hill and close to the river was an eroded ditch, but it was down the river from where the geese were. It would have to do. They crept down the ditch until they were at the riverbank. When they peeked up over the bank, it had worked out just right. The geese apparently had seen them up on the road and drifted down the river, and they were now right out in front of them. They both rose up and shot, but the geese just sat there. Dad and Dale looked at each other, reloaded the guns, and felt they were shooting at someone's tame geese. It turned out that the geese had been sitting there all night, and they were stiff. It took them some time to start honking and flying and, of course, Dad and Dale started shooting. Dad said he shot one big, old goose that was flying right at him, and it didn't fall. He couldn't believe it! When the guns were empty, and the geese were gone, there were only two geese flopping on the water in front of them near the other bank.

Dad told Dale to stay and watch them, in case they came to, and he would go up the river to cross over up around Tripp's Bayou and come down the other side. After Dad left, Dale heard some shooting up river. When he and Dad got back together, Dale heard quite a story. It seemed they had crippled several other geese, and they had dropped back down onto the river when they flew off upstream. They would come flopping out from the bank as Dad came along, and he would finish them off. Dad also found a flock of ducks on one of the ponds up at Tripp's, and he got four ducks off it. They got seven big Canadian honkers that morning and we have a picture of them with Dad, Dale and sister Arlene all holding the geese and me holding the four little ducks.

We had lots to eat, and we made good use of the feathers, too. Mom made a feather tick and pillows of the feathers and down, and Dad made bench-duster brooms out of the wing and tail feathers. Those feather dusters hung above the benches for years, and the pillows may still be in use, too.

※ ※ ※

When I was in grade school, Dad made me a bow. There was an old hickory fence post underneath Grandpa's bench at the shop. Dad cut a blank out of it and shaped it into a long bow. He then brought it home and put it in the cistern in the basement that caught rainwater. Mom used the rainwater to wash clothes and to wash her hair. Anyway, after it had soaked in the cistern for several days, Dad made a form for the shape of the bow. He took it out of the cistern and bent it into the form. When it dried, he put a handle on it and notched the ends to take the string, and I had a dandy bow. I made the arrows at the shop by cutting 3/8th inch square strips of pine and rounding the edges with a ¼ round wood block plane. They worked fine. I had a Schaefer pencil on the end of the arrow for a point, and I even shot a rooster pheasant on the fly with it.

My Dad and I in the boat he'd built in 1942

When Dad would take me fishing, he had a real knack of finessing a chub or big minnow around a stump in the water, and with a lot of patience, he would eventually catch a nice bass or catfish. I would

'Tis Himself

go on to the next stump and I wouldn't catch a thing. He told me I wasn't holding my mouth right. I would hold my mouth in all different ways. I think Dad was the only one that got a kick out of that, as my jaw got sore and I still never caught anything. One time Dad caught a 3-pound catfish when he was fishing alone, and since it was all he caught, he decided to put it on a leash. He tied the fish on a length of line and tied the other end of the line to the stump under water. The next Sunday he was fishing with two other fellows, and they hadn't caught anything when they were coming up on the stump with the tied-up catfish. Dad bet the guys a dime that he would catch a fish before they did, and he came up with the catfish. He told me about it years later, and he said he couldn't take their money as he had the fish tied up. I thought it was a good idea, and I caught two, nice 15-inch small mouth bass below the dam. Since the bass season didn't open until next week, I tied them out like Dad had done with the catfish. When I told Dad about it, he explained it was illegal, and he was not proud of what he had done, and he wished he hadn't told me about it. He said he would take me to the movie if I would turn the bass loose. I agreed, and that night he stood up on the Marion Street Bridge while I jumped across all the rocks and got out to the place where I had left the fish tied up. There were lots of lights on the bridge, and Dad could see me down there when I let the fish go after holding them up so he could see them.

* * *

As stated previously, Walter loved to hunt, and he was a good shot. Of note was the fact that he always carried a Winchester Model 97, 12 gauge pump shotgun. He would have liked to have gotten one of those new semi-automatic shotguns, but he had run a saw blade into the major knuckle on the index finger of his right hand, and that finger would not bend. Consequently, he could not pull the trigger with that finger, so he had to use his middle finger as his trigger finger. The index finger had to be held along the gun's receiver, and it would have been smashed by the action rod of a semi-auto. His "97" had a 32 - inch full choke barrel, and it could reach out and get 'em. He always told me never to miss with his gun as he had broken it in right, and he didn't want me to spoil it.

*　*　*

Walter travelled to several western states deer and antelope hunting, and he went to the Delta Marsh in Canada duck hunting. He went to South Dakota pheasant hunting, and for several years he went to northern Minnesota deer hunting. He also took me to North Dakota two or three years duck hunting. He caught some big fish on a trip into Canada where they stayed 100 miles from the Arctic Circle. Walt always remembered the day his daughter was born, as that was the day he got the mink. His wife remembered it too, as that was the day he didn't come home when Arlene was ready to come into this world. All of us kids were born at home, with Dr. May showing up at the right time, plus Grandma Engel helping as a mid-wife.

*　*　*

Dad told me about the time he and another fellow were laying down beside a pond, duck hunting. A little teal duck came in and lit on the other side of the pond, right across from them. He was within range, and as Dad started to rise up to shoot, the fellow motioned for him to hold up. The guy got out his duck call and made a little quack, and the duck immediately swam right across the pond to them. They scared it up, and Dad shot it. Well, a week or two later, Dad was alone at the same spot, and another teal came in. Dad got out his duck call and made one quack, but this time, that teal jumped right in the air. Dad got him, but he said he must have quacked the wrong word.

*　*　*

Dad and Fred Hilsenbeck were coon hunting one night, and the dogs put something into a hole in the ground. They were sure it was a coon, so Dad went back to the truck and got a shovel. When they started digging, it was taking them too long, so the dogs left to find a new critter to run. When the hole was about three and a half feet deep, the hole opened up on the side, and they hoped the coon was close. Fred leaned out into the hole with Dad holding onto his legs. Fred reached into the hole and grabbed the animal, but it wasn't a coon. He pulled a big skunk from the hole by the back leg, and the skunk shot him right in the face and in his mouth as he was hollering for Dad to pull him up.

When Dad got him up out of the hole, Hilsey was in a very bad way. He could not take a deep breath, and he was foaming at the mouth. It took a long time for him to quit rolling on the ground and to finally sit up and lean back against a tree. Dad didn't know what to do, so he asked him if he would like a cigarette. Fred said he would, but when he took a drag and the smoke went into his lungs, he started gasping and rolling all over again. Dad said it was the wrong thing to do. Hah, I guess!

When Fred was better, Dad shone his flashlight into the hole, and there was the skunk looking up at him. Dad was mad at the skunk and decided to bury him alive. He grabbed the shovel and started shoveling dirt in on the skunk, but the skunk just jumped up on top of the dirt as fast as it came into the hole. Dad doubled his efforts and the skunk just kept on jumping. Dad finally realized this wasn't going to work. As the hole filled up, the skunk was fast coming to the surface of the ground where it could spray him. Dad left the skunk to get the rest of the way out of the hole by himself.

* * *

One moonlight night in the winter, Dad and his hunting buddies decided they would go fox hunting at night since there was deep snow on the ground, and they felt they could see a fox in the moonlight on the snow. When the dogs got to running a fox in the woods, Dad found a broken-over tree that he could climb up on to get a better view. He climbed up, kicked the snow off the tree and found he was about four feet off the ground. He heard the dogs coming his way, and he got ready to shoot. The fox circled around behind him, and Dad was trying to turn around when the fox went right under the tree he was standing on. Dad lost his balance in an attempt to get a shot, and he fell off the log and broke his leg. It wasn't long before he had all the dogs jumping all around him adding to his problems. He had a tough time getting out of the woods and to a doctor, too.

I always got hurt a lot when I was young, and now I see where I got it from.

* * *

Dad used to hunt rabbits in the deep snow using a pet ferret. They would go out into the woods and find a well-used rabbit burrow and put the ferret down into the hole. The ferret would get the scent of the rabbits and go down the hole after them. The rabbits would run out one of the other holes, and the guys would shoot them. During the depression, we ate a lot of rabbits. Every now and then, the ferret would catch a rabbit down in the hole, and he would stay. He would have himself a feast, go to sleep and forget to come out. Dad would have to plug up all the holes and go home without him.

The next day, after work, he would go back and dig out the hole and get the ferret, which would be waiting where he'd put him in the hole. Dad tried lots of different ways to keep the ferret from staying in the hole. He put a collar on him and ran a cord through the collar, but the ferret had to go around lots of roots and rocks and things, so you couldn't just pull him back out. You might be pulling him up against a root and choking him, so you would have to let go one end of the cord and pull it through the ring and back out of the hole. Then, if the ferret didn't come back out in reasonable time, you would be back to filling up all the holes and going home again without him. Dad said it was a good sport if it worked right, but too many times you spent more time waiting for the ferret than you did hunting rabbits.

* * *

When I was in high school, Dad did a lot of work at the library. We put on a new roof and tore off big wide gutters that were getting rotten. I hauled some of the old lumber down to the park and built a duck blind out of it. At night, after the library closed, we would remove all the books from the shelves, move the shelves, take up the old floor covering, put down tile cement and lay new rubber tile. It took us a long time, and it was very tiring as we, of course, worked on other jobs during the day. We did not have to replace the books after we reset the shelves, as the librarian knew we wouldn't get them back where they belonged.

One night, Ralph Simons, part of the crew, found an old radio with a carved wooden top in the next room where we were to redo the floor. He brought it out and plugged it in, and it worked. After we spread the tile glue, we had to wait for 30 minutes or so for it to set before we could put down the rubber tile. We were all sitting there talking, and the guys were smoking, when they started playing "The Irish Washer Woman" song on the radio. Dad jumped up and danced a jig and sang two verses of the dirtiest words that I have ever heard to that song. I had never seen him dance before, either. He never ceased to amaze me. He could quote "Ivanhoe", which he learned in high school, for a long time too. I told him I didn't have to memorize things like that, and he told me he wasn't proud of the way he learned it. It seems when he was bad at school, the teacher would make him stay after school until he memorized a verse. He must have been bad a lot because he knew many verses.

* * *

When I was in college, I came home one weekend to go duck hunting. When Dad came home for lunch, I asked him if he knew a place to go hunting, as the season had been open for a week, and the ducks would be scattered if there were any around. He told me about Blanchard's pond up northeast of the fairgrounds. I didn't know where it was, so he told me how to get there. It was covered with ducks, and I got my limit and was back in half an hour. Dad decided to leave work, and we went back. The pond was out in a pasture with no way to get to it. I had merely stood up, scared the ducks away, and then shot them when they came back in small flocks. There were ducks on the pond, but Dad didn't like my idea of scaring them away. He said we could sneak them, and he had me pull all the long weeds I could find along the fence. He showed me how to make a fan out of the weeds, and holding it up in front of our faces, we crawled to the pond. It seemed to me I must have crawled for half a mile, but it worked and we surprised those birds.

* * *

One day I came home from college, and Dad was in the basement. He had a rope strung up over the water pipe that was fastened to the ceiling. The rope had a loop tied on each end. He had his wrist in one loop, and he was endeavoring to lift his foot up and put it in the other loop. The idea was to get his foot in the loop, step down to the floor and it would raise his arm. He had bursitis in his shoulder, and he couldn't raise his arm without a lot of pain. When I came down the steps, he told me about it briefly, but he didn't tell me about the pain. He said, "Here, take my wrist and straighten out my arm." Well, I was a big stout college kid, and I did just like he said. He turned white as a ghost, and I thought he would faint. He didn't cry out, but I knew I had hurt him something awful.

* * *

Walter and his father, George W. Hansel, worked for many years for A.J. Bruce Construction Company. After the depression, Mr. Bruce owed Walter and George W. a great deal of back wages. When Mr. Bruce died, the business was sold to Walter and George W. for $1,000 dollars and all the back wages. Walter didn't have the money, and he borrowed $500 from his older brother Carl. He paid Carl back in $100 payments as he could. "Hansel & Son Contractors," as they named the business, was successful and they specialized in building residences. They built many fine homes in and around Manchester, Iowa. Walter ran the business at night, keeping the time books, paying the bills and ordering equipment and supplies. In the daytime he worked at the job site, building the houses and being the boss of the crew. George W. worked in the shop and made the kitchen cabinets and put together the windows and frames that came in kit form in those days.

Walter contracted with the Illinois Central Railroad to tear down old depots and build new ones in Manchester and the surrounding communities. He ran three crews at the time: one tearing down the old depot and stock pens; another building the new depots in the shop; and the third putting up the new depot building at the site. The crew in the shop built the depot building and then took it apart into the four walls and two halves of the roof. They would then load the six parts of the building onto flat cars for the railroad to ship to the community where it was to be erected. Needless to say, it kept Walter hopping trying to keep it all coordinated, and that's when he got his ulcers.

* * *

Dad loved tools, both hand and power tools. He would go to the widows of old carpenters who had died and offer to buy the man's tools. He didn't need the tools, but he respected the man and his tools. He once told me he had more tools belonging to dead men than he had himself, which was considerable. He was a real craftsman, and he could make or fix anything. He built his family a house out of the old depot he tore down in Manchester, including saving the 100-year-old slate shingles from the depot and putting them on his house. He built the house strong to hold up that heavy roof.

* * *

Dad made a lot of things that I treasured. He made a pedestal-mounted machine gun that clicked (shot) when you turned a handle. He made many rubber guns and a Tommy gun and slingshots. He made an archery bow from a hickory fence post that was under Grandpa's bench. He and I built a rowboat when I was in high school. He made a gunwale for my Old Towne canoe. He poured a curved concrete front steps and walkway for my house in Wisconsin. I have a walnut chest of drawers he built when he was 17 years old. The cherry Grandfather's clock that he built was willed to my oldest son. I have a walnut Grandfather's clock he started before he died, which I finished and he started two more, for Dale and Arlene, which we also finished. He was a wonderful workman and his joy was in his work.

The seven foot tall grandfather clock Walt crafted out of cherry wood in 1960

My remarkable mom, Alma Hansel

MY MOM

Alma Caroline Johanna Engel Hansel

Alma was born on the 24th of November, 1901, and she died on 7 January, 1995 at the age of 93. She came from good stock. Her father, Gustav Engel, immigrated to the United States in 1893. He could not leave Germany with his family, as he was 19 years old and of draft age. His father hired an agent who smuggled Gustav out of the country on a cattle boat headed for England. From there, they put him on a ship for the U.S. He had a tag on his jacket that gave his designation i.e., Pottawattamie Co, Iowa. He was proud, and he didn't like being treated like cattle, being pushed along and pointed onto the correct train, etc. so he took the tag off, studied it and put it in his pocket. When the next time came for him to board a train, he stepped up to the person in charge and said, "Pottawattamie co Yova." He didn't know that the co stood for county, and in German, "J" was "Y" and "W" was "V" so it came out Yova. They couldn't understand him, so he had to produce the tag, and it was pinned back on. I don't know how you would find your family with just a county for a destination, but there weren't that many people here back then. Later, when people would call him "Gus", he would say "That's not Gus, and that's not Gust, that's Yee-you-s-t-a-wee, Gustav."

Alma's mother, Clara Dorothy Vierck, came to the US in 1884 when she was two years old, and she learned to walk on the ship. She was 92 when she died.

They lived on a farm south of Sutherland, Iowa, and Alma wanted to go to high school. Her folks said it would be all right if she did all her chores before or after school, and she had to get there by herself. She walked to school by road in the summertime, and on the railroad tracks in the winter, as the train kept the snow plowed down. There were no snowplows for the roads, and the wagon ruts were impossible to drive, let alone walk. When in high school, Alma got First Honors in the Junior Four Minute Men Speaking Contest and was selected as the Junior Four Minute Speaker for War Savings Stamps. She received a Certificate of Honor from the White House signed by President Woodrow Wilson for her service during the war of 1917-1918, the First World War.

Alma was a remarkable woman, an absolute wonder, and a pillar of the community in her time. She learned homemaking skills from her mother, but she went far beyond that. She was a wonderful cook, and she could fix a meal from nothing but need. She could fix beets six different ways. During the Depression, she threw nothing away, and she would feed the homeless at any time of the day. She always said no one left her house hungry. She would fix whatever she had. She also baked wonderful bread, which was even sold to the neighbors on Sunday mornings. When I was in college and forgot to eat all the cookies she had sent with me, I would bring back the old, dry, very hard cookies, and she would mash them up with her rolling pin and put them into the next batch. Nothing went to waste.

She cleaned house, washed dishes and clothes, and nursed us all back to health when we were ill or injured. Her kids had the normal childhood diseases: chicken pox, whooping cough, measles, etc. and she treated them with the remedies of the day. I hated cold packs. If we had a deep cough that persisted into the night, she would prepare a bunch of wash cloths with cold water and come into your room, bare your chest and slap on the cold, wet cloths and wrap towels over it. You were instantly awake and the not-so-proud owner of a cold-pack

My Mom

*My Mom made this very special cowboy shirt
for me when I was ten years old*

Mom was also an excellent seamstress. She made all kinds of clothes and coats for her family, and she repaired whatever needed saving. Sister Arlene would stand on a chair or table while Mom pinned up the hem of her dress and she would get upset if Arlene fidgeted around. She made me a two-tone green cowboy shirt with fancy pockets and collar that I just loved and did not want to take off. She also made me a hunting coat just like Dad's, except the shell loops were for 410 shells instead of 12 gauge. It was also green, which was my color. When I inherited a pair of wool pants, I couldn't wear them, as I would break out in a rash. Mom made me an inner liner of silk, and I was afraid someone would see it and tease me. She made Dad a deerskin leather apron for use in his shop. When Dad and brother Dale got seven geese off the river, Mom made down pillows. She also made quilts and hooked rugs with the left-over rags. Like I said, nothing went to waste.

She always had a big garden that she planted, hoed, harvested, and cooked or canned. There were also strawberry and red raspberry patches, too. She raised lots of flowers and decorated the church every Sunday for years. She also sang in the church choir for many years, and she loved to sing in the Messiah, which was staged for the town with imported director and singers from all over. She played the piano to help her in her singing. She was also artistic in other ways. She won the best-decorated house for Christmas one year with her cutout silhouettes of Mary, Joseph, and the shepherds at the manger, which she placed in our front window. They were made of old linoleum and were backlit and very effective. She also stippled the kitchen floor and varnished the dining room floor, which I ruined when I laid down newspapers when I had to come in and go to the bathroom.

Mom was also a very fast reader, and she read most of the books in the library. She loved words, and she took to writing poetry and plays. She would also direct the plays and act in them as needed when they were put on for the community in the high school auditorium. She was voted Iowa Poet of the year in 1976. She always corrected my grammar, which made the high school English workbook a breeze for me and Wayne Condon, who sat beside me. She wrote a newspaper column each week for 20 years entitled "Sure Enough".

She volunteered to help wherever she could. She made and sold sloppy joe sandwiches at the fair for the Am Vets and made sewing kits for the soldiers in World War II. She also cut out articles in newspapers about local servicemen for a scrapbook, and the basement was piled high with the papers. We found that she also saved the papers from which she had cut the articles.

She was also an airplane spotter. She was trained to identify enemy airplanes by their shape, and she manned the observation booth day and night as needed. Yes, and this was in Iowa. She was on the Rationing Board and was a Republican Committee Woman. She was a Cub Scout den mother for me and for others when they couldn't find anyone else to do it, even though she didn't have a son in cub scouts any longer. She went to all the functions at the high school to support her kids and still went to the ball games, plays and music productions even after they had all graduated, just to support the school.

Mom was a special woman. She was witty and wise, generous, but frugal, studious and creative, forceful and caring. She kept her sharp mind and remarkable attitude right to the last days of her life. Manchester was a better place because of her, and I am a stronger person for having had her to inspire me.

Me with Sandy and Sox

DOG TALES

My brother, Dale, had a part-beagle dog named Betts, and he said she was slow on the track, but, if you had the patience, she would bring the rabbit around to you for an easy shot. The rabbit would be just hopping along and not very far in front of the dog. We later had two of Betts' pups, Sandy and Sox. I had my picture taken with them, but I don't remember much about them. Of course Sandy was sand colored and Sox had four white feet.

* * *

Dad had a Terrier dog named Nick that would chase a ball and retrieve it, and he would catch it in his mouth no matter how high Dad threw it, but he was Dad's dog. He would play catch endlessly with Dad when he came home from work, but if I tried to show the other kids what he could do, he tired quickly, and I would have to retrieve the ball.

* * *

My first dog was a beagle. Dad brought him home one day and he was a hunting dog from the "get go". He would run anything that would run away from him and some things that wouldn't. Before I was old enough to carry a gun, I would go hunting with Dad and Jeep. That was the dog's name, Jeep, like the little Army car. I collected the empty shotgun shells when we were rabbit hunting, and I had quite a collection. No one reloaded in those days, but I just wanted the shells. I was interested in anything that had to do with hunting. One time Dad let me hold his gun when Jeep had a rabbit in a hole and Dad was going to try to poke the rabbit out with a stick. I set the butt of the gun in the snow, and I was holding it by the barrel while I watched the action. Dad's gun was a long one, a Winchester Model 97 with a 32 inch barrel. Jeep was barking in one hole, Dad was sticking a switch in another hole, and the rabbit ran out of a third. I raised the gun up to shoot, and Dad looked up just as the barrel was dipping back down as it was too heavy. He said "Shoot", so I muscled the gun back up and pulled the trigger. I didn't see if I got the rabbit, as the recoil sat me down in the snow!

* * *

When we went squirrel hunting, my job was to beat Jeep to the squirrel after Dad shot it out of the tree. Dad had a Remington pump action 22 Special rifle with open sights, and he always shot the squirrels right in the head. When the squirrels hit the ground Jeep would grab them and crunch their ribs as he shook them to kill them. I was to get to the squirrel before Jeep did and hold it up high so he couldn't jump up and get it away from me. If he crunched the ribs it made them harder to clean. One time the squirrel lit in a thicket, Jeep went in underneath and beat me. He began to swallow the squirrel whole as we had been hunting all day and he was hungry. He was gulping like he was gagging. I grabbed the end of the squirrel's tail that was sticking about 3 inches out of the dog's mouth and tried to pull him out. When Dad came up, he told me to let the dog have him as the squirrel was too far down and I'd give the dog a sore throat. Jeep proceeded to swallow that fox squirrel whole, hide, hair, bones and all. I asked Dad how he could do that, and Dad said it would just give him a clean sweep.

* * *

Another fellow that hunted with Dad took to catching the squirrels as they fell from the tree for the same reason. Dad told him he shouldn't as the squirrel might be alive. He said, "Naw, Walt, you always shoot them right in the head". Well, one day a squirrel was just grazed, and it bit the man when he caught it. He didn't do that anymore.

* * *

Norman Anderson and I were hunting back on the river one day. Norman had my 410 single barrel shotgun and I had brother Dale's Remington Model 12A, pump 22 cal. rifle. We were up on a very high bank above the river and there was a little bunch of ducks sitting on the river downstream below us. I knew the ducks were out-of-range of the shotgun, so I lay down on the bank and took careful aim with the rifle. When I shot, I got one of the ducks, a teal, and Norman's shot hit the water about halfway to the ducks. When we got down the river, on the bank next to the duck, Jeep saw it and jumped into the water and swam out and picked it up in his mouth. He looked back at us and since the other bank was closer, he swam to it, climbed out of the water onto a sandbar, dropped the duck, shook himself off and swam back to us, leaving the duck on the other side of the river. Norman was older and bigger, and he could swim. He took off all his clothes, jumped into the river and swam across. He picked up the duck yelling, "Here's your damned duck", and he threw it clear across the river to me. He swam back across and I tried to dry him off with his undershirt. He was shivering big time trying to get his clothes back on. It's cold in duck season!

We went on down the river and we slipped up on a pond to check it for ducks. There were two pintails sitting there, and we shot at them together. I got mine with the rifle and Norman hit his, but we had a problem. That was my last 22 shell and the extractor was broken on the 410 gauge shotgun that I had bought in a secondhand store in Waterloo, Iowa. That pintail duck took off, but it couldn't make any headway. It just hung there in the air flying with all its might, but not moving. If I would have had another 22 shell, I could have hit him easy. Norman was desperately digging at the 410 shell in the barrel with his jack knife. I went and got a small dead tree back in the woods, and came running up to the pond and made a swipe at the duck with the tree to knock him out of the air. The tree was too short and I missed, but the wind I made with the tree managed to push the duck farther out over the pond. The duck kept flapping his wings and getting nowhere. Eventually he got high enough to catch a little breeze, gained altitude and made it up over the trees. I kept running through the woods under him, hoping he would fall or Norman would come with the 410. Eventually I lost track of him. We just knew we should have gotten that duck if things had just worked out.

We had gotten several squirrels, rabbits and the two ducks, and we had to walk right down through the middle of town as we had been hunting up north of town, and we both lived south of town. At the four corners in the middle of town there was the only stop light. It was located right out in the middle of the street on a pedestal. There were two banks on either side of the street. The one on the north side of Main Street had a barber shop under it in the basement. The steps to go down into the barbershop were located in the sidewalk area, and there was an iron pipe railing around the steps to keep you from falling into the hole. Old retired men always sat on this railing when the weather was nice.

There were two or three fellows sitting there when Norman, Jeep and I were going by. They wanted to know if we had gotten anything, and they could see by my bulging hunting coat that we had. Mom had made that hunting coat on her sewing machine, and it was a dandy. It was made of a light green canvas material, just like Dad's. It had a game bag in the back and the side pockets were covered with flaps that also covered shell loops on each side for 410 shells.

Well, I was carrying all the game and the buttons on the game bag gave way right in front of the fellows sitting on the railing. I spilled all of our game right out on the sidewalk. They all laughed and said we had had a mighty good day. I was embarrassed, and I quickly took off my coat so Norman and I could load the game into the coat. We carried it on home like it was a basket. He had hold of the coat's sleeves and I had it by the bottom. We were struggling, carrying that coat full of game, plus two guns and trying to keep Jeep close on a leash. I guess we were a sight, and we had several blocks to go to get out of sight of all the people in town.

*　*　*

One time when I was hunting south of town, Jeep jumped over a fence and the top two barbed wires crossed over his hind leg trapping him. He was held hanging there upside down. I was almost back to town when I heard him calling me. When I got to him, I didn't know what to do to get him loose. He took my hand in his mouth and guided me, and in one quick motion he came loose. Remarkable! Dad didn't believe it, but it's true.

He ran away from me (no leash) in the middle of Franklin Street, and I caught him on Walter Rossman's front yard. I spanked him and yelled at him as several cars had almost hit him. Mr. Rossman was working in his yard, and he chastised me for hitting Jeep. He told me the dog didn't know why I was punishing him. A lesson learned.

Jeep had an animal cornered in a hole one time. The animal bit Ed Frentress' glove off when he reached in to pull out what we thought was a rabbit. We then assumed it was a fox, so we covered up the hole and went home to get a shovel. When we dug him out, it turned out to be an opossum. Jeep never was any good at telling you what he was running. There were many times I wished he had colored lights on his back or something to let you know what he was trailing. We would be tired and we had enough rabbits. We wanted to go home, but we would like to keep hunting if he was running a fox. When he was on a track, you couldn't call him off. You would have to go catch him and put a leash on him and drag him away.

* * *

One day I shot a hawk with my brother's Stevens bolt action 410 shotgun, and the hawk landed in the river. Jeep waded out to retrieve it and when he reached out for it, the hawk grabbed the dog right on the end of his nose. His talons were sharp and Jeep came yipping to the bank and the hawk fell off. Jeep went to find something else and as the hawk didn't appear to be hurt badly, I took him home alive in the back of my green hunting coat. I intended to fix the hawk's wing and have him as a pet. I was at the bench in the basement working on his wing when he grabbed my right hand index finger in his talons. I was holding the hawk with my left hand and he was holding me. It was a standoff, and I was being hurt and scared. I let go, but he didn't, so I ended it with a hammer.

* * *

Jeep caught a big woodchuck one day, but he knew to stay away from the front end. He would hold him by the back end and between bites he would bark to call me. Jeep knew about skunks, too. He would retreat if they turned their rear end toward him, and he would circle around and get in front of them and bark to stop the skunk, and to call me to come see what he had cornered. I shot a big skunk once that was out in the snow which Jeep was baying for me to come see. Of course Jeep left when I was stupid enough to shoot. (See skunk stories.)

* * *

One day when I was going hunting up along Honey Creek, Jeep and I were walking up the street in the north end of town near the box factory. A mean dog was chained to a house that set way back from the road, and he was barking at us and running and jumping at the end of his chain. He managed to break the chain and came tearing down the driveway toward us. I wasn't sure what to do and Jeep wasn't either. The mean dog tore into Jeep as soon as he got there and Jeep, who was much smaller, was trying to defend himself. I was a tall, skinny kid, with big feet in army boots, and I waded into the fight and kicked the mean dog as his owner, a woman, was hurrying down the driveway toward us. When I kicked her dog, the dog hesitated to continue the fight and the lady was able to grab the chain and pull him away from us. She was all upset at me for kicking her dog. She should have been thankful I didn't shoot him!

* * *

I had started hunting rabbits with Jeep with a sling shot or a BB gun, and then my cousin, Don, gave me a Stevens "Little Scout" 22 rifle. During World War II you couldn't get ammunition. The Editor of the local newspaper, Mr. Howard Rann, stood in line for me at the Gamble Store and bought me a box of 22 shells that were being rationed out one box per customer. I went rabbit hunting and got three rabbits. Dad asked me how many times I shot, and he was very pleased when I told him three times. When I then told him I missed twice, he asked how I got the other two rabbits. Jeep caught them.

* * *

One time at the sale barns south of town, Jeep was running something, and I was standing still waiting for what I thought was a rabbit to show up. A big black cat jumped up on top of a fence post right in front of me, and it scared me to death. It was the biggest cat I had ever seen. It turned out that the cat was what Jeep was running, and he holed up in a big stack of straw bales under a shed roof. When I told Ed Frentress, who was hunting with me, about the big cat, we decided to get him. We spent the next few hours moving the bales from one side of the shed to the other. When we were almost done, Jeep told us the cat was now over on the side where we were piling the bales. We were too tired to look any further.

* * *

We ate lots of rabbits and squirrels during the War. While in grade school one year I got a rabbit every day after school for a week. The conditions were just right and I would track them in the snow. When the track stopped by a broken-over cornstalk, I would hit in there with a club and get the rabbit.

* * *

Jeep would point pheasants, too. He would track them until they stopped, freeze until they jumped up. Then he would try to catch them. We were pheasant hunting one day and had just gotten out of the car, when Jeep pointed down in the road ditch. Dad walked over and when the pheasants got up, Dad shot the rooster and Jeep jumped out and caught the hen. Hens weren't legal, but no one had told Jeep. While pheasant hunting, a bunch of us would walk in a line through the cornfields driving the pheasants in front of us. Jeep would be behind us, and if we would drop a pheasant back behind us, we never had to stop and go get it as pretty soon Jeep would be walking right behind you carrying the pheasant. He was a remarkable beagle. It was really great to hunt rabbits and pheasants with Jeep along the railroad tracks. He would go through all the brush in the ditch, and you just walked along the tracks and kept up with the dog. When something jumped up or out, you were right there for the shot.

'Tis Himself

***

Late one winter, a fellow that worked on the railroad told Dad about a slough beside the railroad tracks that was full of rabbits and pheasants. It was a long way from the road, but we decided to try to hunt it. Dad and I and two of the men who worked for Dad, took Jeep and made the long walk. The snow was deep, but we walked down the railroad tracks where it was cleared off. The pheasants saw us coming, and they all flew away long before we got anywhere near them. There was a small creek that went through the slough. It went under the railroad tracks at a timber trestle bridge. Dad told me to stay on top of the bridge and he and the others went off in the deep snow to jump up the rabbits. There were hundreds of rabbits, like there had been pheasants. All of the fields had been harvested bare and this apparently was the only cover for miles. Jeep would jump one rabbit and bark and two more would jump up. He didn't know which one to go after. The guys were shooting rabbits and some were coming my way. I stayed up on the bridge where I could see, and I shot 10 rabbits without moving. Most of the rabbits went into holes in the ground. I had watched a lot of them go into a big brush pile, and when I told Dad to flush them out of there, he found no rabbits, just a hole. We shot 46 rabbits. We ran the dog's leash through their legs and wrapped it around a shotgun. Two men took turns carrying it, and of course, we all had our hunting coats full, too. With our share of the rabbits, Mom pickled them in smoked salt in crocks in the basement. The meat kept for a long time and it was wonderful. Even Mom liked it. We tried for several years to duplicate the process, but we never could.

***

We ruined Jeep for treeing squirrels and retrieving. One summer we felt sorry for him having to spend the hot summer on a leash. We had a chain staked out in front of his house, and it was a poor existence for him, especially when the Renfrow twins, two cute little girls, would stand at the end of his chain and tease him. If he went into his house, they would call him out. If he didn't come out, they would throw clods of dirt in the door. Mom and Dad thought he would like it much better out at Uncle Peck's farm south of Jesup, Iowa. Peck and

Dolly agreed to take him for the summer, and he ran loose with their dogs. He went hunting whenever he wanted, and when he barked treed, no one came to shoot the squirrel. When he caught anything, a rabbit or pheasant, there was no one to give it to, so he took to burying his game. When he would catch a wounded bird or rabbit the next hunting season, I would find him burying it. It was our fault, but I never could trust him after that to bring in a crippled bird.

* * *

One day Norman Anderson and I went hunting, and he brought along a big old coonhound and, of course, I had Jeep. Norman stepped on a rabbit, and he held it down with his foot. He got his shotgun ready, raised his foot quick, and shot the rabbit right into two pieces. It was so mangled up we decided to give the rabbit to the dogs. Well, Jeep ate his half in two gulps and grabbed the other half out of the coonhound's mouth and swallowed that, too. Immediately, we had us a dogfight. Instead of wading in kicking with his feet to try to separate the dogs, Norman dropped to his knees and grabbed his dog by the collar and made a grab for Jeep's collar, just as Jeep was making a grab for a better hold. Jeep got Norman's hand in the deal, and Norman got some deep puncture wounds.

* * *

One day when Jeep and I were hunting northwest of town, in what was called the lower grove, meaning it was smaller and downstream from Coffin's Grove proper, we had a frightening experience. I was carrying my grandfather's double barrel muzzle-loading shotgun and my High Standard HD Military 22 pistol. I would shoot at a squirrel with the pistol when he was still, and if I missed and he ran, I would try to get him with the muzzle-loading shotgun. It was a novel approach and different, which made it fun. Jeep had treed a squirrel and the squirrel ran. I had the shotgun in one hand and the pistol in the other, and I was running through the woods trying to keep the squirrel in sight. I couldn't shoot the shotgun with the pistol in my other hand, so I dropped the pistol beside a tree and kept after the squirrel. The squirrel got away and now I had to go back and find the pistol. It wasn't supposed to be hard, as I had dropped it right by a tree, remember?

Well, there were many trees, and I had run past a lot of them. Jeep went on hunting, looking for another squirrel as I continued to search the base of all the trees for my pistol. I was constantly looking down, and I heard a rumbling that I couldn't place. I cocked my head to one side to listen, and it seemed to be getting closer. All of a sudden, I looked up and there was a herd of cattle running full tilt through the woods, coming right at me. I was in front of a stampede, just like in the movies, and I was about to die. I didn't have time to think of shooting the first one and lying down behind it to protect myself from the others. All of the trees there were small, i.e. no big trunks to get behind, etc. I sucked in a big breath to prepare for the worst, and all of a sudden, there was Jeep running right in front of the herd, looking for me. When he went by me, the cows saw me, and they all slid to a stop right in front of me. Needless to say, I was shaken up pretty badly. The cows all turned out to be heifers, and when they crowded Jeep, he took off running away from them which made them take off after him. After I finally found my pistol, Jeep and I got out of those woods. We were both uneasy, as that was just too close. We both thought that we were about to die. He stayed right with me until we were away from the cattle.

* * *

One time we were hunting in the deep snow out past the golf course, and it was very cold. To warm my cold hands, I used to take off my gloves and put my bare hands under my shirt and in my armpits to thaw them out. When there wasn't any warmth left there, I would put my hands down inside my pants in my crotch to warm them up. When there isn't any warmth left there, you had better start for home as you are cold all the way through. Well, this was one of those days and Ed Frentress' and Norman Anderson's guns had both frozen up and wouldn't fire. My Model 31 Remington 16 gauge would work, but I was just too cold to work it. Norman was using it, and he had shot a rabbit Jeep had run around to him, while I stood there and watched. As we were coming up the lane east of the golf course, a big covey of quail flew up and landed in a small tree. There were so many quail they looked like leaves on that bare tree. Each of us got our guns ready, and we walked slowly toward the tree so as hopefully not to scare the quail. When we got close enough; we all aimed and fired on the count of three. I had stuck my thumb in the trigger guard as my finger was just too cold to feel the trigger. My gun was the only one that went off, but the quail did not fly and none dropped either. We reloaded and stepped a few paces closer and shot again. My gun went off, but nothing dropped again. While we were reloading, the quail all flew. I know I got three or four of them, but they were so cold that they didn't even know they were dead. Blood wasn't flowing that day as it was just too cold!

* * *

Eldon Mangold and I went fox hunting northeast of town one day. The snow was deep and it was cold, too. I attempted to turn Dad's truck around at a farmer's gate to his field. I missed the culvert crossing and got stuck. We walked a long way to the farmer's house to get him to pull us out with his tractor. Up at the house, his wife told us he was in the barn and when he saw me he rushed me back up to the warm house. He proceeded to chew me out because I had frostbitten my nose. It was all white. He said I had been breathing through my mouth and not through my nose. I learned another lesson that day.

* * *

One day when Jeep was running a fox in the snow, we got a shot at the fox and there was blood in the track. We kept following and checking the track for blood, and it was always there, but Jeep wasn't catching the wounded fox. After a long time, we finally realized that Jeep had cut the pad of his foot on the ice and was the one that was bleeding.

* * *

When we moved from the Sandy Flat area on the south of town up to just a block north of the high school, we kept Jeep on a chain fastened to a stake or to the clothesline. When Mom would go to town shopping and drive into the yard, the dog would set up the darndest yowling. She said he would talk to her saying, "Where have you been? I have been here alone all morning. It is about time you got back etc. etc." He would keep it up until she paid him a little attention.

* * *

Jeep had a nice insulated doghouse with a cement sack for a door in the winter. The sack had a piece of chain sewn in it across the bottom to keep it shut. When it was real cold, we would let him sleep in the basement, and he always lay on a hooked rug that Mom had made that was at the bottom of the stairs. One spring when brother Dale came home, he took a shower in the basement and while naked, he stepped on the rug while he was drying his hair with a towel. At first he didn't know what was happening, but hundreds of fleas jumped up and started biting him. He finally realized and got off the rug. The dog hadn't been in the basement for some time, and the fleas had hatched and wanted a blood meal. Dale was most unhappy, and that rug went out the door to be thrown away in a hurry.

* * *

One winter, when the snow was deep, I went out to feed Jeep, and he wasn't in his house. I looked all around as did the folks, but we couldn't find him. Sometime later, a fellow at school told me that Jeep was living under the back porch of the house behind the library. I went looking for him, and sure enough, when I called, he came out from under the back porch through a little hole in the snow. Well, I took him home as he had a nice warm house, and he had run away. The next day he was gone again. He had slipped the collar off over his head. I went back to the house behind the library, and out he came again when I called. It turned out he had a girl friend under the porch, and the folks in the house were feeding both of them. I never did see what she looked like or if any puppies resulted from this tryst.

* * *

When Jeep got old and arthritic and couldn't get around he would stay in his house most of the time. We weren't hunting him anymore and I was busy with all the high school activities. He was going blind and Mom asked Dad to put him down. No one told me, of course, but one day he just turned up missing. I went around looking for him and asked the fellows at school to look out for him, etc. My cousin Don told me that he had probably had a heart attack while doing what he loved best – running rabbits, so I accepted that and quit looking for him. Many years later Dad told me what happened, and I was glad he hadn't told me at the time because I would have been most upset and would not have understood that it was best for the dog. I loved that dog, as we all did, but me especially as we grew up together, and he taught me to hunt. One time when we were hunting, I sat down on the bank of Coffin's Creek to rest. I called Jeep over to me and patted the ground to get him to sit with me. He curled up beside me in the sun and we both took a nap. Neat. We had many, many wonderful days in the woods and fields together.

* * *

Our next dog was also a beagle. You can't go wrong with a beagle. I was now married and in the U.S. Army stationed at Fort Riley, Kansas. Shirley, my wife, and I were living in a little house in Ogden, Kansas, and we had a small fenced-in back yard. We went out to a farmer's house who had advertised he had registered beagle puppies for sale; and we came back with the one that was the most active and inquisitive of the litter. We named him Lineman Riley Rummy. Lineman was the name of his "line", that is, his famous ancestors' and parents' name.

As a puppy, he had a hard time finding his place. He was always getting into trouble. We had a nice new army blanket hanging across the clothesline to dry, up high where we thought he couldn't reach it, but he jumped up and bit it and hung on with his sharp baby teeth until it gave way, and he pulled holes out of it. He also took to climbing the fence and getting out. I put a rope and a drag on him and then, when he would climb the fence, he would hang himself and yell till we rescued him. When he got over climbing, he took to digging out. He was full of mischief!

'Tis Himself

When we took him out rabbit hunting in Kansas, we put him on a rabbit track, and he would follow it just like he did in our back yard when I laid out a track for him, but he wouldn't bark. I called the farmer who sold him to us, and he said, "No problem. Next time you go hunting, come get his momma and take her along. She will teach him to bark on track". It worked like a charm. Momma beagle was baying on the track, and before long, there was young Rummy yipping along with her. Shirley and I got a big kick out of that. Rummy was proud of the whole thing, too.

When I got out of the Army and moved to Wisconsin, Rummy took to running deer. In the area I first hunted, Vernon Marsh, there were more deer than rabbits, and Rummy ran what he could find. I first tried to break him by putting some fowl-smelling deer musk I had bought, on his nose. He didn't like it at all, but after a while it would wear off, or he would lick it off, and he would run deer just like before. I kept putting on the musk like the directions said, but to no avail.

Freddie Welch and I took him hunting pheasants and rabbits at a farm up by Holy Hill, Wisconsin, and Rummy took off after a deer. I took off after the dog, and Freddie went to the truck to get his bow, as it was bow deer season. Rummy ran that deer around that woods about three times before I caught him, and Fred just wanted me to let him run the deer around again, as he had gotten two shots with his bow.

We kept Rummy in an insulated doghouse in the back yard under the canoe, which was up on sawhorses. In the winter, when Shirley and I would get home from work, we would let him come in the house and feed him and let him stay with us until it was time to go to bed. One time Shirley had bought some baby beef liver to fix for supper, as I liked liver and she didn't. She felt if she bought the best, maybe she would try just a bite. Anyway, she went on in the house and put the liver on the table and met me back at the front door as I came in with the dog. While we put our coats in the closet, Rummy ate the liver.

Another time, I brought in the Christmas tree we had bought, while Shirley stopped to let the dog in. I laid the tree on the living room floor, and Rummy ran in, went up to the tree, lifted his leg and watered it good, as he had been in his dog house all day. When son Doug came along, both he and Rummy liked the colored balls that hung down, so we ended up putting the tree in the playpen. It worked pretty well, for when Doug was in bed and the dog back outside, we could let the side of the playpen down and enjoy the tree.

They planted pheasants in Vernon Marsh, and the marsh grass and brush were so thick the pheasants didn't have to fly. Rummy would run them just like rabbits, and if you could keep up, you could get a good shot when the dog finally flushed the bird. Rummy ran a pheasant on that farm up by Holy Hill, and it ran through the woods and out in a slough where I was standing. Shirley, the wife, was standing on a hillside watching the action. I could hear the dog running in shallow water coming right at me. Then the dog stopped not 20 feet in front of me, but I still couldn't see him. About that time, a big rooster pheasant got up and I nailed him. I was very surprised the dog was running a pheasant because he had run in a circle like a rabbit, ran through the woods, and finally ran through water. I mounted that pheasant in 1961, and he has been flying over our fireplace ever since, for forty-seven years now and he still looks great.

One time when we were grouse hunting in Wisconsin, Rummy stood up on his hind legs on a logging road in front of me. He was getting the scent of a deer and when the deer bounded off, Rummy took off after it. I yelled as loud as I could for him to stop, but he kept going, so I dusted his rear end with #8 birdshot. He came right back, and I hoped he had learned his lesson. He had a little BB hole about an inch above his anus that was bleeding like mad. I knew Shirley would have a fit if she knew I had shot him, so I found a puddle of water and proceeded to wash all the blood off his rear end so she wouldn't know and she doesn't to this day.

We camped out one time at the Willow Flowage, and Rummy took off and ran a deer all night long. We could hear him, but we couldn't catch him in the dark. When we were looking for him the next day, a man told us he had seen him out on the road and that he had tried to call him, but the dog ran away. We went to the area and saw him, but he ran away from us, too. He was scared of the cars and strange people. I got out of the car at that point and walked all the way back to our campsite. We went to bed that night just sick, as we thought we had lost him. The next morning, when we got up, he came out from his nest under the canoe. He had hit my track and followed me home. We could hardly recognize him as he was dirty and limping, and his face was all bruised up and his eyes were swollen shut from running in the brush at night.

On two other occasions he got lost running deer. One time he came to a farmer's yard and the man called me to come get him by using the telephone number on the dog's collar. Again, I did not recognize him. He was dirty, full of burrs and with his eyes almost swollen shut. Fortunately, he recognized me. If he hadn't, I would have left him, as I had already told the farmer he wasn't my dog. The third time he came up missing, I put my hunting coat on the ground and urinated near it like the farmer told me to do. When I came back the next morning, Rummy was waiting for me - asleep on my hunting coat. I learned another lesson.

From then on I also learned to take him hunting where there weren't any deer. I had several such spots to hunt him after we moved to Verona, Wisconsin. I was taking care of Craig Malven's beagle dog after his wife and two of his three children were killed in a car wreck. A neighbor and I decided to take both dogs rabbit hunting, and we loaded them into the back of my station wagon and drove to a woods with no deer. I parked beside the road and pulled off as far as I could get in the snow without getting stuck. I told the fellow with me not to let the dogs out yet, as a car was coming. He opened the door just a little, but Rummy was so eager to go, he hit the door with his shoulder, got out and ran around the car and out into the road right in front of the oncoming vehicle. He was killed instantly and was badly broken up. The man stopped and said he was sorry, but we both knew there was nothing he could have done to miss him. I dragged Rummy way off down in the woods beside a little creek and went home and got a shovel. I buried him, after shoveling through the snow and the frozen ground. I had to give Craig's dog back to him, even though he wanted me to keep him. I just couldn't keep him as he reminded me so much of Rummy.

* * *

Later, when we were living in Verona, Wisconsin, we felt every boy needed a dog, so home came another pretty little puppy - a liver and white registered Springer Spaniel male named Doug's Rusty Trigger. We had a nice fenced-in back yard for Trigger to run in. He liked the snow and the water as he was a spaniel. When I would take Doug fishing in the little river south of town, Trigger always jumped in the river. As we walked down the bank, he either waded or swam in the river to keep up with us. When we had the hose out to wash the car, Trigger would jump at the water and even let you squirt him full force in the face. He would open his mouth and try to catch the water. He loved it.

I hunted ruffed grouse with him in Northern Wisconsin, but I never did very well as Trigger was a flush dog. He would trail the birds, and they would run ahead of him until they got on the other side of a pine thicket. Then you would hear them fly but they were out of sight.

When we moved to Nashville, Tennessee, Trigger went along. We didn't have a fenced-in yard, and we went back to putting him on a chain and stake in the yard just off the patio. The man next door had a big white, Husky-type dog that was mean. He kept the dog chained to his house, and that dog was always trying to pick a fight with Trigger. Trigger had never bitten anything in his life, but he had to learn to fight as the big white dog, on several occasions broke his chain and came over to our yard and piled into Trigger and tried to kill him. Shirley went out and turned the hose on them, but that big dog didn't pay any attention to it at all. She was afraid to take after the dog with a broom as the dog would attack her. The only thing that saved Trigger was his collar and chain as the white dog always grabbed him by the neck. Trigger learned to bite back, and he got so that he would growl at you and threaten you if you tried to discipline him with a rolled up newspaper etc. He eventually nipped Shirley twice when she tried to get him to stop barking at the neighbor kids that were always running in the yard, and we had to get rid of him before he bit the kids. He was a good dog, so we decided to find him a good home.

* * *

Our next dog was a house dog. I didn't think we were ready for another dog, and I had never had anything but a hunting dog. You know - a working dog, who earned his keep. Well, a friend and neighbor of Jesse Coles, a fellow I worked with, had to move away, and he couldn't take his dachshund dog with him. Coles told the man he would find the dog a good home, and he kept after me to just take the dog home and introduce him to the boys. I finally gave in, and that's how Fritz came to live at the Hansel House. He was a nice smooth, uniform, brown color with one white spot. Doug and Matt called him their "White Spot Special". He was a good dog for the kids. Both boys played with him a lot in the house and they all got along fine. One of Fritz's tricks was to put his head against you and push. He would put a lot of pressure on you, too. I never saw any other dog do this. He liked to grab the other end of a rag and try to pull it away from you. He would growl and tell you what he was going to do to that rag if he ever got it away from you. If you ever let go, he would look shocked and bring it right back for you to hold onto again. He was strong and the boys would lift him off the ground while he was hanging onto the rag. When he got old and sick, we had to have him put to sleep. We missed that wiener dog.

Our fifth, and at this point, our last dog, was Dixie. She was a Brittany and the first female dog we ever owned. She was liver and white, and she had beautiful long legs. When we brought her home, she was a year old and her name was Nina. We renamed her Dixie, since she was our southern dog. She hadn't been introduced to hunting and I taught her to point using a quail wing tied to a length of monofilament line at the end of an 8-foot fly rod.

We had her spayed and Shirley's driver license number tattooed on her tummy. She was a very loving dog, and she always wanted to please. We enrolled her in a dog obedience class at McGavock High School which met one night per week. We soon learned that the instructor taught the dog handler what to do, and if he did it correctly, the dog learned. Dixie was a fast learner, and she would know what you wanted the first time you did it, providing that you did it right. I goofed one time when I thought she was mouthing a quail she was retrieving, and I corrected her. From then on she would not "fetch". I had to say "Go get 'em" to get her to retrieve.

She was wonderful to train-to sit, stay, down, heel etc. and in the end, she won the trophy for the best-trained dog when she alone stayed in the sitting position the required time, and all the other dogs either moved or laid down. She was beautiful and the only dog in the line that remained seated and alert as required. She was looking straight at me for her next command.

As I've said, she was a loving dog. She would hug you with her long front legs around your neck and snuggle her nose up under your chin, first on one side and then on the other, as she laid in your lap and on your chest in a recliner chair. You could pat your lap and she would jump up into your lap and put her legs on each side of your neck with her ankles curved over your shoulders.

Dixie and I napping after Christmas day dinner 1986

Dixie could tell time, too. Her stomach told her when it was supper time. She would come to you as you were reading the paper, and she would take her paw and scratch at your leg to get your attention. If you ignored her, she would bark at you until you fed her.

'Tis Himself

Shirley's Mom, Mary Hughes, gave us the gift of a fine, chain-link fence for our back yard for Dixie. Dixie loved it, and she ruled her domain chasing cats & squirrels. She would stalk squirrels and birds and even watch them through the window. We had a bird feeder on the window ledge. When a squirrel got into the feeder, you just had to tell Dixie and she would sneak up and stand on her hind legs with her front feet on the window sill. She would watch the squirrel and finally jump at the glass and scare the squirrel away.

She would play with any member of the family using her mouth to catch your hand, but she would never bite. She was quite good at it, and it was remarkable that she didn't ever bite, no matter how fast you were moving your hand. She had a soft mouth on birds, too.

It was fun to watch her, as she was full of antics. She would cross her legs just like folks do. Maybe she got it from watching us, but for some reason, she crossed her legs, too. She also would sleep on her back with her legs sticking straight up in the air. We had a beanbag chair that she thought was hers, and if Matt or Doug would get in it to watch television, Dixie would climb in with them and crowd them out of her chair.

There was a time when, if we would leave her alone so she had the run of the house, she would get into mischief. We fed her dog food that came in a box, and each meal was individually packaged in a little plastic bag. The box full of these plastic bags was stored on the floor of the pantry in the kitchen, and the door to that closet was not always closed tight. Once, when we were away, Dixie got into the closet, stuck her head into the box and took out the individual packages one by one. She didn't open the packages and eat it as she knew she wasn't supposed to, but she hid them all over the house, either to show us she could, or for rainy days. We found them in remote corners, under the davenport and even under Shirley's pillow upstairs in the bedroom, on the bed.

Sister-in-law, Marge, had given us a stuffed, fabric, mallard duck as a door stop, and one day when we came home, Dixie didn't come to meet us, which was strange. We found her waiting for us by the fireplace. She was laying down with that heavy duck door stop between her front legs. She looked up as if to say, "Look what I've got." She didn't chew or tear it up or anything because she knew she shouldn't. She just wanted us to know that she could have if she had wanted to.

One of the fun things of working a young dog is that you get to see her learn. I was thrilled when Dixie pointed her first covey of quail below the house. She trailed them about 40 yards across an open area and across an old road before she froze on point. I did not have a gun as the season wasn't open, but I walked up and flushed them – it was great.

At dog obedience school, many verbal commands are reinforced by hand signals. "Stay," has a hand in front of the dog's face; "Go", has a sweeping motion of the hand and arm, and "Come", a pat on the leg, etc. When Dixie became deaf in her old age, I would converse with her by hand signals only, and it worked fine. When we would be hunting quail and we came to a pond, I would want to check it for ducks. I would hold up my hand for her to stop, and when she saw me and stopped, I would pat my leg to call her, and then we would sneak up below the pond dike with her at heel.

She had been slow to learn to retrieve ducks as she didn't like the cold water, and the first time she went out after a duck, she almost drowned when she got tangled up in some willow branches. She was almost back to the bank with the duck in her mouth, and she swam and swam, she couldn't make any headway as a small willow branch was right across her chest under the water. She tipped up and her front feet came out of the water splashing, and she almost went over backwards. She was scared. I couldn't get to her due to the deep water. She finally dropped the duck, turned around and swam back and got out. Then I tried to retrieve the duck by climbing out on the willow tree, but I ended up in the water and got all wet. She approached the duck from the other side and did go get it while I was wringing out my clothes.

Later, if she was chasing a crippled duck and it would dive, she would put her head under the water and grab it if the water was clear enough to see it. If not, she would swim around in a circle when the duck would dive. When she would get tired, she would look at you and even yip at you asking for a little help. She would say, "Shoot this thing. One of us has got to get some relief". Of course I would have to wait until there was enough distance between them so I wouldn't hit her.

One time, while checking the ponds for ducks at Mr. Robert Carother's farm, I looked over the dike, and a half dozen mallards got up off the far end of the pond out of range. I was about to go on when I noticed two Canada goose heads sticking up out of the weeds where the ducks had been. Since there was no way of approaching within range, I got the idea to send Dixie to see what would happen. I stayed below the dike and waved my arm for her to go. She ran up on top of the dike, but not seeing anything on the pond, she looked back at me. I signaled for her to go on again. She hesitated and then took off over the dike. I couldn't see what was happening, but in a little while, I could hear the geese begin honking. I waited until they sounded close and I looked up over the dike. The two geese were in the middle of the pond swimming toward me and swimming right behind them came Dixie herding them my way. When the geese saw me, they took off into the wind, and I managed to drop them both. Dixie swam up to the first one, grabbed it and started toward the bank. When she reached the bank she couldn't pick the goose up, so she turned around and backed up the bank dragging the goose with her.

When she went for the second bird, it was still flopping its wings a little, and one big wing came down on top of Dixie's head and shoved her under the water. She came up spitting and tried again twice more, with the same result. She was about to give up, and she started to swim toward me, but then, on her own, she went back and finished her job. This time she approached the goose from the front, and grabbing it by the neck, she towed it to the shore and up the bank a little way where I could reach it.

Dixie was a courageous dog. If a wounded duck or quail was in thick brush or briars where other dogs wouldn't go, she would dive right in. She was like a tackle or guard in football. She knew her job was to dive in and get the bird, and she would sacrifice her body as necessary to get the job done. She made me proud of her many times.

She would obey you even if she didn't want to. A squirrel got himself electrocuted at the transformer in front of our house, and he fell to the ground at the bottom of the telephone pole. Shirley told me about it when I came home from work, so I let Dixie out and sent her to retrieve it. When she got there she hesitated, looked back at me, and I had to tell her again. When she finally brought the squirrel to me, much of its hair had been burned off, and it smelled really bad. I didn't blame her a bit because I didn't want to touch him either.

Dixie didn't like cats, and she would chase them and bark at them if they would run away. However, one of our neighbors had a big cat that wasn't afraid of dogs, and it didn't run. It stood its ground when Dixie ran at it, and when she got close enough, the cat slapped her in the face. Dixie didn't know what to think about that, so she became friends with the cat, and they played together after that.

One of her most trying retrieves was late one duck season when everything was frozen up. There was snow on the ground and all of the duck ponds where locked in ice. Rob Raney drove by a pond that was covered with ducks, and the ducks were keeping the water open by their continual splashing and agitating the water. We felt we had better check out the situation, so we made a long sneak and approached the pond from below the dike with Dixie at heel. When the ducks got up, they went every which way and many came back out over us. We got our limit. Most of the ducks landed on the bank and Dixie retrieved what we didn't pick up, but three of the birds were out on the pond floating in the water. Dixie was a pretty good swimmer, but she didn't have heavy fur. In fact her tummy was almost bare and her fur was fine and fluffy. When I told her to retrieve the ducks in that cold water, she looked at me as if she thought I was crazy. I kept insisting though, and after a long time, she finally swam out and retrieved the first one. When she got back to the bank, she rolled and rolled in the snow and grass to try to get the ice off her that had frozen all over her fur as soon as she got out of the water. Needless to say, she didn't want to go get the next bird. I had to talk and talk to encourage her to get back in the water. Rob didn't think I could get her to go in again, but she finally did and she retrieved number two. Of course, we had all the rolling etc. when she got out, and balking on the third retrieve. She finally got that bird too, but by that time it was getting dark. I had a sore throat from all that talking and pleading with her. She was glad to get in the truck as we all were.

Dixie and I with Rob and Daisy after a successful duck hunt

Dixie and I had many, many happy and successful days afield. Over her lifetime we collected 427 ducks and 186 quail. Our best duck year was 1997-98 when we got 68 ducks. Of course, Dixie retrieved lots of ducks that others shot, but we are only talking about what my records show. The best quail year was 1991-92 with 43 in the bag. One time I got three quail with one shot. When the covey got up, I shot at one bird that was flying straight away from me, and he was going between two cedar trees. At the instant I shot, two other birds, one from each side, decided to go between the same two trees and all three dropped. Dixie retrieved them all, one at a time. Another time she retrieved three from almost the same spot, but I had gotten each one with a different shot. Three for three though. We were very lucky to have such a wonderful place to hunt at Mr. Carothers farm.

When we would get home from hunting, I would have to spend 10 or 15 minutes pulling cockleburs out of Dixie's fur. She would also have to have a bath in the sink in the garage as she would get all muddy, and Shirley wouldn't let her in the house.

The quail population is way down around here now. One year I knew where there were ten different coveys on the farm. Last year we only saw two coveys, and there were very few birds in each one. We didn't even shoot at them. Mr. Carothers died last year and his wife and daughters are selling off the land to developers. It was bound to happen, as it is close to the City of Nashville and sanitary sewer became available.

Since Dixie is gone, hunting isn't the same, so I haven't been chasing the ducks and quail. My wife Shirley never did get to see Dixie point a bird, but son Doug did. She pointed a single quail for him, and he got it with this 20 gauge. It was in the woods, too, and not an easy shot.

Dixie was born on May 25, 1984, and she died in my arms on September 2, 1998. at the age of 14 years 3 months and 8 days. I still cry when I think about it. I prayed for God to give me a sign or something as I didn't feel it was right for me to decide when she was sick enough to end her life. The veterinarian had told me I would know when the time had come, but we could still make her feel pretty good with aspirin. God told me he didn't know what the problem was, as I certainly had decided lots of times when to end the lives of many of his animals and birds. The vet said he would put her to sleep and then inject something that would stop her heart. She was a very trusting dog and, at the last second, she struggled and looked at me as if she knew what the vet and I had done to her. I'm sorry, Dixie. It was for your own good.

It was a wonderful time for man and dog. We had her portrait made, and I still carry it in my wallet. An 8 x 10 framed picture helps me to remember how good she looked. She is buried in the back yard under a concrete monument with her name engraved on it. We had a special box made and wrapped her in a pretty colored rug and put her "Best Dog" trophy in with her.

We loved her. Goodbye again, "Long Legged Pup".

FOXES BY THE DOZEN

I want to tell you about the foxes I have taken as a mighty hunter, as they were memorable. My first fox was a grey, and it came from Skinner's woods on the north side of town. Dad, my buddy Chuck Martensen and I were hunting rabbits with our beagle dog, "Jeep", and he was running something. You never knew with Jeep what he was running, as he was some kind of hunting dog. He would run anything that would run away from him and some things that wouldn't. I was standing still like Dad told me, so as to let the rabbit come to me, when I saw a reddish movement in a big tree, and I thought it was a squirrel. I started to ease up on the backside of the tree so the squirrel wouldn't see me and run, when it turned out to be a fox. The fox heard me walking in the leaves, and he jumped to another limb so he could see what I was. I raised my brother's Remington 22 cal. pump action rifle real slow and shot him in the neck. He fell out of the tree, and I yelled for Dad. Since the fox wasn't dead, I picked him up by the hind legs and swung him around in a circle and cracked his head on the tree to kill him. His nose started to bleed, and I thought he was dead. When Dad and Martensen came up, I told them all about it, and Dad told me that a grey fox could climb a tree, but a red couldn't. Since they were on the other side of a fence, Dad told me to throw him over. It was a big task for a small boy, but I grabbed the fox by the hind legs again and, swinging him around, I was able to loft him up over the fence.

Well, the fox landed on his feet and he started to run off through the woods. Dad raised his shotgun, a Winchester Model 97, 12 gauge, and started to shoot him but then he thought that it would distract from my shooting my first fox, and he decided against it. He took off running after the fox and he caught him in about 25 yards and bowled him over with the barrel of his gun. He looked the fox over and decided the 22 bullet in his neck wasn't bothering the fox all that much, so we decided to take him home alive. Dad put the dog's leash on the fox, and we headed for the truck. When we got home, we laid "Willie the Coon's" cage on its side and put the fox in. Willie was a raccoon that my cousin Don had given me, and Dad had built a wonderful two story house for him.

We kept the fox in the cage all that winter, and he made out just fine. The cage/house was on the north side of the garage near the trailer that we hauled the garbage to the dump in, and it always smelled a little around there. When spring came and Mom started working in the yard and garden, she said the fox had to go as the back yard smelled terrible. When we cleaned up his insulated box full of straw, we found the fox had not eaten all we had given him, and he was storing food in his nest. The place was full of rotten food and that was what was stinking up the place.

I was mighty proud of that fox, and Dad told me I would never forget shooting my first fox. He was right, and I have remembered it as if it was just yesterday, even though it was back in 1945 and I was 13 years old. I am 76 now and I remember most all the foxes I have taken and I will try to tell you about each one.

* * *

Where we lived in Iowa it was farm country, and when the foxes got too plentiful, the farmers would complain and the members of the Delaware County Fish and Game Club felt that the foxes were probably catching a lot of young pheasants so the club would organize community fox hunts in the winter on Sunday afternoons. Most of the hunting seasons were over, and in the middle of the winter there wasn't much going on anyway. On a given Sunday afternoon, all the participants would meet and they would be divided up into approximate fourths and assigned to the north, east, west or south of the chosen section of land. In Iowa the land is so fertile and flat that there is a farm-to-market road every mile in every direction. Each section of land usually contained four farms of 160 acres and each farm usually fronted on a different road. The hunters would drive their cars and park along the roads all around the designated section of land. At the agreed upon time, they would get out of their cars, spread out along the road, go through the fence and start walking toward the center of the section of land. All carried shotguns, and as the hunters came toward the center, they got closer together and were supposed to trap any foxes in the center of the circle where they would be shot. We saw no deer on these hunts. At that time there were no deer in that part of Iowa. We did see lots of pheasants, rabbits and a few foxes. The only things the hunters were allowed to shoot were the fox. Most of the foxes would get away as the hunters were careless, they wouldn't keep their interval, and they would be walking in little bunches and talking. The fox would escape up a dry wash or between the hunters, but enough were killed to make the hunt worthwhile.

* * *

On Sunday afternoon February 3, 1946, Dad took me and a neighbor boy, Ronnie Rayborn, along on one of those "party" fox hunts. I was carrying my brother's Winchester Model 12, 12 gauge, as brother Dale was in the U.S. Air Force as a pilot, having enlisted right after Pearl Harbor was attacked. I felt I needed more firepower to kill a fox, and I was right. I used that gun a lot, and Dale claimed I shot up a case of ammunition that he had when he went off to war. I claim there was a box and a half left when he came home. From my records, I bought my first box of 12 gauge shotgun shells on January 19, 1946, and they cost $ 1.19. I was 14 years old.

* * *

Dale's Model 12 didn't fit me when I was small, and it used to give me a fat lip if I shot it very often. One day when my lip was puffed way out, "Jeep" treed a squirrel, and I aimed at it right over my head. When I felt that fat lip on the stock, I pulled my face away just a little and shot. I missed the squirrel I guess, but I didn't pay much attention as my lip split wide open. To this day I have a thick bottom lip, and I have always wondered if that caused it.

Anyway, Dad, Ronnie Rayborn, and I and two other fellows that were riding in our car, spread out and started walking toward the center of the circle. We saw two foxes way across on the other side of the section, so we knew there were some in the net. After a while, a red fox came over a low rise right in front of me. My first shot raked the hair off him, and my second shot broke his hind leg. On my third shot, Dad shot at the same time and the fox went down. As we got closer to him, he would get up and all four of us would shoot, and he would run on a little ways and fall over. We did that several times, and I learned that a fox is one tough customer. When we skinned him that night in the basement, we hung him from the floor joist and the shot just rained onto the paper we had spread out under him on the floor. I count that fox as my first red fox as I was closest and my gun did the most damage, I'm sure.

* * *

My third fox was a grey, and I did not know he was a fox at first. I was hunting rabbits with my beagle dog Jeep, on the north side of the backwater in my hometown of Manchester, Iowa. The Marion Street dam backed the water up through town and it formed a flooded area complete with islands. Senator Rodney Terrill donated the land along one side for Terrill Park. In the early days, the water near the park was beautiful with lily pads and deep pools between the islands and many boats plied the water on weekends, especially Sunday afternoons. I still thought the area was beautiful when I came along, but, as Dad told me, it had deteriorated when the siltation from the river filled in the backwater and weeds started to encroach and plug up the waterways. It was still a wonderful place for a boy like me to grow up, hunting ducks, rabbits, pheasants and trapping muskrats and such.

Well, Jeep was running what I thought was a rabbit, and I stopped on the bank north of the big island that I called Willow Island, and positioned myself near the brushy shore next to an open field where I thought the rabbit would have to run, being pursued by my dog. Jeep ran a long way and made a circle clear over by Bill Tunk's pond, and then started coming back. As the dog's voice came closer, two pheasants ran out into the field and took off, but I was too far for a shot. That day I had my brother Dale's bolt action Stevens 410 gauge shotgun and I was ready should I get a shot. This other dog came out of the brush and ran along the edge of the field. When I checked him out with the binoculars I was carrying, I realized it was a fox and Jeep was on his track. The fox came on along the edge of the field right to me, and as he went by in the brush about 10 yards away, I let him have it with the 410. I shot him again at about 8 feet, and he went down but got up immediately and continued running out of sight. I thought he had gotten away but Jeep soon caught him. I was mighty proud of that fox too, as it was the first one I had gotten all alone.

Due to my hunting with Dale's model 12 Winchester and shooting up his and Dad's 12 gauge shotgun shells, the two of them decided to pitch in and buy me the Model 31 Remington in 16 gauge so I would have to buy my own ammunition! They gave it to me for Christmas, December 25, 1947, when I was 15 years old. It was a wonderful gun, and I didn't miss with it for the first twenty seven times I shot it. I was used to Brother Dale's full-choke gun, and my 16 gauge had a modified choke. We went out to my uncle's farm south of Jesup, Iowa, to visit and to shoot my new gun. Cousin Don took me for a drive to see if we could find anything to shoot at, and we saw a hawk fly up in a tree along the road ahead of us. Hawks were legal then, and while Don drove along slowly, I opened up the car door and shot the hawk. It was sitting, but I was moving, and I had to lead him just right. That was the first shot with that gun.

Later in the day, we decided to see if there were any pigeons in the barn. Six or seven of us lined up out from the barn, below the closed haymow door. The pigeons would come out the slot in the door where the rope went through, and they would swoop down and fly up away from the barn. Cousin Don went into the barn to chase out the pigeons, and I was the first one in the gunner line closest to the barn. Don did a good job, and the pigeons came out one at a time, and I dropped every one. After I had shot about seven or eight straight Dad came up to me and said I should go to the end of the line and let someone else have a shot. I said, "sure," and I still got several more as the other fellows couldn't hit 'em. I couldn't miss with that gun. Dad had cut the stock off and installed a recoil pad to make the gun fit me, but I feel it was the modified choke that allowed me to hit those pigeons.

* * *

My fourth fox was another grey that Jeep was running in the backwater. There was a long peninsula that separated the Maquoketa River from the backwater, and it widened out into a real brushy area that was a good place to hunt rabbits. It was a Saturday morning with no school, and I had been hunting ducks in our duck blind on one of the islands in the backwater. After a limit of bluebills, I went home for breakfast. When I came back, I brought Jeep and let him off over in the brushy area, and I got back in the duck blind. I had left my Dad's homemade cork duck decoys out when I went home for breakfast.

After a while Jeep started running something, and he was telling me about it. About then, a bunch of mallards came in, and I managed to get four by waiting to shoot until two swam together. I got two on the first shot and one each on the next two shots. I had my limit of four with three shots. There was a plug in my Remington Model 31 sixteen gauge pump, of course, limiting it to hold only three shells due to the Federal Migratory Bird law. I rowed the boat out (Dad and I built the boat in his shop) and picked up the ducks. I laid them out on the back boat seat and smoothed the feathers down. Big red-legged, mallard drakes from Canada are so beautiful I just had to display them properly.

I rowed the boat over to the bank, and Jeep was still running in the brush on the other end of the peninsula. I knew that whatever he was running had to come back by me, so I just stood on the path along the riverbank and waited. Suddenly there was a fox coming straight at me, but he saw me as soon as I saw him, and he jumped into the brush and took off back down the peninsula. I knew I had goofed. I knew the fox would circle around again with the dog after him, but when he came around again, he would be looking for me now. I went down the river a few yards and climbed a tree and went out on a limb that positioned me right out over the path. I was standing on two limbs and holding on to another with my left hand while holding the gun with my right. Before long I could see the fox coming back on the path, and holding the gun with one hand, I shot him as he ran under my tree. I was thrilled, as I had "outfoxed" the fox.

I climbed down out of the tree, and when Jeep quit worrying the fox, I put him in the bushes and went to get the boat and rowed it closer. When I stepped out of the boat onto the bank, a rabbit jumped up and ran straight away from me. I shot him at about 15 yards and it scared me to death because a man was standing right there where I shot the rabbit. I had not seen him, but he had heard me pulling the boat up on the bank, and he had started my way. He was hunting also and he was very impressed with my four mallards, a grey fox and a rabbit all laid out on the back seat of the boat. That was one of the best days hunting that I ever had.

* * *

My fifth fox was a red fox that I surprised. I was duck hunting along Coffin's Creek out west of town. I was now old enough to drive, and I had driven the folk's car out to Dr. Wayne (Hickory) Hall's farm that backs up to the creek and woods that we called the lower grove. That differentiated it from Coffin's Grove, which was a big woods, and it was upstream. There were several ponds along the creek and, early in the duck season, there were often wood ducks or teal on these ponds. One year I shot a drake redhead duck on one of Hickory's ponds. It was the only redhead I have ever shot.

Down the creek a short distance, there was a big tree that had blown down across the creek making a natural bridge. I crossed the creek on the tree, and when I came up a rise to the flat land on the other side of the creek, I saw something moving at the base of a tree. It was small and black, and it was going up and down right at the base of the tree where the trunk flared out for the roots. I stood there watching it for a couple of minutes until I finally figured out what it was. It was a fox's ear! The fox was lying in the morning sun on the other side of the tree, and he was licking the dew off his legs. As he licked, his ear was the black thing that was going up and down at the base of the tree. I got my 16 gauge up and aimed at the spot, and I whistled. When the fox looked up at my whistle, it was the last thing he ever heard.

* * *

'Tis Himself

My sixth fox was a called shot. It was a warm day, and the snow was melting. Dad had come home for lunch at noon, and I had decided to go rabbit hunting with one of my buddies that afternoon. While I was talking to Dad about where I should go, I had a feeling that I was going to shoot a fox. It was a perfect day for Jeep, the beagle dog, to run one, and I told Dad that I was going to shoot a fox! He said, "Just like that, huh." I said, "Yup", and we laughed about it. Well, that afternoon the dog hit a track, and I got up on a stump so I could see better above the brush. As nice as you please, a grey fox came right to me, and I made my prediction come true.

* * *

My seventh fox, a grey, was taken at night, south of my home town of Manchester. Two of my hunting buddies, Jim Malven and Bert Retz and I were hunting in the folks' 1950 Chevy. I had purchased a predator call from Burnam Brothers in Texas, and it made a scream of a dying rabbit. We would drive to a likely spot in woods near a field and try to call up a fox. This particular night, we were in the woods. We had had the car lights on and a spot light out each side, but we couldn't see very well from inside the car, so we got out and climbed up on the car with our feet on the hood and our seats on the top of the car. I had Dad's Winchester Model 97, 12 gauge, with a full choke and 32 inch barrel. A grey fox came out of the brush in front of us. I dropped him I was sure, but it took me a long time to find him with a flashlight. Looking back into the car lights, I couldn't see a thing. Somehow, we got too far onto the top of the car and "plunk", the top bent in. I lay down in the front seat and was able to pop it back out with my feet on the ceiling! It didn't show unless you knew where to look.

We were able to get several fox at night by calling them in, and we paid for one of our spotlights with the bounty the fox hides brought. On two separate nights, a reporter from the newspaper went along, hoping to do a story about us, but wouldn't you know- we didn't have any luck when he was around!

My eighth fox was another red, and I was proudest of him because I outfoxed him. It was 1956 and brother Dale was home from the Air

Force on leave, and I was on leave from the Army. He and I and a high school buddy, Wayne Condon, were going pheasant hunting south of Masonville, Iowa, where we had been duck hunting and had seen a lot of pheasants in the morning. Pheasant season didn't open until noon. We were driving down the road, and a red fox ran across the road up ahead of us and went into a slough, a thick wet area full of long grass and bogs. I knew the fox wouldn't stay in the slough, and if we went in after him, we would never get close enough to get a shot. I yelled for Dale to stop the car. I quickly told him to let me out, that I would run along the fence and get up on the little wooded hill on the other side of the slough. He was to drive slowly up to where the fox had crossed and give me some time to get to the hill before he and Condon spread out and started through the slough toward me.

I was standing real still and quiet, and wondering if I was in the right place, when, all at once, I could see the fox's black feet coming toward me under the bushes. When he topped the hill and broke out of the brush, he was close, and I dropped him with my 16 gauge Remington Model 31. At the sound of the shot, a big rooster pheasant got up and I threw two shots at him in vain. Dale was surprised to see me coming carrying the fox, for when he heard the three shots he figured I had missed him. He was a beautiful big male red fox. We skinned him and Dale took his pelt home with him to show his boys.

Many, many years passed before my ninth fox appeared. I had graduated from high school and college and served two years in the U.S Army. I had worked six years in Milwaukee, Wisconsin, and six years in Madison, Wisconsin, and it was now 1970. I was working in Nashville, Tennessee and I had just moved into a new home in a new subdivision near J. Percy Priest Lake. The area behind the house was an undeveloped cedar woods, and it had been a poor, hard rock farm years ago. The fence posts could not be dug into the ground due to the rock, which was right on the surface. The farmer had held the fence posts up by piling rocks around the posts and the fence wire ran through the rock pile. It was a queer sight for a fellow from Iowa where the black topsoil ran deep. It was very ingenious of the farmer though. He used what he had available and that was a lot of rock!

'Tis Himself

* * *

On Thanksgiving Day, 1970, while wife Shirley was cooking our turkey dinner, I took my 16 gauge shotgun and our Springer Spaniel, Trigger, and went out behind the house to look for a quail. We got one quail and a grey fox, number nine. After dinner, my eight-year-old son Doug wanted to go hunting with me. We went out into the cedar glade again, and we found a woodchuck about six feet up in a little two-inch diameter tree. I asked Doug if he wanted to shoot it, and when he said he did, I gave him my 16 gauge shotgun. At a range of about 10 feet, he shot it right out of the tree. It was a good day. I skinned both critters and tanned their hides with the hair on, and they are hanging on the wall in the office/game room, right now. It is 2009, thirty-eight years later. It seems like a long time ago. Doug is working in New England now.

* * *

A couple of years later I was hunting ducks on the shores of the lake below the house in a snow storm. I saw a red fox coming toward me along the water, and I got down behind some rocks to wait for him. When he got close enough, I dropped him with my 16 gauge and I got a rabbit with the same shot, as the fox was carrying it in his mouth! That fox's hide and the rabbit skin are on the wall, too. That was number 10.

* * *

My eleventh fox was taken with nephew Roger Raisch's 12 gauge, single barrel, single shot, 3 inch magnum, turkey gun. I was not familiar with a 3 inch magnum, and when we saw a grey fox that was on a rise too far away for a shot, he said his gun would take that fox. I didn't believe it, but he let me try, and that fox dropped dead in its tracks. I was impressed.

* * *

My twelfth fox was taken at a boat ramp on J. Percy Priest Lake when we were duck hunting. Like Dad told me, I have never forgotten any of the foxes I have shot.

* * *

Two other foxes of note that I should tell about I didn't get, but their stories are of interest. Dad missed a fox one snow covered cold night when he was hunting by moonlight with his hounds. It was before I was born, and Dad kept both coon and fox hounds. He and his hunting partner were out in the woods in the dark, but they could see pretty well with the full moon on the snow. Dad had climbed up on a tree that had blown down, and the trunk of the tree still rested on the stump. The trunk was level with the ground and about 4 feet up and covered with snow. Dad kicked the snow off under his feet and was standing there listening to the hounds run a fox, when they circled around behind him. He could see the fox coming through the woods, and he was trying to get turned around, when the fox ran right under the tree trunk Dad was standing on. Dad's foot slipped, and he fell off the log and broke his ankle. Sometimes the fox wins! Dad and his buddy had a hard time getting Dad out of the woods and back to town.

When I was in grade school and living on South Brewer Street in Manchester, Iowa, the next-door neighbors to the south were Fred and Eunice Hilsenbeck. Fred hunted and worked with Dad when Dad needed a good brick or block layer. One day Fred brought home a live red fox that he had gotten, and he put a collar and leash on it and tied it to the clothesline. The clothesline was a length of #9 wire that was stretched between two trees. The fox eventually became quite tame and would eat out of Eunice's hand. It would play with our terrier dog "Nick", and they would roll and chase each other as far as the clothesline would let the fox go. Nick would come back, and away they would go again.

The fox dug himself a den under our concrete garage floor and Dad got upset because when he looked under there, he could see way back under the floor about eight feet. He felt the floor would give way under the weight of the car. He got Fred to run the clothesline to another tree where the fox couldn't reach the garage, and the two of them attempted to fill the hole back in. They couldn't tamp the dirt in good enough to pack it under the concrete slab to adequately support the floor, but they tried hard.

Well, one day the fox slipped his collar and ran across the street and was out behind the Reedy's chicken coop. The chickens were upset, and when Mr. Reedy showed up, the fox went into a hole under a willow tree that was back there in the fencerow. Mr. Reedy didn't know at first that it was the Hilsenbeck's fox, and he was trying to get it to run out so he could shoot it. The neighbors told him that Hilsenbeck's fox had gotten loose, and they went to tell Eunice that the fox was in the hole. When Eunice arrived, there were several men there and a bunch of kids including me. She tried to call him out of the hole, but he was scared of all the people and he wasn't coming. She got down on her hands and knees and started to reach into the hole. The men tried to stop her, but she said that the fox was tame and wouldn't bite her. She reached way into the hole, and the fox clamped down on her hand big time. She was caught fast. She was hollering her head off, and all the guys were helpless as they couldn't get close to the hole because she had it blocked. They tried beating on the tree trunk, but the fox just held on tighter. Someone finally worked his way around Eunice's arm and took the barrel of a shotgun in with his hand. When he knew he would hit the fox and not Eunice's hand he told someone to fire the gun. The fox let go and Eunice went to the doctor.

* * *

A pseudo fox's hide is also on the wall in the other room. It is one of my "trophies". It is a coyote that I got with a bow and arrow when I was up in a tree stand, deer hunting. He came up the hill right at me so fast that I didn't have time to get my bow ready until he had passed right under my tree and continued up the hill. He turned 90 degrees and headed off to my left without stopping. When he got to my 30 yard marker, a piece of blaze orange plastic lying on the ground, I whistled. He stopped, and I immediately shot, as my orange sight pin was right on his boiler room. The arrow flew true, and I saw him flinch, but he took two jumps and he was over the hill. I waited a few minutes and got down and went to look for him. There was no blood, but I kept quartering back and forth in the direction he had been heading, and I eventually found him by the smell. That's right. I could smell him. He was lying just below a log he had jumped over, and without that coyote odor, I would never have found him.

One less coyote, taken with bow and arrow in Garland's woods 1989

MY DEMISE

I almost died several times. I got hurt many, many times, and for a while, people said I was prone to injury. Right now I want to tell you about my coming close to death!

There were two different occasions when I almost drowned. Once when I was with a bunch of kids at the beach at the Backbone State Park, I was floating around in a red rubber inner tube. I ventured out toward a floating raft where the big boys, who could swim, were playing around. The water depth at the raft was over my head, but I never felt I was in any danger as I was in a boat - a rubber tire tube. One of the older boys got up from lying on the raft, and he jumped and cannonballed into the water close to me. The inner tube tipped over, and I sank to the bottom. I literally was sitting on the sand bottom and looking all around. I wasn't scared. The water was kind of an eerie green color, and it was light and bright off to my left. The noise of all the kids was also to my left. To my right it was dark and silent – the deeper water). I stood up and started walking to the left toward the light. After taking a few steps, my head started to come out of the water and I was able to jump up and get to shallower water. I got back onto my inner tube as if nothing had happened.

* * *

When I was a kid and out to Uncle Peck's on the farm, we all went swimming in the creek under a bridge where the water was deep. I couldn't swim, but that didn't matter, as I wouldn't wade out above my waist, and not that deep if I could help it. Someone found an old railroad crosstie and the kids were using it as a boat. They would get astraddle of it, and others would push it out into the water. You tried to stay on all the way under the bridge. Cousin Don put me on, against my better judgment, and he gave it a big push, but the "boat" quit going right out in the deepest part. When I turned around to look back, I lost my balance. Of course, I fell off and sank to the bottom. I was only under for a minute or two, and I can remember it was very dark in the water under the bridge. I felt a swirl go by, and then an arm hit my shoulder and someone grabbed my hair. Don pulled me up, and I grabbed the railroad tie. He swam us to shore. I did a lot of sputtering, but I don't remember being scared. Both times I didn't try to breath and didn't swallow any water. I wasn't smart enough to know I was in danger so I hadn't panicked.

* * *

One day the car wouldn't start, and I was helping Dad push the car out of the garage. There was a workbench along the north wall, and as the car started rolling, I gave up pushing and started walking along beside the car, between it and the bench. Dad was pushing at the driver's side door and steering with his arm through the window. He thought the car was too close to the north side of the door, so he turned the steering wheel, which made the front of the car pin me between the car and the bench. The car was rolling down the incline up into the garage, and it came to a stop. Dad saw my predicament just before I passed out. I was squeezed so tight that I could not cry out. I also saw all the things that I had done in my life pass before my eyes, so I know that story is true.

Anyway, Dad came to the front of the car, and taking the car by the bumper, he slid the car sideways and got me out. I was like a rag doll. He carried me out into the yard. Mom called the doctor, and by the time he got there, I had come to, but they wouldn't let me move. I didn't feel like moving anyway. The doctor checked me over and said that I'd probably live, so I did.

* * *

One time, when I was in college, I came home and drove down to South Brewer to visit with the Renfrows, my cousins. They were all sledding on the little hill across the street from where I used to live. The snow had melted, but they had poured water on the trails so you could really go fast on the resulting ice. The trail went down the hill, between two bushes and curved around between two buildings, over the plank walkway to the chicken house and off toward the garden. Well, I waited at the top of the hill and asked Cousin Chuck if

I could use his sled. When he said I could, I took a long run to build up a lot of speed and belly-flopped onto that icy trail. I made it down the hill and between the bushes, but I was going too fast to turn on the ice to go between the buildings. I hit the closest building broadside, and it stunned me so bad I couldn't speak or move. The kids all came down and stood around me and talked about what to do. One said, "Is he dead?" I could hear everything, but I couldn't speak. Slowly, I came out of it, but another lesson was learned, I hope.

* * *

When I first got to Fort Riley, Kansas, as a young Army lieutenant, a colonel moved into the BOQ right across the hall from me. He was to be the Chief Surgeon, and he had done a lot of work with plastic surgery on soldiers who had been wounded. Since we were both new on the post, we did a lot of things together and we became friends. Of course, I was a Sanitary Engineer and he a doctor, so we didn't see each other during the day. One night he invited me to come to his room to see some slides. He had invited lots of doctors, so the room was packed, and I ended up sitting in a back corner on a stool. The slides were gruesome to me as they depicted tube grafts etc. and young men with no lower jaws etc. Anyway, I passed out, but I didn't fall down. I just fell into the corner and remained on the stool. One of the doctors close to me heard me hit the wall, and after a bit, he checked on me again. Finally, he realized I wasn't watching, and he called a halt to the proceedings, and they got me onto the floor. He told me I was a long time coming to, but that I couldn't have been in a better place, as the room was full of doctors. If he hadn't laid me down to get the blood back into my head, I would have been brain-dead instead of just brain-wounded.

* * *

In June of 1996, I had just returned from working on the roof up at church, and I was sitting on the back porch. Shirley, my wife, was at the dentist, and I was reading a new sportsman's catalog that had come in the mail. I suddenly had the feeling of impending doom. It wasn't affecting me, I didn't think, as I felt fine, but I felt the dentist might be hurting Shirley or that she had a wreck on the way home or something. Maybe one of the boys had something happen to them? I even looked up above my head to see if I had a black cloud above me, but all was clear. I just couldn't understand what this great big, overwhelming feeling was, but it was doom, for sure.

Finally, I got the feeling that I was going to faint, so I realized it was about me. I scooched forward in my chair, and got my head down, and the feeling went away. I went on reading with no more problems until Shirley got home. She sat down beside me, and I was telling her all about it when, all of a sudden, I felt like I was going to faint again. When I told her that, she wanted to feel my pulse. Like a dummy, I gave her my wrist when I should have been getting my head down. I passed out while she was looking for a pulse. She couldn't get me out of the chair by pulling on my arms because I was limp. She slapped my face, pulled my hair and generally had a ball, but that isn't the way she describes it. She said she looked into my eyes, which were open, and there was no one home. When I came to, she insisted I go to the hospital, and as I had a little nausea, I agreed. Anyway, the doctors at the hospital couldn't keep me going to their satisfaction, so I now have a pacemaker, which keeps me ticking along.

LES AND SKIN HAPPENINGS

Les Shaw and "Skin" Hines worked for Dad as laborers, and one day he had them down in a dark basement with the task of breaking out a concrete wall. Les was a big fellow, and "Skin", as the name would imply, was a thin, wiry man. The only light was a bare bulb hanging from a twisted pair of fuzzy, cloth-covered yellow wires.

They proceeded to beat on the wall with sledge hammers, in an attempt to locate a weak spot where they could concentrate their efforts. Every time they hit the wall, a little concrete dust would puff out, and, with no ventilation, the room was soon full of concrete dust, making visibility near zero with the bare bulb.

Now and then they would take a break, and search along the wall for a crack or any sign of weakness. Les was looking at the wall, and he placed his hand flat on it and said, "I think if we'd hit it about here", and that was the moment that "Skin" did just that. A nine pound sledge on a full swing can make an awful mess of a man's hand. It ended Les' life as a laborer, and he became a truck driver.

Speaking of "Skin" Hines, I came upon him at the mouth of Coffin's Creek one day when we were both hunting. He was in a terrible fix. He had an old double barrel shotgun with 36 inch barrels, with big wing hammers on each side. Somehow, one of the hammers had cut his right hand between the thumb and first finger, and he was attempting to tie a blood-soaked bandana around it with his left hand and his teeth. He was glad to see me as he needed help, and he was a long way from home. He unwrapped this hand, and I looked in the cut, and I could see way into his hand between the meat of his thumb and his finger. It was an eerie sight, with little bubbles down in there. I wrapped it up for him, and as I had a car at the Quaker Mill, I gave him a ride home.

Many months later, I asked him about it, and he said his wife had poured whiskey into the hole and filled it up. He howled and walked the floor all that night. He never did go to a doctor, and it needed stitching. He kept his hand closed, and it eventually healed, but it was a long time before he got any use out of that hand.

* * *

When I was little, we didn't see many beavers, but the population grew steadily. When they finally opened the season on beaver, no one had any traps big enough to catch them. Skin Hines said you couldn't kill a beaver with a shotgun as he had tried it, and he never found the beaver. Dad told him you could kill an elephant with a shotgun if you were close enough and shot him in the right place. Anyway, since it was late fall and the pelts would be prime and worth good money, Skin said he had come up with a new way to catch them. He was going to snare them. He put a screw eye on the end of a long pole and with a light cable made for hanging pictures, he made a small loop to hold a big loop and then he threaded the cable through the screw eye. He would climb out on a tree that the beavers had dropped into the water and wait until dark when the beavers would come back to cut off the limbs for their winter food supply. By moonlight, Skin would maneuver his snare around a beaver, then he would jerk the snare loop tight and hold it while he or someone else would hit the beaver on the head with a small wooden baseball bat.

One night he got the snare around a really big beaver, and when he jerked the snare, the beaver dove and pulled Skin right off the tree and into the river. The beaver was on one end of the pole and Skin was on the other. The beaver would dive and pull Skin under, and then one or the other would come up for a breath of air. Skin yelled for his helper to come with the bat, and the guy waded out in that cold water in the dark to where the beaver had been, and when he reared back to hit it with the bat, it was Skin that came up as the current had carried them downstream. Skin hung on, and they eventually got the beaver. Some said it would weigh 60 pounds, but it didn't get weighed. I only saw the tail, and I could hardly believe it. I had trapped several beavers with cousin Don's #2 fox traps, but I didn't think beavers got that big.

THREE IOWA MUSKETEERS

Jim Malven, Bert Retz and I were always together. We once hunted pigeons with tennis rackets at night, while skating on ice skates under a bridge west of town. We came close a couple of times, but no pigeon. There was snow on the ground, and they could see us comin'.

We hunted crows at a big roost west of town, but the crows had been shot at lots of times, so they sat out in a pasture until well after dark before they started coming in to roost. We could hear them landing in the pine trees up above us, and when we thought we might hit one, we would shoot up in there, but nothing ever fell out.

In the summer, we would go up to the Quaker Mill after work and sit on the dam with a bar of Ivory Soap and take a bath, because we were dirty from working in construction. Then we would play football with a rubber football. The guy on the dam would pass the ball to the other fellow as he ran and leaped out over the water from the flood gates on the west side of the dam. The idea was to catch the football and hit the water with it in your arms and then come up with it. We always fumbled, as the water took the ball away from us every time.

When it got dark, we would go cat hunting. Because wild cats killed pheasant chicks, baby ducks, rabbits and songbirds, we didn't like them. We kept good records of the cats killed, rabbits seen, etc. The record was 40 cats in the month of July. I gave a speech about that when I was in college. Once, when we got hungry, we pooled our money and sent Bert into a store to buy supper. When he came out, he had a loaf of bread and a quart of milk. He said, "You want a jam sandwich?" When I said I did, he handed me one and I said, "I thought you said a jam sandwich." He said, "That's what it is – two pieces of bread jammed together!"

Sometimes, on Saturday nights, when we didn't have to get up and go to work the next day, we would sleep out and get up early the next morning and go fishing or crow hunting. One time we camped below the Fish Hatchery, and during the night we slipped into the

Hatchery and caught a few trout out of the concrete fish ponds and put them in the creek for someone else to catch. We kept three or four for breakfast, but, as I remember, they were kind of soft. They were on a stringer in the creek in front of our campsite, and they died during the night.

We hunted fox at night with a predator call and spotlights. One night, we were trying to get to a place in a woods southeast of town, when I took a wrong turn in the dark, and we found ourselves stuck, going down a washout. We didn't have a chance to drive out, so I walked the three and a half miles to town and got Dad's truck. When I got back, I set the brake and hitched up the 50 Chevy with a tow chain and tried to pull it out. No go! I tried and tried until I finally found that I had left the parking brake on. We finally got out, but I had burned the clutch out of the truck by then. Dad found out about it the next morning.

We tried to spear fish one night up on Coffin's Creek, but it began to rain and we couldn't see the fish. When we quit, I had caught a big crawfish that was in my flashlight beam, and I put him in my hat. When I was driving back toward the Quaker Mill, I tried to reach around Jim and put that crawfish down Bert's shirt collar. I didn't watch where I was going, and I ran off the road and into a ditch. We went to a farmer's barn and borrowed some hay to try to put under the wheels, as everything was mud due to the rain. When that didn't work, we walked to another farm where someone was home and called my Dad. He came with his pickup truck, and we connected up a tow chain and Dad began to pull with the truck. We weren't getting anywhere, so Dad got way over on the other side of the gravel road to try to improve the pulling angle. He ran off the other side of the road and was also stuck in the soft mud. We now had two stuck vehicles chained together, and the chain was stretched tight about a foot above the roadway. It was three in the morning and Dad said, "If someone comes along, they probably won't stop, so you boys make yourselves scarce, as when they hit that chain you don't want to be around!" We finally got both vehicles out. Fortunately no one came along, so all was well.

As you can see, there was never a dull moment when we were out on the town. We did lots of stuff and had great fun in the doing of it. If the three of us could get together again, we would remember other happenings, and we could go on reminiscing for a long time. Like Bert said, we could have another jam sandwich and a quart of milk for supper.

Two musketeers: Bert Retz and Jim Malven

MY FIRST PIZZA

Believe it or not, there was a time before pizza was known as a good thing to eat. In 1952, I was a second semester freshman in college, and my roommate was Harry Nelson from my hometown. He had two buddies, Maurice Buresh and Frank Buckwald. They became my buddies, too. Anyway, they were all about to graduate, and Harry had decided to join the Navy. He had signed up and needed to go to Des Moines, Iowa, to take his physical and take the oath, and whatever else was involved. We all decided to go with him. We had heard of a tavern where a certain waitress could deliver 6 mugs of beer to your table, carrying two mugs in each hand and the other two on her ample chest.

When Harry had done his thing, we went to the tavern to see the sights. They had pizza on the menu, and our waitress said it was very good and suggested we order it. We said, "Okay, bring us four pizzas." She hesitated, and asked if we had ever had pizza before, and when we said, "No," she felt that two pizzas would be plenty for the four of us. The guys were drinking beer, but I never could, as the carbonation didn't agree with me.

When the pizzas arrived, we were shocked. They were two big round things on two big platters. They were thin and looked like someone had spilled a can of tomato soup on them and poured some whitish stuff on top of that. We didn't know how to eat it, or if it was fit to eat. We tried spooning the liquid stuff off and eating that, but it didn't taste good and it sure didn't look good. We looked around to see if there were others eating pizza, but since it was the middle on the afternoon, we were about the only customers. Well, the guys were drinking their beers and I was hungry, per usual, and I kept picking at the pizza. Eventually, I ate most of it by myself. It was a learning experience. When I am hungry, I can eat most anything!

Lieutenant Hansel - 1956

KANSAS MEMORY

When Shirley and I were first married, I was in the Army Medical Service Corps stationed at Fort Riley, Kansas. My clerk was a young man named Ron Maas. He and his wife, Joyce, were both from Kansas, so they knew their way around the area. I did a lot of fishing and hunting with Ron, and since we were newlyweds, the girls often were along. Joyce and Ron's folks had farms which we visited, and we fished their farm ponds and nearby streams.

One weekend, when the four of us were out looking for a good duck hunting spot, we saw a likely-looking place. Ron and I got ready for action and proceeded to slowly and carefully climb a hill, concealing ourselves all the way. When we got to the top and looked over the dike, we were surprised to see – nothing. It was an empty pond!

When we got back to the girls in the car, Joyce scolded, "You big dummies – sneaking up on a dry hole!" As we didn't know it was dry when we sneaked it, we thought she was pretty hard on us, but, after all these years, we still remind each other not to sneak up on a dry hole.

My army buddy, Ron Maas, and I with a good catch in Kansas

Fishing in a lovely lake in Canada - 1962

MY CANOE

I have always loved the water, i.e. sloughs, swamps, creeks, rivers and lakes, also Indians and their way of life and their method of transportation on the water. When I had to write a book report in grade school, my Mom found some books at the library that I just loved. They were the Altsheler Series, "The Young Trailers". It was all about the adventures of Henry Ware and his three buddies and their interaction with the Indians. So I loved canoes even before I was in one.

Doctor Wayne Hall had a nice aluminum canoe that was stored beside his garage, which was about three blocks across Terrill Park from the Maquoketa River and the backwater from the Marion Street dam. He said I could use it whenever, and I would tie his paddles across the thwarts for a carrying yoke for my shoulders, and off I would go, carrying it to the river. I also hunted ducks out of it up in North Dakota when Dad got up a couple of duck-hunting-trips for me, and Dr. Hall would go along and bring his canoe. It was great to paddle out among the bull rushes in a canoe.

I got married in 1957, got out of the Army in 1958, and went to work in Milwaukee, Wisconsin. Shirley and I bought our first canoe that same year. It was second or 35th hand, and it was an Old Towne canoe with wooden ribs and planking; however, the canvas covering had been replaced by fiberglass. It had painted gunnels which we found out later were rotten, but Dad made us some new ones. It was a very nice canoe, except being stored outside on top of the doghouse in the winter, the wood would shrink, and the fiberglass would crack, making it necessary to repair it every spring. In the spring of 1961, we not only repaired the fiberglass, but we took all the old dark varnish off the interior ribs and planking.

When we had it newly varnished, it was beautiful. We had fixed it up to sell, as we didn't want to repair the fiberglass again. On April 6, 1961, we traded it in for a 16-foot Alumacraft canoe with a rocker keel, and we also purchased a carrying yoke and a motor bracket. The bill was $285, less $135 for the Old Towne canoe trade-in, so it cost us $150 for the new one, which was a lot of money for us back then.

Another couple, who lived behind us, Dick and Jerry Miller, went with us to the boat store and bought another Alumacraft canoe just like ours. We did a lot of camping and canoeing with them in Wisconsin, Michigan, and in Canada. Shirley and I painted Indian designs on it for several years so I could be connected to the Indians. Later, Andy Peck, a fellow from work, won a 3 Hp Evinrude motor in a drawing, and since he didn't hunt or fish, I bought it from him to go with our canoe.

I absolutely love this aluminum canoe. It is now 48 years old, and it is as ready to go as ever. It has been repaired many times. I have put in new rivets when the rocks and gravel bars, etc. wore off the old ones. The seats have been broken and fixed, and the dents in the bottom have been pounded out with a rubber hammer. The motor bracket has also been repaired many times. I have installed seats for comfort, and the front one even swivels to help in fishing and duck hunting. The area above the water line is painted the same color as the logs and driftwood on the bank to camouflage it, and I have a cover I made out of two Army shelter halves if you really want to hide it. It is very stable, as it is heavier than most aluminum canoes, and all the folks want to go in my canoe for comfort and stability. Me, too!

When Shirley and I first got it, we took it out to see how difficult or easy it would be to tip it over. We put our swimming suits on, and we both leaned over on the same side, but we could not, or would not let it tip over. Now, don't you believe it can't tip over, as I will relate a few times when it did.

Fred Welch and I were going fishing in Muskego Lake, south of Milwaukee, and the wind was blowing much too hard for canoeing on a lake. However, this lake is full of tall weeds, and we were sure we would be okay once we got out into the weeds. We first had to cross a bay. We were in the trough of the big waves, but we were doing all right until we were approaching the bank. We noticed a boat right in front of us. This boat had 4 passengers and only about 3 inches of freeboard. I was running the 3-horsepower outboard motor, and

My Canoe

instead of slowing down, I turned into the big wave upwind on the right side of the boat. When the wave raised the front end, the motor, which was on the left side of the canoe, pulled us over, and we were all-of-a- sudden swimming. All of the floatable equipment was immediately blown away - the gas can, the two life preserver seat cushions, etc. The canoe was mostly under the water as the motor on my end was holding it down. The front end was sticking out of the water, and that was where Fred was hanging on. I was holding the boat with my feet to keep it from tipping over and losing all our stuff. As it was, I lost my fish pole and favorite reel and a shirt, and Fred lost a small tackle box. A man in a motorboat came to our rescue. He went way downwind and picked up the gas can and other things, and then he approached us from downwind so he wouldn't run us over. We were very thankful, as we needed rescuing. We came back the next weekend and managed to snag my shirt and fish pole in about 15 feet of water, so all was not lost.

Another time Fred and I were duck hunting on a little river that ran through a marsh. We saw a hen mallard land upstream from us on the right side of the little river, and we went after her. The duck got up on the right side of the boat just as we were opposite of her, and we both tried to shoot. Fred was shooting one handed, as he couldn't swivel around that far. When both shotguns went off, the boat rolled out from under us. Fred lit on the bottom on his back with his shotgun on his chest, and his hat came floating down to me. With my long legs, I had just stepped out and I only got about a cup full of water in the top of my waders. The canoe didn't even get any water in it.

Fred and I got in trouble again in the canoe on that same little river. We were going duck hunting on the marsh, and since there was a nice little woods, we felt we would hunt deer with bow and arrow during the day when the ducks weren't flying. We put out decoys and hunted ducks until mid morning. Then we took up the decoys, unloaded and encased our guns, paddled to the woods and started bow deer hunting. The encased guns were left in the canoe. When late afternoon came, we went back to duck hunting. When we quit hunting, we had to paddle upstream to get to the car. When we got there, we were met by a young, seasonal game warden. He watched us unload our gear, and he saw Fred's bow and encased gun in the bottom of the canoe. After verifying ownership, he wrote Fred a citation for archery hunting deer while in possession of a gun. When he saw my gun and bow in the trunk of the car, he was going to give me a similar ticket until he called his boss, Jim Amundson, the real game warden. He was told that the weapons in the car were in transit and that was all right. We tried to tell him that both in the canoe were also in transit, but no one would listen. He confiscated Fred's gun, bow and one arrow, and we all parted, but not friendly.

We then noticed that the citation was for the wrong month. This was November, and the citation was dated October. It said we were hunting deer while possessing a gun, but the temporary warden hadn't seen us hunting at all, just unloading the boat. Well, Fred made some phone calls to the Chief Warden, Commissioner, etc. and Jim Amundson eventually brought Fred back his cleaned gun, and his bow and arrow. We were now on a first name basis with the game warden, and whenever I would see him, he would ask me, "How's your buddy Fred?"

Fred and I had another notable experience with the canoe up on Petenwell Flowage. We were trying to hunt deer and ducks at the same time. When we found a long peninsula of land, we would post one man where the peninsula met the mainland and the other fellow would canoe down to the point and make a drive toward the "poster." I was the driver, and I pulled the canoe up on the bank on the leeward side of the peninsula and proceeded toward Fred. When I reached him, we started walking back to the canoe and noticed that the wind had pushed the canoe off the bank. I ran as fast as I could, but the canoe was gaining speed fast as the wind caught it. What to do? Petenwell Flowage is a large body of water, and we were a long way from the car. The canoe was headed across the flowage! We walked to the car, drove way north to a bridge and got on the correct side of the flowage and proceeded downstream to each and every vantage point where we used binoculars to try to locate the canoe. We stopped many times, then kept going and when we did spot the canoe, it was almost to the bank. We ran down to it, and Fred's shotgun was still in it, and there was a paddle laying across the gunnels, even in all that wind! When the canoe hit the bank sideways, the next wave filled it with water. Wheeooo! We were extremely lucky.

Fred drying his handkerchief over the campfire after hunting with a bad cold

When we moved to Tennessee in 1970, we found a perfect place to canoe. The Narrows of the Harpeth River was located west of Nashville. The river makes about a five mile loop and comes right back to within 100 yards of itself. It is an historical place where Montgomery Bell built a tunnel through a solid rock ridge to connect the river. He then built a gristmill there when he couldn't get the government to help him build an iron forge. The roads were bad, and the government backed out. Anyway, you only need one car to canoe this stretch of river; it was perfect. Now it is a state park with all kinds of restrictions on its use, but it's still a beautiful float.

※ ※ ※

Walter Collins, a fellow from work, and I were hunting ducks on the Harpeth River in the canoe, and we slipped up on a bunch of wood ducks. He was in front in the shooting seat, and he got his limit. A cripple flew downriver in front of us. We changed seats, as it was now my turn to shoot. We continued down the river, and the crippled duck got up on the left side of the boat and went back behind us. I swung my shotgun back that way, and Walter decided he wanted to get out of the way, so he leaned out to the right and over we went. He was upset because he lost his shotgun, but I managed to find it with my toe as the water was only about waist deep. We pulled the canoe over to the left bank, tied it off and scrambled up the steep bank where we promptly built a big fire.

We stripped down to our birthday suits and proceeded to wring the water out of our clothes. We hung the clothes on branches downwind of the fire, and we stood there freezing as the water was cold. It was late in the fall, and the wind was blowing. After an hour or so, we had seen a little steam come out his jeans, but as far as we could see, nothing was getting dry. We decided we were going to have to put on our cold, wet clothes and paddle like the devil and get out of there and into a warm car. We got dressed, and I went down the steep bank to get the canoe ready while Walter doused the fire. I was holding the canoe at the bottom of the slope when Walter, a fairly heavy boy, stepped up to the edge of the bank above me and he said," Hey, Hey, Hey." in his very good imitation of Fat Albert. I laughed so hard I almost fell out of the canoe again.

We have caught some big fish out of my canoe. The biggest was a 34-pound carp that Fred Welch caught on a 6 lb. test line. That fish towed us all around Mauthe Lake, in Wisconsin. I caught a 25-pound rockfish in the Caney Fork River in Tennessee. Shirley caught a 6-½ lb largemouth bass, which is mounted on our wall, and I have caught three brown trout that were 5 and 6 pounders. The longest trout was 26 inches.

* * *

After I retired, I loved to hunt ducks on the Harpeth River during the week when the competition was less, but I didn't have any buddies that could get off work when I dropped my hat. Therefore, I bought a moped to take me back to the truck. I would hide the moped at the downstream bridge and float down to it and ride it back. I built a

My Canoe

frame in the truck to keep it upright and a ramp to roll it up into the truck bed. It all worked very well, and I could go alone. I caught small mouth bass; shot ducks, geese, turkeys and even a big dog coyote that was slipping up on a flock of geese.

* * *

Dr. David Denny, my dentist friend, and I have spent the most time in the canoe. He has arthritis, and he loves to sit in the front seat with shotgun, fish pole or both, and be ready for something to happen. We canoed both the Harpeth and the Caney Fork Rivers, but most of the time we were on the Caney Fork. We had it down to a science. It gets hot in Tennessee in the summer, so we would go trout fishing on the Caney Fork early in the morning about daylight. The cold river water kept the air comfortable, and we would fish until about noon when we would get to the downstream bridge where his car was waiting. By then the sun would be high enough to reach us down in the river valley, and it was time to get in the air-conditioned car. We would go at least once a week, during the week, and we caught lots and lots of trout each summer, fall and winter. You can fish all year in Tennessee, don't you know? We always released the trout if they weren't hurt bad, so we could catch them again. There were two years when we caught over 450 trout, but we went fishing a lot those years. We always kept track of who caught the first fish, the biggest fish and the most fish, so we could see who the best fisherman was. Like I said, the canoe is out back right now, ready to go. Wish I was!

A good day's hunt with David Denny

CAMPING ADVENTURES

The first camping trip with Shirley was shortly after we moved to Wisconsin in 1958. It was a four-day weekend, so we left Milwaukee and headed north. We ate lunch at a roadside park, a nice place with a stream, however it started to rain while we were eating, and it never let up. At about 3 p.m. we arrived at Little Spider Lake and then went on to Manitowish Waters and the Vance Lake Camp site. There were 4 other tents pitched at that site and it looked mighty wet and crowded around there! We went on to Candy Lake and set up camp at a very nice place that a friend had told us about where there was only room for us. I set up our tent and ditched it, which proved to be a wise move.

It continued raining all the time and was so wet that we had to rig a shelter over the fire since the rain kept putting it out. We were cooking over a campfire since this was before we had a Coleman stove. We managed to have supper and head for bed. We were sleeping in an Army surplus pup tent, with Army surplus mummy type sleeping bags, on Army surplus air mattresses, so we managed to keep warm and dry.

The next day it had quit raining, but the wind was coming off the lake so hard we couldn't even start a fire. I took down the Army poncho we had used for a shelter over the fire and erected it as a wind buffer on the side, to keep the wind from blowing the flames away from the frying pan so Shirley could cook breakfast.

It's a wonder that I ever got Shirley to go camping again!

Still in love after the first camping trip

We became "every weekend" campers and gradually acquired more equipment. One weekend, Shirley and I camped up on the Willow Flowage in Wisconsin. We had a beautiful spot all to ourselves, because we drove way back in to get there. We put up our umbrella tent right close to the water where we could launch our canoe. During the night, we were awakened by a loud growling sound, right close to us. We couldn't figure it out. It was loud and growling and gnawing, and we were quite concerned. I finally got up and took a lantern out to see what it was, and, would you believe it, beavers were attempting to cut down a big tree right in front of us. I was amazed that they could make that much noise with those big buckteeth. The beavers left, but then, when it got to be daylight, we didn't get up very fast as it was cold out, and we were warm in our nice sleeping bags. We heard more strange noises! Thump, thump, thump, up the side of the tent and thump, thump, thump, down the other side of the tent. The sun was shining on the tent, and a chipmunk was having a ball running up and down on the warm canvas. He kept it up for some time for our enjoyment. We could see his shadow through the canvas tent.

* * *

We camped quite often on weekends at Mauthe Lake, which was not too far north of Milwaukee. There was a campground there, but it was almost always full. They allowed the overflow campers to pitch their tents in a grassy field right next door, and many did. We arrived quite late one Friday night, and we were relegated to the field. Not wanting to disturb the other campers when I drove my tent stakes, we went farther out in the field than necessary, and pitched our tent. Come morning, the ground started shaking, and there was a clomping noise all around us. I got up, unzipped the door and stuck my head out. There were horses and riders all around us. We had pitched our tent on the bridal path, and they were all laughing at us!

* * *

We loved to camp and fish the Shaky Lakes in the upper peninsula of Michigan, but one year the mosquitoes were so bad we had to take evasive action. To launch the canoe, I would get it on my shoulders while Shirley got all the other gear-paddles, cushions, fish poles, etc., and then we would run to the water. We had to cross a place with high grass, and the mosquitoes would swarm up out of there in a cloud. We would get the boat in the water, get it loaded with our gear and us, and paddle as fast as we could to get out on the water where the wind would blow the mosquitoes away. It worked, except that now we had a boat full of mosquitoes that were down out of the wind, and they were biting our rear ends and legs with a vengeance. We would use a bug bomb to spray inside the canoe and under the seats, and another cloud of mosquitoes would come out and be blown away with the wind. From there on it was fine, except we knew we would face it all again when we got back.

When we came into a hidden bay, we saw a deer out in the water, and he was facing away from us. I wanted to see how close I could get to him, so I paddled quietly right up to him. He had mosquitoes all over him, too, and every time he would breathe in, he would have to snort to blow the mosquitoes out of his nose. When we got real close, Shirley looked back at me to see if she should touch him with her fish pole. He sensed her movement, made a run for the bank, and promptly gave us all his mosquitoes. Out came the bug bomb again.

* * *

One trip, we were camping in the fall when the weather turned really cold. We were sleeping on the ground in our umbrella tent and we had Rummy along. We were worried about him out in the cold under the canoe, so we let him in the tent with us. We were in our Army sleeping bags and had one of Alma's quilts under the bags on top of the air mattresses and another quilt on top. It was seriously cold! It wasn't long until Rummy nosed his way under the top quilt and between us. We learned that a dog is as good as a hot water bottle. We were nice and warm all night.

In the morning, George decided to light the Coleman lantern, which was hanging on the center pole of the tent. We hoped it would warm the tent up. We waited and waited to feel the heat, but nothing seemed to be helping. We finally just had to get up, and when we stood, it was like sticking our heads in an oven. The lantern put out heat all right, but it all rose to the top of the tent and didn't help us down on the ground at all.

* * *

We camped one weekend on Petenwell Flowage with the Welchs. We had Walt's truck and they used our tent. They had their three children, we had our two, and we had a big mosquito problem there, too. We were in a little wilderness campground with no frills, and lots of brush and undergrowth to protect the mosquitoes. We played in the shallow water and the kids had a ball catching leeches. We found out later that due to paper-making upstream, there was no oxygen in the water, so the leeches were dying and therefore easy to catch. Fred and I didn't catch many fish either. Anyway, toward evening, we heard this high-pitched whine and wondered what it was. It was a trillion mosquitoes waiting for us to come back to camp. It was terrible. We built a fire and put pine branches on it to make smoke, and Fred and I stood in the smoke all except our heads, but the mosquitoes would just rise above the smoke and eat our heads. The authorities came through with a fogging truck in an attempt to kill the mosquitoes, but the bugs again just rose above the fog and settled back down when the fog blew away. Fortunately, the tent and the truck were mostly mosquito-proof, so we survived that camping trip in spite of the evil insects.

SHIRLEY'S LUNKER

When we were newly married and just out of the Army, Shirley and I were living in Milwaukee, Wisconsin, where George worked for the city in Sewer Engineering. Shirley was working at Schuster's Department Store as a receptionist for an optometrist. Each weekend we would leave the city and go camping somewhere. We were driving our '57 Buick with our Old Towne Canoe on top. We had purchased the car new from Shirley's Uncle Guy, and the canoe was a second or fifth hand.

We often camped at Mauthe Lake north of Milwaukee, and we would canoe up the Milwaukee River that fed the lake. We were camping in an Army pup tent and cooking over an open fire. We were roughing it at first. Later we bought a Coleman stove and an umbrella tent from Milwaukee Tent and Awning. Both of them saw many years of service.

If conditions were right, we would catch some nice bass in the Milwaukee River. We would sneak up the river and position the canoe on the inside of bends of the river, and hold the canoe by sticking the paddles down in the mud. We would cast across the river and fish just off the bushes that hung over the water. On August 17, 1958, we were so positioned, and Shirley was in the front of the canoe. She was using an eight-foot fiberglass fly rod and a Goodall spinning reel that looked like a fly reel, except it used monofilament line. She was using a rubber worm for bait, as we were out of night crawlers. She hooked a 6 pound 3 ounce largemouth bass that was 21 inches long. She was having a hard time holding the fish with the fly rod bent double over her head. When she tried to reel the fish in, the handle of the reel got caught in her shirt. As she tried to get it undone, the face of the reel came off and fell in her lap. I couldn't help from the other end of the canoe. She managed to fight the fish and keep him out of the brush by holding onto the line and the fly rod with one hand and getting the reel put back together with the other hand. It was nip and tuck, but she persevered. We took the fish to a little grocery store to see if we could get him weighed. They weren't too happy about it until they saw the fish. That is a big bass up in Wisconsin! We packed him in ice and took him home while we decided whether to have him mounted.

Well, we scraped up the money (a dollar per inch) to have him mounted by a man who had retired from the Milwaukee Museum. Now, 40 years later, that fish still swims on our wall. We have enjoyed him on five different walls, and he still looks good. I mounted the worm she caught him on, too, and had it dangling out in front of him on a little wire, but 40 years were too much for the worm. So now, it is just the fish.

Shirley's 6 pound 3 ounce largemouth bass caught in 1958

THE GREENFIELD FIRE DEPARTMENT

Back in the early 1960's, we lived in Milwaukee, Wisconsin, on the southwest side near the intersection of Oklahoma Avenue and Forest Home Avenue. The city limits' line was right there, separating the City of Milwaukee and the City of Greenfield.

There was a small sporting goods store on one side of Forest Home run by a fellow named Chuck Mork, and across the street was a restaurant that specialized in grilled steaks. I was in the sporting goods store, which was actually a converted mobile home setting parallel to the street, and I was talking to Chuck, when he called my attention to the grill in the eating establishment which had flared up with a grease fire. There were lots of flames shooting up off the grill, but the cooks in their white floppy hats just stepped back to let it burn out. It was a pretty good fire, but everyone sort of ignored it as it was confined to the grill. The sporting goods store manager and I went back to talking, and after awhile, he noticed the building across the street was smoking, and all the people were filing out and standing around looking back at the building. The fire had apparently caught the grease in the hood over the grill on fire, which had ignited the roof. In just no time, the fire spread across the ceiling, and by the time the fire trucks arrived, there wasn't much they could do as the entire building was engulfed in flames.

It burned to the ground, and the firemen stayed and sprayed the ashes until they were satisfied it was out. They then packed up and left the scene. Some of the patrons were still standing around when way off in the distance we could hear the "ding, ding, ding" of a fire engine. It was coming up Forest Home Avenue from the south. It was an old, red antique fire engine with wooden spoke wheels, and the driver and the copilot were sitting on an uncovered bench seat. The copilot was jerking on a short piece of rope that was attached to the silver bell. No sirens, just ding - ding -ding. This was the Greenfield Volunteer Fire Department.

They pulled up to the curb in front of the burned-out restaurant, and several men jumped from the truck, ran around to the back and came running forward carrying a fire extinguisher. No one could understand why on earth they were running, for the fire had long since been put out. The firemen ran to the front of the engine, threw up the side engine covers, and we saw that the engine was on fire. They had brought their own fire with them! They squirted the fire out with the fire extinguisher, started her up again, climbed aboard and away they went, amid laughter and cheers from the onlookers.

Well, it seems the City of Milwaukee Fire Department sent the City of Greenfield a bill for their efforts in putting out the restaurant fire, since the restaurant was located across the city limits line. The City of Greenfield refused to pay the bill, so Milwaukee told them not to call them again, because they would not respond.

Some time later, the Sporting Goods Store caught fire. Both fire departments were called and the City of Milwaukee Dept. did not come. This was a busy intersection, and soon there were many spectators. Every one kept asking if anyone had called the fire department and several assured us they had been called. After a while away off to the south, we could all hear a distant "ding - ding - ding".

Up drove the old spoke-wheeled engine and they pulled into the paved parking area. The Captain jumped off the truck and shouted for everyone to stand back! Locating a fire hydrant off to the north in front of the truck, he shouted for one of the firemen to throw down a hose. One of the firemen climbed up on top of the truck, and slid a big roll of fire hose off onto the ground. The Captain pointed one man toward the fire hydrant with one end of the hose, and another in the opposite direction toward the building with the other end. I was standing near the front door of the store and just as the man with the hose nozzle reached the door, he was violently jerked backwards and fell down. The man going to the fire plug was likewise jerked backwards. It seems they had just pulled an enormous knot in the middle of the coiled-up fire hose at the truck! The hose was hopelessly tangled, and the Captain yelled at his men to forget that hose and use another.

Meanwhile, one of the firemen came up to the Captain and asked if he should get up on the roof and chop a hole to vent the fire. The

Captain yelled that he should, so the man left and went to the rear of the building. Back there he found an old used wood ladder laying behind the building, and he went back to the Captain to ask if he should use that old privately-owned ladder. The Captain yelled at him to, "Get up on that roof!" and "Yes, use that ladder". Two men in bulky raincoats, hip boots and fire hats finally leaned the ladder against the building and climbed up on the roof. It was a pitched roof, built over the mobile trailer, and it was made of plywood sheathing on wide-spaced rafters and covered with tarpaper and tar. One of the firemen had a brand new red painted fireman's axe, which he swung high over his head and brought down with a mighty chop! The plywood bounced that axe right back as fast as it had come down, and it almost upset the fireman standing on the pitched roof. He caught his balance and tried 4 or 5 more chops, to no avail. Then the other fireman took the axe. When it bounced back on him, he turned the axe head around, and using the pointed spiked end of the axe, he struck a mighty blow. The point went through the roof up past the handle, and the axe stuck fast. Both men tried to get the axe out, but it held tight while they jerked it this way and that.

Meanwhile, they had gotten the hose hooked up to the hydrant and into the building. Some smoke now could be seen coming out the front door, and the water was on the floor. The Captain called from inside the store for someone to bring a mop. One of the firemen ran to the truck and returned with a mop with a brand new white fluffy mop head. He ran in the front door and out of sight, but in just a minute he came running back out with the mop in front of him. The white fluffy head of the mop was on fire! That was the only fire we ever saw, and he could have put it out if he had put the mop on the floor, as water was now running out the door.

The fire turned out to be in the window air conditioner, which had smoked up the building. They never got a good hole in the roof, but the roof required repair. The water damage inside was worse, and the smoke stunk up the place. The firemen replaced the old used ladder, loaded up the knotted hose and retreated from the scene. A great time was had by all the spectators, and they applauded as the Greenfield Volunteer Fire Department departed in all their glory.

SHIRLEY'S BIGGEST CATCH

In about 1958, Shirley and I were fishing for bass in the Milwaukee River, upstream from Mauthe Lake, which is North of Milwaukee where we lived at the time. On weekends, we would camp at Mauthe Lake and canoe up the river. We had some fine times on that little stretch of river, catching fish and watching wildlife. Shirley caught a 6 ½ pound largemouth bass one day, and we got our limit of 2 - 4 pound bass another day. Once we had a North American Bittern (a very shy shorebird) sneak out of the reeds near us and make the strangest call. His head went up and down, and the sound he made was like that made by an old long-handled pump, pumping water.

One morning we were situated on the inside of a river bend with our paddles pushed into the mud to hold us there, and we were fishing beneath the bushes on the opposite bank of the river. Shirley had cast a little too far, and she had caught the bushes. We did not want to disturb the fish in the clear water under the bushes, so we did not go retrieve her hook. She was letting me continue to fish to see if I could catch one before we got her unhooked and moved on.

We heard a commotion down the river and, would you believe it, a man was sailing a boat up the river! He had his wife and four dogs in the boat with him, and due to the wind and the bends in the river, he was running into the bank at regular intervals. When they passed us, we all said "Good morning," and they continued a little way up the river. In a short time, they turned around. When they came back, he ran right into the bushes that we were fishing under. After he pushed off and started downstream, Shirley noticed her line was going out. Her rod had just been laying in the bottom of the canoe since she had that snag in the bushes, and they had sailed right over her line on the way up the river. When she saw the line being pulled off the reel, she realized the boat had apparently caught her line. When she told me about it, the sailboat was 15 yards downriver and moving away with the current. I told her to pull back hard to see if she could break the line before she lost all the line on her reel. She heaved back on her 8-foot fiberglass fly rod, and the sailboat slowly came to a stop.

Shirley started pumping the rod and reeling in as she could, and she brought the sailboat back upstream.

We didn't say anything, and the man was at a loss as to what was happening. He couldn't see the monofilament line, and he was moving upstream, maybe due to an ill wind. When Shirley got him reeled back up to us, he realized what had happened - that he had caught on her line. We didn't know it, but the line was still caught on the bushes, and it was just around his mast. The springy bushes and the whippy fly rod allowed the monofilament line to stretch and not break. We were all apologizing, and before we figured out what the problem was, the man untied a rope and dropped the sail right on top of his wife and dogs. He then crawled over his wife and dogs, and dismantled the mast right in front of us. He freed Shirley's line, put the mast back up, hauled the sail up, and away they went down the river.

We were stupefied while all this was happening, with the man's wife and dogs looking out from under the sail, but, to this day, Shirley is the only fisherperson I know or have ever heard of, who has gone fishing and reeled in and landed a sailboat!

STUFFED STUFF

In the fall of 1960, Fred Welch and I were hunting ducks, and we found a drake mallard duck lying in a cow path. The duck had apparently been shot, and when he died, he had left his body on the cow path and had stuck his head into the grass at the side of the path. I picked him up, and we looked him over. We couldn't find any injury, and every feather was in perfect shape. He was beautiful, and I didn't know what to do with him. We couldn't take him home and eat him as we didn't know how long he had lain there, but he was too pretty to just leave him there. Fred told me I should take him home and mount him. He said, "With all the skinning of game and birds that you have done, you wouldn't have any trouble at all." I told him that I didn't know how to tan the skin, etc. He said that it was easy. It seemed that Fred had been a graduate of the Northwestern School of Taxidermy since he was 12 years old. He explained that you had to remove all the meat and then treat the skin with borax. He said all you had to buy when you mounted birds were the eyes and the form, but you can make your own form.

I decided to try it, and I was going to use buttons for the eyes as Shirley had lots of black buttons and some were round, just like eyes. I skinned out the duck by cutting him down the breast, and I opened up the muscles in his wings by cutting the skin on the underside. It was tedious because all the muscles were connected to tendons, and they extended into the joints. I rubbed borax into the skin and everywhere it was needed, and left it to dry. I had to cut the skin on top of his head, as his skull was too big to come through the neck.

I mixed up a handful of plaster of Paris and imbedded five wires in it, one for the head and neck, one for each wing and one for each leg. I next wrapped carpet underlayment around the plaster of Paris until it was about the size of the duck's body. I threaded the wires through the wings, the feet, the head and neck. I then filled the neck with the carpet underlayment, and I sewed it all up. It looked pretty good. I had used the duck's skull, and I set the button eyes in the eye sockets with clay. I positioned him for hanging on the wall with one wing up along the wall and the other wing sticking out into the room. I curved his head and neck, and it looked like he was just taking off of the water. My sister Arlene took a liking to him, and he is still flying on her wall up in Iowa Falls, Iowa.

Shirley with Rummy and the nice pheasant he ran to us in Holy Hill, Wisconsin

The next year, 1961, I shot a big rooster pheasant near Holy Hill, Wisconsin. Shirley was with me, and I was standing in a slough waiting for the dog, Rummy, to run past me whatever he was trailing. I heard the critter running in the water underneath the slough grass, and it stopped right out in front of me. When the dog arrived, this big pheasant took off, and I shot him and didn't mess up his feathers very bad, so I decided to mount him. He is flying over the mantle of my fireplace right now, 47 years later. He has jumped down two or three times, but I have always been able to put him back.

When Dick Miller, who lived behind me, saw my mounted pheasant, he had to have one, too, and he went to Iowa on a pheasant hunt.

He brought back a nice rooster, but one wing was all shot up. I told him I couldn't repair it, so he went back and shot another and brought me its wing. I put it all together, and it turned out fine.

About then, Russ Simonas, a fellow from work, shot a 5-point buck, and he asked me if I had ever mounted a deer head. I told him that I hadn't, but that I would like to. He said his deer wasn't nice enough to have a professional mount it, but if I wanted to mount him, he would pay for all the supplies, etc. I decided to try it. I ordered the eyes, form, ear inserts and the pickling solutions from Herter's. I skinned out the head and the hardest part was skinning out the ears. At that time, the procedure was to skin out the ears and put a plastic insert inside each ear to keep it from wrinkling or drying crooked. The Styrofoam form they sent me was way too big, and I had to trim it down with the aid of a big sharp knife. I sawed the horns off the skull, leaving a little shelf of skull on the horns so as to position them correctly; they fit on the shelf on the form. I put it all together, and it looked fine until it started to dry. The skin shrunk and pulled out my stitching on the back of the neck. I had to cut hair from the unused cape and glue it into the half-inch wide split.

The pickling crystals cure the hide, but they don't tan it. The directions said when the skin dried, it stuck the hair tighter in the skin than it was originally. I used it to treat a deerskin that I had, and it worked fine as I flattened the skin. When it dried, it was put on the wall as a backdrop behind my archery display which holds my bow and arrows.

Since that time I have mixed up tanning solutions and have tanned all kinds of animal skins. I have tanned four deer hides with the hair intact, but I only worked hard enough on one to get it soft, and I had to cut the neck skin off as it was too thick to allow me to break up the fibers. I later learned that I should have shaved the skin down so it wouldn't be so thick. I have two raccoon skins on the wall, and I made a raccoon skin hat out of one of them. Both were given to me by others as road kill when I wanted a young raccoon just big enough for a hat. Likewise, I have three mink on the wall, all road kills. There is also a woodchuck hide from the first thing my eldest son shot out of a tree when he was eight years old.

'Tis Himself

* * *

On January 7, 1973, while hunting along Priest Lake in a snowstorm, I got a red fox and a rabbit with one shot. The fox was carrying the rabbit and both are now on my wall. There is also a gray fox and a coyote hide on the wall. I got the coyote with my bow and arrow, which made it a trophy. There is a muskrat skin, a beaver skin and the soft deer hide in my office, or "road kill room" as some like to call it. This room is where we had a favorite niece-in-law sleep, much to her chagrin. We later learned that she is a PETA member.

* * *

I went on to mount several more birds or parts of birds. My eldest son Doug shot a nice wood duck drake that is flying right over me with his wings cupped, his tail flared, and his neck turned as he is coming around for another look. I have a green wing teal flying in the same room and a drake mallard flying over my bed. I also mounted a drake pintail duck in the same pose as my first mount with one wing up the wall and the other sticking out into the room There are two ruffed grouse tails on the wall as well as pheasant tail feathers. There is also a rattlesnake skin from a big snake that had 18 rattles and a button.

There are two nice turkey feather mounts. One contains the wings, tail, and beard, and the other one has just the tail, back feathers and the beard. In addition, I put a six-point buck's horns on a plaque with his tail hanging down. The last critters I mounted were a wood duck drake sitting on a cedar crotch, and an alligator head from Nephew Lynn.

There are half a dozen sets of deer horns and two big cow skulls with horns on the garage walls. Under the house in the crawl space where I practiced my taxidermy, are several ducks and a cow skull that didn't suit me. The ducks got ahead of me and dried too fast for me to get them positioned to suit. Other items that could be classified as taxidermy include two gun racks made of turned up deer feet, some standing turkey feet, a turkey spur necklace and a necklace made out of a skunk skull with a wired lower jaw that works.

Stuffed Stuff

On the wall of the family room is the 6-pound largemouth bass that Shirley caught and Mr. Big, a 12-point buck that was professionally mounted. In my office there are two mounts that I got from my Grandfather. They are the horns from a 10-point buck and the horns of two buffaloes, each mounted on matching oak shields. Howard Rann's daughter gave me the very old 6-point deer head mount that I petted as a kid. It was all fun and I enjoy every one of them to this day.

The Pheasant I mounted is still flying over our mantle

GUARDIAN ANGELS

I was bow hunting for deer in Central Wisconsin, and I had found a tree with a bent-over limb that made a natural seat, about eight feet off the ground. At that time, it was illegal to construct elevated deer stands, and there weren't any of those fancy commercial contraptions that are available now. You could hunt out of blow downs or other naturally elevated places, so I was very fortunate to find a comfortable perch on a ridge that had a good deer trail.

After I had been in the tree about an hour, a couple of grouse hunters drove in below me, and when they got out of their car and slammed the door, they spooked a doe up onto my ridge. The deer blew at them constantly and started down the ridge toward me. She continued to blow, so I knew she was coming, and I got all ready.

She came into view and was distracted by the grouse hunters, so she wasn't looking up at me. She ambled down the trail just perfect to give me a good, close, wide open shot. I drew back, took aim, and let go an arrow straight as a die right at her heart. That arrow was so true that I was reaching back to get my skinning knife from my belt, when, all of a sudden, when the arrow was about four feet from the doe, the deer's guardian angel reached out – stopped that arrow in mid-flight and gave it a little flip and dropped it on the ground, while the doe and I watched. We looked at each other, then at the arrow, and then she went on down the ridge, strutting haughtily.

I climbed down and looked for branches or twigs that I could have hit to make the arrow act like that, but could find nothing. The arrow was in fine shape, showing no ill effects, so it just had to be the deer's guardian angel. Do they leave fingerprints?

* * *

One time my buddy Craig had me located in a big pine tree on a Wisconsin stand about 10 feet off the ground. A Wisconsin stand is a carpet-covered board that is held to the tree with a rope, and if you don't move, the rope won't squeak to give you away.

Well, Craig had been scouting the area, and he knew deer were walking right under this big pine tree every day, going back and forth to the swamp. I had placed two markers on the ground - one at 20 and the other at 30 yards. These markers were blue and orange 4-inch plastic squares, and they matched the pins on my bow sight. I took a shot at the blue 20-yard marker while I was up in the tree, and put a broadhead right through it - I was ready!

The next morning I heard a noise, and looking around the tree, saw a big doe coming toward me. I waited and the deer went right under me and continued down the trail toward my 20-yard marker. I slowly began my draw, since her back was to me. As I got my bow back to half draw, a deer snorted just behind my tree. The doe in front of me looked around, right at me. I froze at half draw, knowing if I moved, it would all be over. It turned out the doe had two fawns with her. They had seen me move, drawing the bow, and warned mom. The doe was looking at them, but I thought she was looking at me. We all stood there looking at each other until I couldn't hold the bow back any longer, and I had to let it down. Miraculously, they didn't spook, and she finally turned her back and continued down the trail.

I attempted to pull the bow back again, but my arms failed me. There was nothing left – my muscles simply refused. The deer walked to my 30-yard marker and stepped on it and stood there a few seconds. I finally put the bow down along my legs, and by bracing it, I managed to get it drawn, but when I attempted to shoot at the deer, the arrow just barely went in the general direction. I was beat from holding that compound bow as long as I could at half draw. A doctor friend said I depleted my acetylcholine, but I relate the incident to the "Guardian Angel" principle.

CLAY BIRDS GET EVEN

When son Doug was 12 years old, he and I went clay bird shooting in the woods out behind our house. I had bought him a Steven's double-barreled 20-gauge shotgun, and we were practicing with it. We would take turns shooting and throwing the clay pigeons with our hand trap. When it was my time to shoot, Doug threw the bird, but he hadn't put the leather wrist strap on, and the thrower came out of his grip, and it hit me right in the face. It broke my glasses frame and one lens. I quickly closed my eyes tight, and I carefully dropped the loaded gun on the ground, pointed downrange. Would you believe it? The gun went off, both barrels!

Without my glasses, I am as blind as a bat and Doug didn't know how to drive, but I felt around and found what was left of my glasses, put them on, and I was able to drive home using one eye. I spent several days in Vanderbilt Hospital, healing up with my eyes completely bandaged. They finally brought me something to eat, but no one offered to feed me, so I ate it all by myself, by sticking my finger into each bowl and eating whatever I found there.

When they finally took the bandages off, we found that I could see, and that was a relief! The only permanent damage was to the pupil of my right eye. It does not contract down as far as it is supposed to, so I sneeze whenever I go out in the sun or a bright light hits me in the face. That is my shooting eye, so I was glad it was all right, and I didn't need to learn to shoot left-handed. What a scare for both father and son!

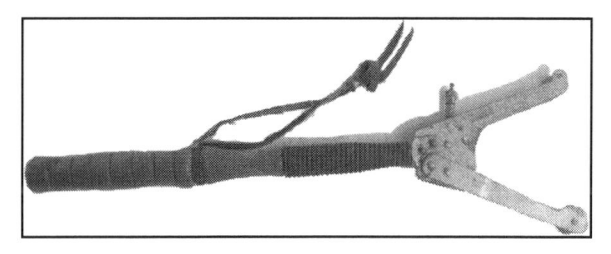

The clay bird thrower that Doug will never forget.

At Moose lake, the start of a big adventure in the Boundary Waters Canoe Area

BOUNDARY WATERS ADVENTURE

August 1981

Since our whole family loved canoeing, we decided to tackle a "real" canoe trip. We drove to Ely, Minnesota, and arranged a trip in the Quetico National Canoe Wilderness between Minnesota and Canada.

After meeting with the outfitter, we opted to take a trip through many lakes with many portages. The canoes were provided and were aluminum, but, fortunately, not heavy like ours at home. We were set up with six 40 pound, big canvas packs containing a tent, sleeping bags, ground pads, cooking utensils and food. In addition, we carried a Coleman lantern and fuel so we could have light at night. Of course, we also had to have life preservers and canoe paddles.

We started out at 7:30 on a lovely morning, all set for our grand adventure. Doug and Matt were in one canoe and Mom and I in another. We soon learned that when you are paddling across a big body of water, it is really hard to see that you are making progress. We paddled and paddled and paddled, and finally got to the first portage where we had to unload the canoes and load up for the climb. I carried one pack and a canoe, Doug carried another pack and a canoe, Matt carried 2 packs, one front and one in back, and Shirley carried one pack and the Coleman lantern and fuel. That left one pack which someone had to go back for.

We soon learned that a portage is not just a walk down or up a path, but a major trek over huge boulders and roots and washouts. The first one was 35 rods into Splash Lake – that's almost 200 yards! Ugh! We were sure glad to finally make it and then be able to reload the canoes and start paddling again!

We had been told that the water in these lakes was pure and that we could drink it safely. We found that hard to believe, but as there was no other water, we had no choice. We had been shown a way to get a drink of water while paddling - by lifting the paddle out of the water and letting the water drip down the paddle and then off your thumb into your mouth. We all managed it, but Doug was really good at it. He had a sliver on his paddle and when he wanted to get a knife to trim it off, Matt said "Here, use mine," and tossed it toward Doug. It fell into the drink, and Matt's knife was no more.

We paddled and paddled and thought we were lost. We had been given a map, but we couldn't figure it out. There were lots of islands that were not on the map. Finally we got oriented and stopped for hot dogs and soup on an island. We paddled and paddled toward the next portage, and soon found that folks had taken the portage signs as souvenirs. We might never have found the spot, if it had not been for other people ahead of us. We learned to watch while we were in the middle of the lake for folks disappearing into the woods. That must be the place!

That portage was 53 rods – almost 300 yards up and down. Mom was panicky because we hadn't tried to get a campsite on Ensign Lake, but the boys and I wanted to push on to try to get away from people – Hah! We paddled and paddled again, and finally came to the portage into Ashigan Lake. There were many people there, but we hurried and got out ahead of them. As a result, we managed to get the last campsite on Ashigan. You have to stay in established sites. We heard the lakes ahead were all full before 3 p.m., so we learned we must start early and stop early again.

The water in Ashigan was not good - there was suspended matter. So much for pure enough to drink! We had a great meal of steak and corn on the cob. We put potatoes in the coals and cooked them to death, so that wasn't so great. As we had been told we must do, we tied the food packs up between two trees to defeat the bears. There are supposed to be many. We had met one party that was headed back because, even though they tied up their packs, the bears pulled on the rope and managed to drop the packs and totally destroy everything.

We set up our tent and went to bed with the sun still up. The pads were only half size and didn't help a lot on the rocks, and we missed our pillows. That was just day one!

The next day was a rough one. There were many portages –7 or 8 in a row. We spent so much time loading and unloading the canoes that we didn't get far. We did find a campsite on an island and got the tent set up with no problems – except that the ground was hard as a rock – it <u>was</u> a rock, and it sloped downhill.

Matt got a little lesson in ax. He went looking for firewood. Everything near the campsite had been picked clean. After a while, Matt came back with wood, but said he'd had a little accident. I asked, "What kind?" and he said he hit himself with the ax! He peeled down his knee socks and there was about an inch-long slice right on his shin. I got out my first-aid kit and started to prepare my suture needle. Matt asked what I was doing, and I said, "I can put a stitch in." He said, "Why?", and I said, "Because if I don't, you'll have a scar." He said, "I'll take the scar!"

We were all worn out because of all the portages, and were thrilled when we actually found one we could paddle up! We didn't have to load and unload. The boys went swimming. It was cold, but they claimed it felt good. The wind had blown, and so the bugs were no problem. They hadn't been bad except on the portages.

The next day we were up and going after a big bacon and eggs breakfast. Cooking over an open fire is a mess. We finally wrapped foil around the pans and that helped keep them clean. The good thing was that everything we ate made the packs a mite lighter. Our first portage that day was only 25 rods – a piece of cake! Then after paddling and paddling and paddling again, we came to a portage of 179 rods – Ugh! That's almost a thousand yards! It was also a steep uphill with big steps, and then up and down, and finally down a mountainside! It was rough! Because no one wanted to make the trek twice, Matt carried three packs, Mom one, and Doug and I each one, with the canoes. It was as much as we could do.

To make the day rougher, the wind was in our faces, and strong. We really had to work to paddle against it. We decided on an early camp since we were worn out, and found a nice one with a table even! Matt swam a bit and Doug and I fished – no luck. The loons were fun. They are used to canoeists and got close to us before they dove. Of course, they laughed at us all night, too.

The next day was rough again. The wind was in our faces, and the last leg got really tough. We decided to try to make it in ahead of time. There was a 105-rod portage that was bad up and bad down, but the middle was easy. The paddling was hard again with long hauls against the wind. Sometimes we were so tired of paddling we were glad to get to a portage, and then when we saw how rough the portage was, we sure wished we could get back in the canoes.

The hardest thing was knowing that we had no choice but to go on. There was no way out except by our own steam. It was scary when we realized what a bad situation we could be in if one of us should be hurt or ill. The portages were so bad that we don't know how we escaped without one of us falling. We had been told that a plane flies over and watches for a smoky fire indicating trouble, but we never saw one. Of course, we were busy, paddling and paddling!

There were seven portages on the last day, but somehow they didn't seem so bad. Doug claimed it was because he could smell home! Even though we were on our last legs, we kept going and made it in. We decided that if we did it again, we would do it with a Coleman stove and air mattresses and no lantern! We lugged that lantern all the way and never lit it. We were always in bed long before dark. If I had known it was going to be this rough, we'd never have tried it. Now, we look back and see it was a great experience, but during it, if we could have quit, we would have!

SAILING

Shirley once bought a sailboat at a garage sale. It was a little boat –for just two people at the most, but the price was hard to resist, so we became the proud owners of a sailboat even though we knew nothing about sailing.

Shirley went to the library and came back with a book called, "How to Sail," and by trial and error; we learned how to run the thing – sort of. Matt and I decided to camp out at Poole Knobs campground on Percy Priest Lake. We got the campsite all set up and decided to take the sailboat out. We got the sail up and started across the inlet, but promptly ran into the shore. We started again and tried to go the other way, but ran into the bank again. No matter what I did, I couldn't seem to get anywhere. Finally, we decided that this was no fun and pulled the boat up on the bank and got out. There on the ground in front of us was the dagger board! Without that, we were essentially just sitting in a bathtub, blowing around. Lesson learned!

Another time, Matt wanted to take a girlfriend out on the lake in the sailboat. With misgivings, Mom delivered them to the boat ramp and off they went. After a while, Shirley realized that a storm was blowing up, so she drove back to the ramp hoping to see the kids coming in. They were waaay out and not making it back. Much to Matt's embarrassment, she prevailed on a fisherman who had returned to the ramp to go out and tow them in.

We played with that sailboat for several years and felt we got our money's worth, even if we never felt we really knew what we were doing.

THINGS ALONG THE WAY

Rob Raney and I were bow hunting one day out at Leo Garland's ranch. Leo raised Appaloosa horses and his daughter raised Siamese cats. She made more money from her kittens than he did from his colts.

It was real early in the morning, and Rob and I had split up to go where we were each going to hunt. I was walking along in the dark with my metal tree stand over my shoulder. I had my bow in one hand and a flashlight in the other. I heard two of Leo's horses following along behind me. When one of them got close, I hurried up, but so did the horse. Finally, I stopped and shined my flashlight on the horse, which blinded him, and he ran into me and knocked my tree stand off my shoulder. The horse jumped back, but was soon following me again. When he again got close, I stopped and this time, I shined the flashlight on me. The horse came up, we said hello; I scratched his forehead, and we parted friendly.

* * *

On May 1, 1982, I saw a Canadian goose in a nest on top of a duck blind in Old Hickory Lake! We were fishing and moving with a trolling motor. The goose just let us go right on by her as she sat up there on her eggs. On that same day, Jake Syler, the chief maintenance man at work, saw a robin catch a bumblebee in his yard. The bee apparently stung the robin, since the bee flew off and the robin flopped around on the ground like a chicken with its head cut off. The robin eventually died.

* * *

On May 2, 1982, Rob Raney and I went fishing on J. Percy Priest Lake. I was watching a bikini as I pushed the boat away from the shore, and we had a minor boating accident. We bumped another boat is all, but we certainly wouldn't have, if it hadn't been for the bikini. That day we also saw a snake that had caught a mud puppy (water dog), which was approximately 8 inches long. The snake was about 3 feet long. This was southeast of island number two, which is downstream from the Hobson Pike Bridge. The snake took the mud puppy to the bank, but it had quite a time as the mud puppy was very much alive, and he could hold onto things and try to pull himself back into the water. We suppose the snake finally won, but it was a struggle either way.

* * *

While fishing the Caney Fork River for trout, Rob caught about a 10-inch rainbow on a white rooster tail spinner, but his hook was not in the fish. One of the hooks of the treble hook on Rob's lure caught the front wire loop of someone else's spinner, which was in the trout's mouth. Can you believe that? I can't, and I was there and saw it!

* * *

David Denny caught about a 14-inch trout while fishing out of my canoe on the Caney Fork. I was in the back seat and landed it in the net. While I was endeavoring to take the hook out for David, the fish was slipping in my left hand, and I tried to hurry and jerked the lure. I managed to jab one of the treble hooks through the skin and into the big knuckle of my right index finger. I couldn't let go of the fish as he would flop and make things worse, so David paddled us to the bank and then came back to help. Using the monofilament line method of hook removal, he snatched the hook out. It had been in way past the barb, but the skin was loose there, and it hadn't apparently done any damage. I put some ointment on it from the first aid kit in my tackle box, and by the time we got off the river, I couldn't find the wound. I had used that finger constantly, too, in spin casting and had no ill effects or pain.

While canoeing the Harpeth River, I hooked a good fish, and he broke my line, and I lost my black spinner. We decided to fish that spot a little harder, so we pulled over to the bank and walked back. I tied on a yellow spinner, cast out, hooked and landed an 8# buffalo, and, would you believe it? He had my black spinner in his mouth, so I got it back!

David and I with all the crappie we could carry

I was hunting down in the scrub oaks below Manchester along the river, and there were big rapids there that didn't freeze up when the rest of the river did. It was always a good place to check for ducks late in the winter when everything was frozen up. I was walking along a path on top of a high bank before I got to the rapids, and I heard a commotion in the thick brush beside the path. I stopped, and was just standing there, when a rabbit came out of a little tunnel in the brush right beside me. It stopped in the trail in front of me. He looked up at me, and then ran down the trail ahead of me. I didn't want to shoot, as it would scare any ducks up ahead, so I just stood there and watched him run away. Just then, a hawk came running down the same tunnel to me, and it, too, came out in the trail. The hawk looked at me and then took off and flew away. I had never seen a hawk run a rabbit on the ground, but it had worked, as he had flushed that rabbit out of the thick brush. He might have had him, except for the tall guy standing there.

* * *

I was quail hunting at Robert Carothers's farm where he had a very large bull. Usually the bull left me alone, but this time, he started walking toward me. He made no outward sign of aggression, but he was huge, which alone was scary when he got close. I didn't know what to do, so I just stood there. The bull came right up to me, and when he stopped, I scratched his forehead. We also parted friendly. When I told Robert about it, he laughed. It seems that Robert had raised that bull since he was a calf. He was always friendly, but on several instances that Robert knew of, the bull had really scared other hunters on the property when he would try to walk up to them. He was better than a No Hunting! sign.

* * *

One weekend we were fishing the Shakey Lakes in Michigan's Upper Peninsula, and I was out in the canoe all by myself. A good bass missed my plug, and he saw me when he did. He was living under a dead tree that stuck up out in the lake and there were thick weeds all around his house except on one side. I tried for 15 or 20 minutes to interest him again with all sorts of other lures, but he was too wise for that. Finally I gave up and went on to fish other areas of the lake. About an hour and a half later I was heading back to camp, and I positioned myself upwind of the dead tree and let the wind carry the canoe soundlessly toward the bass's lair. When I got in range, I pitched my plug near the tree, and that 6-pound bass was mine.

* * *

On February 20, 1995, Rob Raney took me fishing on Old Hickory Lake northeast of Nashville, Tennessee. I only caught one fish, but it was a good one. A six and a half pound largemouth bass that was 23 inches long took my crank bait as I was pulling it near a log. Rob groused that he took me to his Honey Hole and I caught his Honey!!

Trophy brown trout from the Caney Fork river

A DUCK HUNTING SURPRISE

One day, David Denny and I decided we would go duck hunting on J. Percy Priest Lake, which is in Nashville, Tennessee. The lake is a large man-made lake that has several reasons for being. One of them is for flood control. In the winter, the Corps of Engineers, who built the dam and lake, pull the water down 10 feet below summer pool, to store spring rains. They release the water when the rivers downstream won't be flooded. This procedure is not good for duck hunting, as the vegetation is now 30 yards from the water's edge and there is little chance for ducks to find food.

We had seen some ducks hanging around a sheltered bay over by the Hobson Pike Bridge. We decided to put out some decoys there, cover the boat with a canvas tarp, and use it for our blind. We were headed that way in the wee hours before dawn. I was driving the boat and David turned his seat around so his back was to the wind, as it was cold. I was using the red lights on the top of the big electrical transmission towers to guide me as I pulled into the bay. Suddenly the motor made a lot of noise, and as I turned back to look, we ran right out on the bottom of the lake. When they dropped the water, the bottom would be visible, but I hadn't seen it in the dark. We ran aground, and a long ways! The boat stopped about 25 or 30 feet from the water's edge, and the motor was tipped up and still going full blast. David said, "I think you can turn the motor off now", but I was so shook up, I didn't know how to do it at first. We stepped out of the boat and wondered what we should do next. Since it was still dark, we put out some decoys and covered the boat with the tarp. We were visible from Hobson Pike and we were embarrassed for anyone to see us.

When it got light, I walked to a corner store, called Shirley, and had her come pick me up and take me to the boat landing so I could get the truck and boat trailer. When they built the lake, they piled up big mounds of dirt at the ends of the roads that used to go across the lake, so people could not drive into the lake. I just went to the nearest road and drove my pickup up over the dike. Then I was able to drive right up to the boat. I backed the trailer up to the front end of the boat, put two sheets of plywood under the prow, tipped up the trailer and winched the boat right off the rocks and onto the trailer. According to the insurance people, my boat was totaled.

Later I took the big motor off the boat, took out the seats, put two block and tackles on the ends of the boat, raised it up and turned it over so I could work on the underside and fix it. I had to re-fiberglass the keel, but we used it for many years after that, and I never ran it out on the bottom again!

The boat high and dry – December 21st, 1981

AFRICA - 1997

Doug had tried to convince us to join him in Africa, but we had resisted. He finally prevailed and on the 20th of February, we boarded a plane at the Nashville airport and taxied to end of the runway and sat for 20 minutes as there was a backup in Chicago. When we got to the Chicago airport - our airplane had mechanical problems and we had to wait while they brought up another plane and got it ready. We were late!

We flew overnight into the sun, and arrived at London where Doug had arranged for Alan, the taxi driver. He had waited for us which was fortunate. He took us to Danesfield House, a converted mansion on the Thames River with a formal garden. It was a lovely place to stay overnight.

The next day, we visited Windsor Castle and toured St. George's Chapel. Alan took us to the Castle and retrieved us and delivered us to the airport for our flight to Johannesburg. The next morning Doug met us at the airport, filming. With a rental car, we went to the Balalaika Hotel and repacked our suitcases. We also went to a market. It was exciting to be in a scene just like in a movie.

We left Jo'burg early on the 24th and drove 4 hours to Kruger National Park. Immediately we saw warthogs, giraffe, monkeys, impala and crocodile. We settled in at Skukuza Kamp where we were staying in Rondavel – nice round buildings with thatched roofs. They had indoor plumbing and even air conditioning. There was no kitchen inside because of animals and critters, but there was an attached kitchen area outside and a braai (grill) so you could cook. We then went on a drive where we saw a leopard in a tree right over the road, zebra, hippos, crocodile, giraffe, eagles, waterbuck, duiker, wildebeest, lizards, baboons, bushbuck, elephants, buffalo, big black rhino and kudu. Doug cooked us dinner on the braai. Our adventure was already a marvelous success!

The next morning we checked water holes and saw 6 or 7 species at a time; elephant, lion, zebra, wildebeest, ground hornbill, sable, giraffe, false mongoose and a big baobab tree.

On the 26th we drove to the Satara Kamp and saw more and more animals. We had a problem on a night drive – when we stopped to photograph a giraffe that was right near the road, the car wouldn't start. Since we had been warned not to get out of our cars because we are food to the animals, we didn't know what to do. Fortunately, a local man came along and got out of his car so we figured we could too. He found the trouble to be that some one had jerry-rigged a fuse. By pushing down on it, we were able to get going again. A good thing too, since we wouldn't be able to get back into our enclosed area at the camp and wouldn't have liked to spend the night out with the lions and so on.

The next morning we were surprised to see that there had been a big storm during the night. There were leaves and branches all over the road. We slept right through it. The thatched roof is wonderful insulation.

We tracked an elephant on the road and eventually found him. We saw a herd of elephants with young and lots of zebras.

We drove from Kruger to Londolozi Game Reserve, a really nice private reserve. We checked in, and because they didn't have many guests, were upgraded to a really nice room set in the trees. We went on a game drive with our ranger, Byron and tracker, Regiment. We observed up close three male lions, and a leopard with a cub. The mom had killed an impala and dragged it right to us. It was amazing to see. It seemed like she felt we could give them protection while they ate.

The next morning, February 28th, we were up very early for a game drive. We saw 3 leopards, 2 male rhinos, 2 elephants, and a hyena. When we got back to the camp, some of us had impala liver for breakfast. We went for a walk with an armed tracker and saw dung beetles, learned about the toilet paper tree and the toothbrush tree. He showed us the difference between hippo and rhino tracks. While having an afternoon rest, we had a vervet monkey come to visit us on our balcony. He drank out of Doug's cup. We went on a night drive and saw a herd of about 30 - 35 elephants as well as rhino, buffalo etc.

The next day we toured again and saw a female leopard with her grown daughter, had an exciting encounter with 6 lionesses on the road, saw more giraffe, hyena and mongoose. We toured the Londolozi village where the employees live and gave small gifts to the children. We returned to Jo'burg shopping along the road on the way. We had to repack our suitcases since we would be restricted on a small plane flight later. We would be able to leave some suitcases along the way to be collected later. We found we had a frog decomposing in the handle of our borrowed cooler. What a smell!

On March 2nd we boarded a plane for a trip to Zimbabwe, and arrived to see armed men watching as we went through customs. The Victoria Falls Hotel is very nice. We walked to the falls and took frune pictures of the falls, rainbows and critters. It is an amazing place and the falls are a mile wide. Really beautiful! That night we went to see a tribal dancing show. The next day we were picked up for an hour drive to our next stop, Imbabala Game Reserve, which is on the Zambezi River. We had to swerve around elephant dung on the road. We were the only guests and had nice cabins with thatched roofs.

During a night drive in a range rover, our guide, Steve, took us to an area where elephants come down to the Zambezi River in the evening. We were thrilled when 33 elephants walked right by us and went into the river. Some just drank but others took a bath and others went for a swim. They rolled around and splashed and squirted each other like kids playing in the water. Steve said that in the dry season sometimes as many as 400 elephants come to this place at one time.

After some time as it was getting dark, they started to leave. It was full dark when the last one passed us going up the hill. When Steve started the land rover he announced that we had a flat tire. I didn't understand what he said, but then he said "Sit tight", and with a big jack he had on the back end of the rover, he changed the tire all by himself in the dark.

The next day, we went out on the pontoon boat and saw lots of hippos, even right under the boat. Steve cooked an English breakfast on the boat – everything, even bacon, cooked in oil in a wok. After our return, we went for a game drive and Steve showed us where 4 countries come together – Botswana, Zambia, Namibia and Zimbabwe. He told us about their war 20 years ago. That evening we went out in the pontoon boat again and saw lots of hippos. We learned that they kill more people than any other animal. It rained a lot during the night and in the morning, but we went out in the boat anyway. The motor quit and Steve had to use my knife to fix it. We later learned that it was water in the carburetor. Glad he could fix it since we were in the river above the falls!

After another pontoon boat ride and another breakfast on the Zambezi when the motor quit again, we were taken back to the airport for a flight to Hwange and Kariba by Air Zimbabwe and then a small plane to Tiger Bay on Lake Kariba. The runway was just a dirt track. The "cabins" are open completely – no door or windows – anything could come in. Shirley has said this is one place she wouldn't come back to. We were taken out in a pontoon boat and saw a hippo out of water, elephants, lots of waterbuck, etc. We took a much-needed siesta. The evening boat ride was special because of the fabulous sunset. We have lots of pictures.

The next day, a neighbor offered to take Doug and I out fishing for the famous tiger fish. He had brought his own boat. We went out early and after much hard work I managed to catch a really small one. In the meantime, Shirley went to the eating area for breakfast. When we got there, another guest said "Have mums raise her feet." "What?" "Never mind, he's gone." "What's gone?" "The snake!" It turns out that there was a skinny green snake that slid right under Shirley's chair and up the wall. We were told it was a boomslang snake – a very poisonous one. That was the last straw for Shirley! She couldn't wait to get out of there. The next morning we went out in the boat again and the guide fed fish eagles. We saw crested cranes and had an old elephant charge us. Then it was time to pack and fly back to Victoria Falls.

Africa - 1997

When we arrived there on the way home, we met some folks who told us that we should go to the market as the vendors were dealing (barter system) on souvenirs and they would trade you for the shirt right off your back. We needed some money and as I was ready to go I went down to the bank in the hotel to cash some traveler's checks and 20 dollars US for Zimbabwean dollars Shirley informed me that I needed my passport to cash traveler's checks so I stuck it in my back pocket with my billfold. We bought a lot of things at the market. To make a long story short, when we got back to the hotel and changed clothes, I found I didn't have the passport. What a scare! We searched everywhere and were told I would have to go to Harare to get a new passport before I could leave the country.

The next morning as we were having breakfast and trying to figure out how I could go to Harare by myself, get a passport and get back to Jo'burg to meet them for the flight home, Shirley checked her purse and there was the passport! We don't know how it got there, but we were sure glad it did.

This was the adventure of a lifetime and nothing can ever top it!

Shirley, Doug and I on safari in Africa - 1997

THE ORDEAL

Way back when I was young, we didn't have much, due to the depression and all, and I was called upon to help out by keeping meat on the table hunting small game such as rabbits and squirrels. There was no big game to speak of in Iowa at the time.

One particularly bad winter, I was having trouble finding any game, but I was out there looking every chance I got as I dearly loved to hunt. One day I got caught in a big blizzard, and when I tried to head home, I couldn't see my hand in front of my face for the blowing snow. It turned real cold, too, and my hands and feet were about frozen. Sloggin' through the deep snow and squinting my eyes, I vaguely saw something in front of me. I took a couple of more steps, and out of the swirling snow there appeared the shape of a big elk. His head was down and he was facing into the wind and broadside to me. Well, don't you know, I raised my rifle and dropped him right in his tracks since the range was about 15 feet.

I started to field dress him, and, as he was warm, my hands soon warmed up, and I just felt wonderful kneeling there before him in that snowstorm. When I got all his insides out, there was a nice warm cavity inside him that was out of the wind and mighty inviting. It was a fine shelter, and since I was going to have to go get Dad to help me get the meat home, I decided to crawl inside to wait out the storm.

It was nice and warm in there, and before I knew what happened, I fell asleep. When I woke up, the storm was over, but I was in a bad way. The elk carcass had frozen stiff, and there I was - trapped inside. To make matters worse, a pack of wolves had found the elk, and they were proceeding to eat it. I had left my rifle leaning against the carcass, but the wolves had knocked it down, and I was afraid to try to reach out and get it for fear that one of them would bite my arm off. I yelled as loud as I could to try to scare them away, but they paid no attention. They were making a lot of noise growling amongst themselves and fighting over the carcass. As I lay there wondering what to do, I suddenly panicked. They were going to eat right through that frozen carcass, and then they were going to eat me. My mind was going a mile a minute. I finally decided to try to grab one of the wolves. He might think one of the other wolves had a hold of him, and he might bite the wolf next to him. Then he would bite him back. If I could get a wolf fight going, they might kill each other, and I might be saved.

I finally got my chance when one wolf's tail came close to the slit I had made in the elk's belly. I reached out quick and grabbed his tail. He yelped and tried to jump away, but I held on tight. I was surprised at how strong he was as he actually moved the carcass. My idea of starting a wolf fight worked fine. The wolves stopped eating and all joined in. The one I had by the tail was holding his own. Due to him being snubbed up against the carcass, none of the others could get at his rear end, and they all had to face his snappin' jaws head on. He was biting and growling something fierce. The other wolves didn't much care for whatever he was saying, and they started to gang up on him. One came in from the side, and I got a chance to reach out and grab him by the tail, too.

He yelped and tried to jump away, too, and when they jumped together, they actually moved the whole elk carcass. The snow had frozen, and it was like ice up on top of the snow. The two big wolves were scared of what had them by the tails, and they were also scared of the other wolves. Soon they were dragging that elk, with me inside, up on top of the snow, and then off across the ice, hell bent for leather. I found that if I let them have a little slack, they could run much faster, and by pulling one in a little, he couldn't pull as good as the other one, and lo and behold - I could steer them.

To make a long story short, I drove them all the way home. Dad came out and shot them both. He then heard me yelling, and he got the axe and chopped me out. We had meat to eat and wolf hides to sell and things were a lot brighter around there that winter. Oh, yeah, Mom was glad to see me as I had been out in that big blizzard and hadn't made it home, and she had been "some worried".

(Apologies to all who have told this tall tale through the years. It was always a favorite yarn of mine.)

Folks say I could spin some big yarns

IOWA FALL TURKEY HUNT

For those of you who love hunting, I offer this story – one of many similar adventures.

In October of 1989 David Denny and I joined Nephew Roger, "The Turkey Pro" for a hunt in northeast Iowa. We were up very early the first morning and ventured into the woods in the dark. We were instructed to walk from tree to tree up a wooded valley and, believe it or not, we were to beat on the larger trees with a tree limb bat and to yell," Shoo birds!" The idea was to flush roosted birds, count how many flew and determine if they flew off in all directions indicating they were scattered.

I flushed a half a dozen and went off to find Roger to report. He had flushed a dozen or more and really scattered them, so we decided to set up at the location the birds had roosted, await daylight and try to call them in. As it started to get light there was turkey talk all around us. I had never heard so much calling, and we felt sure of collecting a turkey or two. Unfortunately the turkeys regrouped on the other side of a deep draw and we saw nothing. We again attempted to scatter them, but they flew off together.

After lunch we decided that Roger and I were to drive a wooded draw between the two hay fields in search of turkeys and David was to take the car to the farmhouse where the draw ended in a cornfield. Roger suggested I climb the left bank and get up on top as there was little use for both of us being in the narrow bottom. I had heard him call a couple of times and had answered him from the top, when I heard him yell. I came out on a point and he said he had jumped some turkeys as they were resting on a deadfall. He suggested I go 100 yards or so ahead and set up and call. He was going to go get David.

It turned out the gate to the cornfield was closed, so David had not gotten to the end of the draw, but had entered right where some of the spooked turkeys had landed. He called and three turkeys came running to him. He shot one and shot at another that had flown up and landed in a tree. Roger and I heard the shots, and I assumed he had missed as there were 2 shots.

As I eased forward, I heard two young birds kee-keeing, and I set up to call in front of a huge old tree. The birds would answer my kee-kees, but they responded to my yelps much better. Another turkey answered much closer to me out in the field, and he soon walked in on me at about 12 yards. I never saw his body as he was in high grass and weeds with just his head showing.

When he went behind a hickory tree I raised my gun, but he must have seen me because he wouldn't come out from behind the tree. I knew he was still there as I could just see his bill sticking out. He eventually tried to sneak off back through the grass, but I could still see his head, so I was able to shoot him. It happened that neither David nor Roger had heard me shoot as they were in the car heading back.

I figured my shot would have spooked the other birds, so I continued up the draw toward where David had shot. I stopped to call, and always heard answering turkeys up ahead of me. Soon I recognized Roger and David calling from two directions behind me and I answered them with kee-kees and yelps, but I kept going, as I could not hear turkey talk except in front of me.

Shortly thereafter was another shot and I figured David had gotten his bird. I stood up and started walking back the way I had come. Suddenly three turkeys got up to my right at the edge of the hayfield and flew off across the field. I stopped, and looking over that way saw a turkey standing in the field. I shot it and two more took off and flew out over the woods in front of me. I shot both of those too, so I had 4 birds for 4 shots. David had gotten two and missed one with his three shots.

We took pictures and pictures back at the cabin, and then Roger and I cleaned the birds before we all went out to try to roost some so we could try our skill at bagging a turkey with the bow and arrow.

Roger and I walked into the woods and right in on several turkeys that flew up to roost right over us. He had seen five on the ground, and motioned for me to lie down. All were gobblers and one bird with a 6 to 8 inch beard roosted right above me. It would have been a great shot but I didn't have my bow - I was carrying the blind.

I fell asleep waiting for dark when we could scatter them. We finally yelled, scattered the birds and set up the blind. The next morning all three of us were in the blind with bows and arrows, but the turkeys regrouped on the hill behind us. We saw two birds, but they were 80 yards off. We finally called it quits and headed back by way of a scenic tour of the farm. We packed up and left our host Roger, Thanking him for a most memorable hunt.

The mighty hunters – David, Roger and I with 3 good turkeys

Roger and I with Mr. Big at Roger's ranch – 2007

"MR. BIG"

My Lifetime Whitetail Deer Trophy
October 2003

This story actually started several years ago when my nephew, Roger Raisch, "The Turkey Pro", and his friend purchased a 500-acre farm in northern Missouri. They bought the farm at an auction. HUD had foreclosed on the last farmer to live on the property, and the farm had, unfortunately lain dormant for 12 years. During that time, vandals had broken into the farmhouse and trashed it, breaking the doors and windows and kicking holes in the walls. The fields had grown up with volunteer cedar and other trees and bushes, making them impossible to cultivate. In order to be able to lease the property for farming, the fields had to be cleared. This was done by pulling up the trees with a chain and a 4-wheel drive Bronco. The trees that they could not pull up were cut down at ground level. It took a lot of work, but eventually they were able to lease out the cultivatable fields. They purchased a tractor and a bush hog, harrow, plow, etc. and Roger began working up six or eight food plots, which he planted with winter wheat, rape, clover and rye in an effort to attract deer and turkey.

Over the years, he has increased the deer and turkey on the property, and he has also seen pheasants, quail, coyotes, bobcats and wood ducks. He has invited me out there each spring and fall, for turkey hunting and archery deer hunting. He has turkey blinds and deer stands in strategic places throughout the property. I have always had chances at does, and last year I should have shot at an eight-point buck. I hadn't scored on deer, but we always got our turkeys because Roger is an expert turkey hunter and caller.

On October 17, 2003, I drove out to Roger's Ranch from Nashville, TN. Roger met me, and we began fall turkey hunting in the mornings, and I bow hunted deer in the afternoons. He had planned the hunt, and he wanted us to get our turkeys early so we could concentrate on the deer toward the end of the month, when the moon would be right. During the first morning, while in my ground blind, turkey hunting, we had a black opossum with a white face come out of the woods to us. We first thought it was going to be a skunk, and we were a little nervous, as it came right to us. I wish I had jumped up and captured the opossum so we could have taken some pictures of it, but we were calling turkeys, and Roger would have frowned on any movement at that moment.

During the first part of the week I was there, I was unsuccessful in bagging a turkey although I had two or three opportunities. On Thursday morning, October 23, Roger located two turkeys that he was able to flush, and they flew off in opposite directions. He came and got me, took down the canvas blind I was in, and moved it to where the turkeys had been. He set the blind up in a neck of woods next to a wheat food plot he had planted. He checked his watch and said we had about 30 minutes more to wait, as it would take the turkeys an hour to get back together. We were sitting on two little folding stools talking quietly when he said the hour was up, and he made a kee-kee call and got an answer. In no time, we had a turkey enter the woods and present us a 15-yard shot. Roger had all his camera gear set up to film the turkey meeting its demise, but the one in the woods was not photogenic. The turkey dropped at the shot, and we just sat still in the blind.

Roger whispered it would take about 5 minutes for the woods to settle down after the shot, and he checked his watch. When the 5 minutes were up, he made another call and the other turkey answered, and he was coming from the other direction. I looked out of my window of the blind, and there was the turkey, standing right in front of me in the woods at the edge of the wheat field. I asked Roger if I should shoot him, and he said I should let him come out into the wheat field so he could get him in his camera's viewfinder and take his picture. The turkey walked out into the field, where we had our decoys placed, and while Roger was filming, he told me to shoot him. I couldn't even see him out of my window, so I put my head out of the 10-inch diameter window and looked to the left. The turkey was about 12 yards out and walking away from me. I stuck my Benelli Super Black Eagle, a 12 gauge magnum shotgun loaded with 3 ½ inch number 4 shot, out the window and put my right arm out, but I couldn't put the gun to my shoulder, so I put the butt stock in the crook of my arm on my bicep. Then I put my head out and found the turkey in my scope sight and pulled the trigger. The gun kicked me so hard I sat back down in the little chair and said, "I think I have broken my nose". Roger was watching the turkey flopping around on the ground in the camera viewfinder and had no idea what had happened. I had my hands up to my face and repeated that I thought my nose was broken. He finally looked at me, and not only was my nose bleeding, but also my eyebrow. The nose pads on my glasses were mashed flat, and my right arm ached, too. I had often heard and read about a "scope eye", and now I had one. The wounds were superficial, and I healed up fine, but my arm was black and blue for a long time.

We got the birds to the check station, and would you believe it, Roger pointed out to the man that the bird I had shot was a young jake, and it had 4 beards each ¼ inch long. He was a trophy, or would have been if he had been allowed to grow up.

That afternoon we were putting a roof on a porch, and I decided not to get in a tree stand that evening for deer. Several times I had does right under me, but I hadn't seen a buck yet. Just before dark, we decided to try to roost some turkeys as we each could harvest another one. We each went a different direction. I walked to the North Honey Hole and Roger took the 4-wheeled ATV to the 18-acre field, which was planted in beans. As he walked up the edge of the bean field along the woods and started to top a low rise, he saw several deer in a patch of rye he had planted, between the bean field and the woods. He got out his binoculars and counted 8 does and 4 bucks in the rye food plot. There were two fork-horn bucks and two six-pointers. While he watched, two eight-point bucks walked out of the woods and joined the others. A few minutes later two big bucks, 10 to 12-pointers came across the bean field from the south, and when they got to the other deer, the two big boys started to fight. Roger said they had a real big-time fight but he could only hear most of it as they stirred up so much dust he could not see the deer. The two big bucks eventually ran back across the bean field, one chasing the other.

When we got back to camp, I told him I hadn't heard or seen anything, and he related his deer story to me, and announced we were going to hunt those bucks tomorrow evening. In the morning, Friday, Oct. 24th we tried turkey hunting, but we could not locate any birds, even though we tried long and hard.. We went back to camp and worked on our porch/deck project, but quit early so we could prepare for our deer hunt.

Roger said we were each to take a shower with non-scent soap. To a half-gallon milk jug, ½ full of cold water, he poured in a ½ gallon of hot water from the teakettle. He said you shake it up to mix it, and then you pour half of it over you to get wet. You then soap up with the non-scent soap and pour the remainder of the water over your head and body to rinse off. It worked surprisingly well, although I about scalded myself, as I didn't shake it up enough. I then dressed in my ScentLok (charcoal) suit, put on my rubber boots, and sprayed the boots with non-scent spray. While Roger showered and dressed, I shot at his archery target at 10, 20, and 30 yards and was satisfied that I was ready.

When Roger was ready, we loaded all his camera gear, archery gear and a deer decoy onto the 4-wheeler. When I started to look for a place to put my bow, he said that I should ride the second 4-wheeler as we would need it to haul the deer back to camp. —Well, duh – yeah sure!! We parked about 200 yards from the rye field and walked up the north edge of the bean field, carrying all our equipment. Roger was going to get into a canvas blind on the edge of the rye food plot and take digital movie pictures of the deer that came out in the rye. He had his bow, should the big bucks show up. He told me to go south across the bean field and get up in a ladder tree stand he had placed on the edge of a clover food plot. That was about where the two big bucks had come from and returned to the night before.

When I got to the clover, it was lush and green, and I paced off 10, 20 and 30 yards from the tree stand and placed small blaze orange range markers in several directions. I had de-scented the range markers and was wearing rubber gloves when I handled them. I also put out a few drops of "Active Scrape" at two locations 20 yards out. One such doctored- up spot was where Roger had put out some mineral for the deer, and it was a bare spot in the clover.

"Mr. Big"

When I got up in the stand I found, as Roger had told me, I had to stand up on the seat to see over the trees and brush and have shooting lanes. The tree had two forks, and I put up a camouflaged screen across one to conceal me from the west. I got out my grunt call, binoculars, etc. and hung them on branch stubs left for the purpose, and fastened my war bag around the tree. I put my safety belt on the tree and me, and pulled up my bow. I got a drink of water and checked my watch. It was 4:00 pm. The stand was fairly comfortable, as I could semi-sit on the tree and take the weight off my feet.

At 5 o'clock, I looked east to the end of the clover plot, and there stood a big deer just at the edge of the woods. He was about 100 yards away, and I was looking through tree branches with many leaves on them. I got my binoculars on him, and he was one of the big bucks – a 10 or 12 pointer! He stood there for a few minutes, looking over the field, and finally he walked out into the field and started to feed on the clover. He was eating just like a cow, munching three or four times to get a mouthful, then looking up and all around as he chewed it up and swallowed it. He ate and ate in the same place for a long time. Finally a smaller buck, a six pointer, walked out into the field and started to feed. At one point, the smaller buck walked up to the big one, and when they were face-to-face they touched noses. There was no aggression. They were just saying hello – maybe, "Hello, Dad".

Eventually the big buck started down the edge of the clover field in my direction. He had a long way to go to get to me, and he was walking very slowly. The wind had come up, and it must have been blowing 15 to 20 mph out of the north. It was partly cloudy and the temperature was about 62 degrees F. Due to the strong wind, my tree was moving and all the leaves were rattling, big time. When the deer was about 60 yards away, a noise in the woods caused both deer to stand and stare in that direction, but they soon kept coming. The big boy was right along the edge of the woods coming right to me, and the smaller deer was out in the center of the clover patch. As the big buck got closer, I could see how really big he was. Where all the deer I had seen before were light, quick and graceful, this big boy plodded along like an old bull. He was old, too, as his face was white.

'Tis Himself

When I could see I was probably going to get a shot, I located 4 holes in the foliage, one at 10 yards, one at 12 yards, one at 15 and one at 20-just depending on how far out in the field he was when he got to me. He plodded along on his big feet, his big legs and his big body, and he was coming into the 12 yard opening when I drew back, put the pin on his boiler room and released my arrow. He took two jumps away and stood there looking at the brush at the edge of the field. I just knew I had hit him, so I watched him closely and was waiting for him to fall over. He eventually started walking away from me, and it did not appear that the arrow had fazed him. I couldn't believe that I had missed him at 12 yards.

He walked up to my 20-yard marker and started smelling the "Active Scrape" scent I had put on Roger's old mineral lick. He was offering me a 20-yard broadside shot, and his broadside was big. The tree trunk was in the way, but there was a crotch in the trunk through which I might be able to get off a shot. I stood on my tiptoes and got my bow up and through the crotch, but when I attempted to get enough of me through there so I could get off a shot, there was no way I could come to full draw. Fortunately, the wind covered my movements, as when I tried to let the bow down, the bow jerked, the nock came off the arrow, and it was laying on the arrow rest. I put the nock in my pocket, and I dropped the arrow straight down to the ground 2 feet from the ladder. I took another arrow from my bow quiver and placed it on my arrow rest and knocked it.

The big buck continued to walk slowly north, away from me and toward my 30-yard range marker. I assumed he was going to keep going across the bean field and go over where Roger was waiting in his blind. When the buck got to my 30-yard marker, he stopped, looked around, and then turned 90 degrees and continued walking to the west. Soon he was coming out from behind the tree trunk, and he was going to offer me a measured 30-yard shot. I got my bow over the camo netting and waited. When he was clear of my tree, I drew back the bow and put the green 30-yard sight pin on the center of the deer just behind his front leg. At that time, the sun suddenly broke through the clouds and illuminated the field and the deer. It surprised the big buck, and he stopped, took a ½ step backwards and stood there in the sun, 30 yards away and broadside. I checked that my bow was clear of the tree and the camo netting, and that I was looking through the peep sight. Everything checked out, and the green sight pin still was steady as a rock on the deer. I thought at the time that I had never held so steady a sight picture in my life. When you hold a 60-pound pull bow, the sight drifts around, and you try to release the arrow when the pin gets to where you want it. This pin didn't move. There was no drifting around. It just stayed in one place. It was higher than the deer's heart, but I thought that it must be where I was supposed to hold. When I released the arrow, the buck tucked his tail and ran straight ahead about 20 yards and entered the woods. He stopped just out of sight and stood there for 10 to 15 seconds, and he make a strange vocal sound. It wasn't a snort, a wheeze, or a grunt, and I didn't recognize it. About that time, he ran south, parallel to the clover plot, and I could just see him in the woods as he ran. He stopped again after running about 15 yards, but I couldn't see him. While he was standing there, out of sight, he made the same sound three more times.

I decided to wait the suggested 30 minutes before going to look for him. I relived the shot and marked in my mind about where he entered the woods. I prayed that I had made a good shot, that he would die quickly, and that I would find him. After 15 minutes, I couldn't wait any longer, so I took down my camo screen and put all my gear back into my shoulder bag. I lowered the bow back down to the ground and climbed out of the stand. When I was on the ground, I replaced the nock-less arrow into my bow quiver and went to look for my first arrow, which must have missed the buck at my 12-yard shot. The arrow was not sticking in the ground as I assumed it would be, but half of the arrow was lying on the ground beneath some branches. The carbon arrow had shattered or splintered, and I only found the front end with the broadhead. One of the replaceable blades was missing, but there was no indication the broadhead had hit anything. I guessed the shaft of the arrow had hit a branch, but I didn't stay around to look. I put the remnant of that arrow in my quiver and picked up my 10, 20, and 30-yard markers as I retraced the buck's movements. When I got to the place where I had shot at the deer, I didn't spend much time looking for the arrow as the clover was thick, and I didn't see any arrow or blood. I hurried to where the deer had entered the woods and looked for blood on the leaves. There was no blood! I kept looking, and then went south to about where I felt the deer had run. When I got to the point where the deer had stopped the second time and make the strange noise, I found a plate-size area of blood. So I had hit him!

The blood trail from there was easy to follow. It turned a little to the west and crossed a shallow swale, and then it came out into an opening that headed toward the bean field. I felt if he went out into the bean field, he wasn't hit as hard as I hoped, or he wouldn't be going out into the open. The trail immediately turned back into the woods, and when I looked up, there he was. He was the biggest deer with the biggest rack that I had ever seen in the woods. There was a very large area of blood just above where he lay, so I knew he had stood there before he fell over. I searched his body and found the entrance wound. It was a little higher and a little farther back than I would have wished, but it had done the job. I was elated, and I said a prayer of thanks. When I tried to turn him over so his belly was down-hill, it was not an easy task. His horns caught in the dirt and his rear legs flopped back. I had to turn his head first. I got out my walkie-talkie and called Roger. I told him of the big 12-pointer that I was standing over, and I don't think he believed me at that time. He didn't want to leave, as he had deer out in front of him in the food plot.

I got out my knife and field-dressed the deer. My arrow had gone clear through both his lungs, and I finally understood what the noise was that he had made. He had coughed 4 times. Roger came over after it got dark. We admired the buck and dragged him up to the edge of the bean field. We both walked the length of the bean field and got the two ATVs and rode them to the buck. We had quite a time trying to get the big buck up onto the ATV. It was very hard to lift him, as we couldn't get a hold of him in the center where he was the heaviest. I finally climbed up on the 4-wheeler and pulled him up by the horns while Roger kept lifting and getting the legs clear. We eventually got him loaded, and his feet and horns tied up so he wouldn't drag on the ground.

When we got to camp, we loaded the deer into the back of my pickup truck by dragging him right off the ATV so we didn't have to lift him anymore. We got him to the check station at 7:15 p.m., which was 15 minutes after they had closed. Mr. and Mrs. Kenneth Bosley at the Spickard, Missouri check station, were gracious and let us check him in, as I was to head for Tennessee in the early morning. They congratulated me and Mr. Bosley said, "I passed up a lot of deer that size while looking for a big one." He put a transportation tag on the buck, and though we couldn't get him weighed, Mr. Bosley guessed his weight at about 250 pounds. Even the taxidermist back in Tennessee felt he would weigh that much and he only saw his head. I could hardly wait to get his mounted head back and on my wall. We have eaten some of the summer sausage we had made from him, and it is good. When it warms up, we will grill the tenderloins.

Mr. Big looking important on our family room wall

As I think back on this hunt, there were so many instances where God was helping and watching over me. I could really have broken my nose or lost an eye when I shot at that turkey. The strong north wind blew my scent away from the buck, and it covered the noise I made when I hit a branch with my first shot. Then He turned the deer 90 degrees at my 30-yard marker, and then stopped him, illuminated him, and steadied my aim. He <u>gave</u> that old deer to me, an old man. I am 71 years old and very, very thankful.

A SPECIAL HAPPENING

On April 25, 2008, on a Southwest Airlines flight landing in Las Vegas, I was praying silently that God would grant us a safe landing. I do this every time I fly. I pray for a safe take-off, flight, and landing and I do it maybe a dozen times a year. However, this time it was different. When I opened my eyes – God was there. He was all around me; the airplane was full of God. I looked around and I could see the inside of the airplane, the walls, the seats, the passengers but the air around and throughout was God. A presence of God. We landed a short time later and I knew it would be a safe landing.

This sense or presence of God lasted maybe 6 to 8 seconds. I felt no spirit enter me, I saw no holy smoke or fire, no ghost, I didn't see God or his face but I knew he was there – He was everywhere – All around us. <u>The air was literally filled with God.</u> Now, I have no doubt that God is with us at all times. He allowed me to feel or rather sense his presence. It was very real. I have been thinking of this for months now and I do not know what to do about it. I do not feel qualified to talk about it, as I cannot satisfactorily put the feeling into words and I do not know why it happened. What do I do about it? If I tell it, folks will think I dreamed it, or made it up. Maybe they will think I am crazy, or bragging or looking for notoriety etc. etc. I do feel privileged, as I have not heard of anyone else who has had a similar experience.

Should I just suppress it, ignore it or am I missing something? Is there a message that I should tell others of this experience? Could I convince others that God is everywhere – all around us? I can't prove it. It's my word only. My wife was sitting right beside me and she felt nothing. So, I am embarrassed to bring it up.

Now 3 months later I am facing a life and death situation with my cancer diagnosis. This immediately brings up other questions. Could it be that the cancer started to grow in me during that flight into Las Vegas? Did God allow me to sense his presence to say to me, "I am here with you to heal you or take you home with me?" In either case he gave me insight, strengthened my faith, and He comforted me. I am ready, come what may, because I know <u>God's Will be Done</u> and I am so thankful!

IN CLOSING

George lost his battle with gall bladder cancer on May 20, 2009. He had been given 2 – 3 months to live, but survived 10 months. During that time he continued to write stories, and if he had not passed, he would still be remembering more things he wanted to tell about. His book was a long cherished dream and we are so sorry he was not able to see it become a reality. His family hopes that through these stories you will see he lived a life full of joy and happiness. George always had fun and loved sharing that with his many friends, so read this book with a smile and perhaps with a tear, as you get to know, "Himself."

Matt, Doug, Shirley and I in the Smoky Mountains – 1993

In Closing

My grandsons Lowan and Kaelen and I pausing for lunch on a canoe trip in NH

Made in the USA
Charleston, SC
29 October 2010